THE COLOUR OF JUSTICE

Policing Race in Canada

the COLOUR of JUSTICE

Policing Race in Canada

DAVID M. TANOVICH

Published in 2006 by

Irwin Law
Suite 206
14 Duncan Street
Toronto, Ontario
M5H 3G8

www.irwinlaw.com

ISBN-10 1-55221-119-3   ISBN-13 978-1-55221-119-9

Editor: Rosemary Shipton
Design: Heather Raven

Library and Archives Canada Cataloguing in Publication

Tanovich, David M.
    The colour of justice : policing race in Canada / David M. Tanovich.

Includes bibliographical references and index.
ISBN 1-55221-115-0 (bound)
ISBN 1-55221-119-3 (pbk.)

1. Racial profiling in law enforcement—Canada. I. Title.

HV7936.R3T35 2006   363.2'3'08900971   C2006-900085-9

The publisher acknowledges the financial support of the Government of Canada
through the Book Publishing Industry Development Program (BPIDP) for its
publishing activities.

We acknowledge the assistance of the OMDC Book Fund, an initiative of Ontario
Media Development Corporation.

Printed and bound in Canada.

1 2 3 4 5   10 09 08 07 06

Contents

Introduction

THE COLOUR OF JUSTICE in Canada is White. The unequal impact of our criminal justice system begins with police surveillance.
If you are not White, you face a much greater risk of attracting
the attention of law enforcement officials in public spaces such as
the highway, street, border, or airport. While it is true that many
Whites experience an unwanted encounter with the police, social
science evidence reveals that racialized individuals experience
far more of these encounters. In 1994, for example, 17 percent of
Black residents in Toronto reported having been stopped on two
or more occasions over the previous two years, compared to only 8
percent of White residents.[1]

The evidence further suggests that this increased police surveillance is triggered by appearance, not behaviour. In 2000 a survey of Toronto high school students revealed that Black students
who were not involved in criminal, deviant, or other activities that
would attract police attention were nevertheless four times more
likely to report being stopped and six times more likely to report
being searched than similarly situated White students.[2] In October 2003 thirty-six Black police officers in Toronto met to discuss

their lived experiences with racial profiling. A majority of the officers reported having been stopped and questioned by a fellow officer for no apparent reason other than the colour of their skin. Three officers described instances where they were stopped more than once in the course of a week, while six officers revealed they had been stopped more than twelve times in a single year.[3]

The experience of racialized individuals in Canada is also very different in terms of the degree of intrusion and risk of harm that follows an initial stop. Racialized individuals are at a far greater risk than Whites of being searched, assaulted, and even shot following a stop.[4] Moreover, being White guarantees that you will not be picked up by the police and taken on an Aboriginal "starlight tour" and left for dead on a cold winter night in Saskatchewan, Manitoba, or British Columbia.[5] And being White ensures you will never have to fear being sent to a country to be tortured when you are stopped at the airport.[6]

The impact of the colour of justice in Canada extends beyond surveillance. Because racialized individuals are more likely to be stopped, they are also more likely to be arrested than Whites who engage in similar activity. For example, 65 percent of self-identified Black drug dealers in the Toronto high school survey reported having been arrested, compared to only 35 percent of White high school drug dealers.[7] Once arrested, Black and Aboriginal accused are more likely to face the prospect of being overcharged, of not being released by the police or on bail by a justice of the peace, of being tried by a trier of fact who looks nothing like them, and, ultimately, of being sentenced to jail.[8]

The colour of justice in Canada is largely driven by stereotypical assumptions about crime and those who commit it. These assumptions, which are perpetuated in police intelligence materials, popular culture, and in the media, have served to place the burden of suspicion almost entirely on racialized communities. Over the last few years the use of race, ethnicity, and religion as an indicator of suspicion by the police and security officials has come under scrutiny. The focus, however, has largely been on the American experience. Although exposure of the problem in Canada has been increasing, no comprehensive study of the policing of race in this country has been done. This book is an attempt to fill this gap. It seeks to provide as broad a picture of the situation as possible. Although much of the recent attention has been on the Black, Muslim, and Arab communities, all racialized individuals in Canada have been and continue to be victimized by racial profiling. The number of potential victims is staggering. According to the 2001 Census, 4,960,150 racialized individuals, including 976,305 Aboriginals, live in Canada.[9]

This book seeks to provide answers to six fundamental questions about racial profiling in Canada. When should policing be characterized as racial profiling? Why does it occur? How pervasive is it? What damage does it cause? Is it ever reasonable? How do we stop it? The goal is to foster understanding and reform. Although there is growing recognition of the existence of racial profiling by police forces in Kingston, Montreal, Ottawa, and Toronto, a general unawareness of its scope and pervasiveness remains. In the context of security policing, claims of denial and necessity can still be heard. This current state of affairs stems largely from a misunderstanding of the problem. Many see racial profiling in blunt or overt terms – where race is used as the sole reason for the police investigation. However, racial profiling is essentially a systemic problem, and these overt cases have more to do with expressions of hate by the "bad apples" than "good faith" attempts to enforce the law.

Cases where race is the sole reason for the police encounter likely make up only a small number of all racial-profiling cases. Usually, other factors trigger an officer's suspicion, including age, gender, location, clothing, and time of day, or, in the security context, religion and place of origin or status of citizenship. In these cases, most officers probably believe they are not using race in a discriminatory fashion, or, if they do, they think it is reasonable because it is based on criminal profiling or differential offending rates, and not on racialized stereotypes. The problem is that, in these cases, the decision to investigate is not premised on objectively suspicious criminal behaviour, which is the hallmark of reliable and constitutional policing, but rather on a stereotypical perception of the usual offender. That is what racial profiling is all about. Even where officers believe they are investigating criminal behaviour, there is a danger that racialized stereotypes or guilt-by-association reasoning has converted innocuous conduct into suspicious circumstances. That, too, is a form of racial profiling.

The misunderstanding extends beyond the police. Lawyers remain reluctant, generally speaking, to raise the issue, and courts are often hesitant to reach the conclusion even in the face of compelling evidence. Canada also lags behind the efforts of the police and politicians in other countries where there are laws banning racial profiling and requirements that the police document those they stop, question, and search. This inaction is attributable not only to misunderstanding but also to a lack of appreciation of the harm caused by racial profiling. Those who have never experienced it, or who have been stopped only once or twice, likely see police stops as a minor inconvenience. The damage is, however, significant. For example, conduct that most of us take for granted, such as driving a car or walking down the street, can suddenly become a volatile and potentially deadly activity for racialized individuals. Enormous psychological damage, as well as the engendering of a mistrust of the police and the justice system, often occurs after multiple experiences of being stopped and harassed by the police. And, as a pragmatic matter, profiling can serve to hinder law enforcement and perpetuate the very violence that it seeks to address.

Given that misunderstanding is the major problem in Canada between the justice system and the affected communities, the best way to stimulate remedial action is to identify and expose the common misperceptions surrounding this complicated and politically charged issue. This book uses social science evidence, judicial decisions, commission findings, government and police documents, narratives, and media reports to shed light on the flawed assumptions behind the myths surrounding racial profiling. It attempts to provide the reader with the necessary tools to understand the nature and scope of this social problem and, ultimately, the courage and motivation to do something about it.

TERMINOLOGY

As the Ontario Human Rights Commission has observed, "[t]here are inherent challenges in finding ways in which to best describe people. Terminology is fluid and what is considered most appropriate will likely evolve over time."[10] In describing people collectively, this book uses the term "racialized" rather than "visible minority" or "person of colour" because it more accurately reflects that race is a social construction and not a biological identifier. The process in which race is constructed by the dominant groups and institutions in our society is referred to as "racialization." The *Report of the Commission on Systemic Racism in the Ontario Criminal Justice System* defined racialization "as the process by which societies construct races as real, different and unequal in ways that matter to economic, political and social life."[11] To reflect the point that race is socially constructed for reasons of both privilege and subordination, the terms "Black" and "White" are both capitalized.

[*Part One*]

UNDERSTANDING RACIAL PROFILING

What Is It?

A RITE OF PASSAGE

IN THE EARLY MORNING hours of October 22, 1993, Dwight Drummond, a popular Citytv assignment editor, and his friend, Ron Allen, were driving home in Drummond's blue Volkswagen Passat. They were young Black men and about to experience, as Drummond would later call it, a "rite of passage"—an unwarranted encounter with the police. This time, the stakes were particularly high. Before they knew it, their vehicle was boxed in by two police cruisers near the intersection of Dundas and Sherbourne streets in Toronto. With the officers assuming a defensive position behind their vehicles, one of the officers used his loudspeaker to order Drummond and Allen to raise their hands and exit the vehicle. A high-risk take-down had begun. The two men were ordered to take three steps back, go down on their knees, and lie on their stomachs with their arms stretched out. As Allen was exiting, one officer thought he heard a metal sound, reinforcing his opinion that there was a gun in the vehicle. This assumption immediately made a tense situation even more tense.[1] With one of the officers "covering" Drummond and then Allen, two other officers approached and handcuffed them. They were searched and placed in the cruiser.[2] When no gun was found, the officers let them go. What was a routine ride home from work and a meeting of friends suddenly escalated into a situation where Drummond and Allen faced the very real possibility of joining the many other young Black men who have been shot by the Toronto police under troubling circumstances.[3]

Drummond filed a complaint with the police against the two officers who had initiated the take-down. Allen refused to do so because he felt the "outcome was predetermined"[4]—a sentiment shared by many in the Black community. As Cecil Foster, one of Canada's most highly regarded writers on race relations, put it in his book *A Place Called Heaven: The Meaning of Being Black in Canada*, "the complaint would amount to a case of the word of a black man against a white policeman, and everyone knew the likely outcome."[5] The complaint was dismissed.[6] Deputy Chief Robert Kerr was troubled by the incident and intervened. He took the unusual step of having the officers charged with discreditable conduct under the *Police Services Act.*[7] Kerr's decision sparked a controversy at 51 Division, where the officers worked.[8] On January 26, 1995, Constable Craig Bromell, who would later become president of the Toronto Police Association, advised his superiors that the division's fifty officers would not be going on patrol that day and that the station doors would be locked. For the next eight hours, Toronto witnessed the first police strike in its history.[9]

Why were Drummond and Allen singled out? At their disciplinary hearing, the officers testified that there had been two 911 calls reporting gunshots in the area. Although they were in that neighbourhood, the officers had not heard any gunshots.[10] They felt that Drummond and Allen were acting suspiciously. When their vehicle passed the officers' cruiser, it appeared to slow and, as Drummond put it, "we broke the unwritten rule and made eye contact."[11] The officers felt that the men were looking at them "intently" and as if they were going to "bolt." They also saw Allen bending down to put something under his seat, as if to hide it.[12] What they likely thought was a gun turned out to be chicken that

Allen had just bought at George's BBQ, a well-known restaurant in downtown Toronto.[13]

Finally, the officers claimed to be acting on a tip they had received from someone they thought was a prostitute. Apparently, a woman had approached them out of nowhere and asked, "Are you guys looking for the guys with a gun? They are getting into a blue car from the parking lot of George's [BBQ]." She even used police lingo in describing them as "two male blacks."[14] The officers were unable to provide a name for this mysterious woman, and, when they advised dispatch that they were planning on stopping two "male black" suspects in relation to the gun incident, they failed to mention the "tip." Moreover, they provided no description of her to the other officers on the scene, made no attempt to locate her, and, ultimately, she never surfaced.[15] In her cross-examination of the officers, Jean Iu, counsel for Ontario's police complaints commissioner, suggested that the tip was a fabrication: "You never got any information from a woman," she said. "You were acting on hunch, only a hunch." The officers rejected this version of events.[16] In her closing submissions, Iu "made it clear that she thought the officers and their supervisor had lied about an alleged prostitute informant."[17]

The three-member civilian Board of Inquiry, which included one Black member, dismissed the disciplinary charges.[18] It held that while it was aware of the "perception held by some members of the public that black motorists are randomly and arbitrarily stopped by police officers for no reason other than the colour of their skin," this was "not a case for such a determination."[19] It was satisfied that the officers' conduct was warranted in light of the "suspicious activity" of Drummond's vehicle, the lateness of the hour, and the lack of vehicular traffic.[20] In addition, the board observed that "[w]e would be hard pressed to presume that these officers would go through such a complex, military, precise technique as the high-risk take-down, involving several police officers, *with the motivation of racial bias or harassment*."[21]

In so concluding, the board gave no weight to its own observations that this purported chance meeting with a mysterious informant was "puzzling" and "intriguing."[22] It simply concluded that it was "not necessary to enter into the speculation as to whether the street walker did in fact exist" because the officers' conduct was justified even in the absence of the tip.[23] But surely this issue was relevant to the credibility of the officers? Moreover, was the board as sensitive to systemic racism as it believed itself to be?[24] It did not, for example, address the issue of whether the officers had unconsciously or unintentionally relied on race to convert innocent into suspicious conduct.

Drummond was angered by the decision: "Throughout my life," he said, "I've been going through this thing, day in — day out. It's been a rite of passage for me. It's not the first time I was stopped and it probably won't be the last time.... I think it's open season on young black men in this city."[25] The notion that racial profiling is a rite of passage for young Black men in Toronto is a common refrain.[26] Hamlin Grange, for example, a current member of the Toronto Police Services Board, observed in recounting his own experience with profiling that "[i]t is a rite of passage that most young black people in this city have been through."[27] The decision of the board was upheld on appeal.[28]

A DEFINITION

UNTIL RECENTLY, THERE WAS no generally accepted definition of racial profiling in Canada.[29] This deficiency has proved to be a problem in seeking a remedy and in otherwise moving forward. As University of Toronto law professor Kent Roach has observed, "[a]ny debate about profiling that is not guided by a clear definition is bound to be a recipe for frustration and bitterness."[30] We saw first hand in the Drummond case the problems of not having a clear definition. What we need is a concise definition that captures the issues that make this practice discriminatory. It is not good enough to claim "I know it when I see it" because not all of us are looking at it with the same lens. Racial profiling occurs when law enforcement or security officials, consciously or unconsciously, subject individuals at any location to heightened scrutiny based solely or in part on race, ethnicity, Aboriginality, place of origin, ancestry, or religion or on stereotypes associated with any of these factors rather than on objectively reasonable grounds to suspect that the individual is implicated in criminal activity.[31] Racial profiling operates as a system of surveillance and control. It "creates racial inequities by denying people of color privacy, identity, place, security, and control over [their] daily life."[32] It shares many similarities with previous systems of control such as slavery and segregation, both of which had a long history in Canada.[33] As one scholar has pointed out, "[r]acial profiling is best understood as a current manifestation of the historical stigma of blackness as an indicator of criminal tendencies."[34]

Defined in this way, racial profiling is both unlawful and unconstitutional. It violates our constitutional right to be free from arbitrary detention as guaranteed in section 9 of the *Canadian Charter of Rights and Freedoms*.[35] It also violates our section 15(1) *Charter* right to equal protection of the law, a right that serves to protect against "the violation of essential human dignity and freedom through the imposition of disadvantage, stereotyping, or political or social prejudice."[36] Finally, racial profiling is a violation of human rights.[37]

SYSTEMIC RACISM AND STEREOTYPING

THE DAY-TO-DAY RACIAL PROFILING that occurs in Canada today is primarily about stereotyping rather than the expression of animus or overt racism. Those few that target out of hate, such as officers who target Aboriginals and leave them for dead in the middle of winter in the outskirts of town, are truly the "bad apples."[38] But we need to be equally concerned about the much larger group of police officers who use racialized stereotypes consciously or unconsciously on a daily basis. Overt racism, the intent to treat individuals differently based on a belief in the superiority of one's own racial group, has been largely overshadowed in Canada by a more subtle and yet equally pervasive form of racism known as systemic racism.[39] Systemic racism is the "social production of racial inequality in decisions about people and the treatment they receive."[40] It occurs through a process called racialization:

> Racialization is the process by which societies construct races as real, different and unequal in ways that matter to economic, political and social life. It involves —
> - selecting some human characteristics as meaningful signs of racial difference;
> - sorting people into races on the basis of variations in these characteristics;
> - attributing personality traits, behaviours and social characteristics to people classified as members of particular races; and
> - acting as if race indicates socially significant differences among people.[41]

For the most part, racialization is largely unintentional. As the Ontario Human Rights Commission observed in its 2003 racial-profiling inquiry report, "[p]ractical experience and psychology both confirm that anyone can stereotype, even people who are well meaning and not overtly biased."[42] In other words, most police officers probably do not even realize that they are engaging in inappropriate conduct when they conduct race-based stops and searches.

Where does this racialized "usual offender" stereotype come from? In part it comes from our history of overt racism, a history that has made us far less likely to be critical of the suggestion that crime can be linked to certain racialized groups. It also comes from the people the police see most often in court or in high-crime areas. As Jacques Lelièvre, assistant director of the Montreal Police, candidly admitted: "Officers see street gangs ... [t]hey see some black people doing wrong. They get used to that, and myths develop. So when they see a black guy in a Lexus, they assume he's in a gang."[43] A similar admission came from Ottawa's Deputy Police Chief Larry Hill: "Do stereotypes exist? Yes. Do things happen because we stereotype people? Yes. So if we're going to call that racial profiling, then, yes, it certainly occurs in our police force as well as [in] other police services."[44] Racialized usual-offender stereotypes also come from "the misinformed anecdotal musings of associates, inaccurate media information or a misunderstanding of information, reports and studies etc. disseminated by police or governmental agencies."[45]

A MISNOMER?

ALAN YOUNG, A LAW professor at Osgoode Hall Law School and author of the provocative book *Justice Defiled: Perverts, Potheads, Serial Killers & Lawyers*,[46] has argued in a *Toronto Star* commentary that it is a "misnomer" to use the term racial profiling to identify what is going on when the police improperly use race as a proxy for criminality. He believes that we have mischaracterized the problem. "We are not dealing with racial profiling," he writes; "we are dealing with racism, the same racism that infects our schools, our courts, our legislatures and our homes."[47] What is the basis for Young's misnomer argument? He argues that "properly understood ... [racial profiling] is not an established police practice.... Such a practice would mean there exists some training manual instructing officers to consider racial features in determining whether to investigate an individual." He goes on to state: "If our police have been secretly relying on an express racial profile for criminal investigations, then the only solution would be armed insurrection." But rebellion need not occur, he concludes, because "we have mischaracterized the problem."[48]

But does Young's misnomer argument withstand closer scrutiny? As a factual matter, there are official police and government materials in Canada that racialize crime and, in doing so, fuel the targeting of racialized groups. For example, some intelligence reports explicitly link drug trafficking and gang activity to particular racialized groups. The 2004/2005 Annual Report of Criminal Intelligence Service Alberta provided quite detailed information to Alberta police officers:[49]

Jamaican Organized Crime

In 1999/2000, a CISA funded Joint Forces Operation in Edmonton, Project Kalcium, revealed that groups of Jamaican males were bringing cocaine from Jamaica to sell in the city.

Asian Criminal Groups

There are a large number of groups comprised of Asian criminals who, collectively, dominate the distribution of cocaine and marihuana.

Self-Identified Criminal Groups

... The Indian Posse and Redd Alert are comprised largely of Aboriginal males who carry out criminal activities relating to drug trafficking and violence at the street level. These groups cause considerable harm to rural and First Nation communities....

According to statistics, single-parent families (with children under 18 years of age) in Canada are earning 40 percent less than two-parent families. This is disproportionately impacting Aboriginal children where 32 percent on reserves live in single-parent families and 46 percent in urban areas. Forty-one percent of Aboriginal children in Canada live in poverty (as do 42.4 percent of immigrant children).

Aboriginal people are disproportionately impacted in the criminal justice system. They represent three percent of the population but 18 percent of the federally incarcerated population—an increase of nine percent in 20 years. They are more likely than the average Canadian offender to be incarcerated for violent crimes. The Aboriginal "baby boom" will have a profound impact on gang activity and incarceration rates. Aboriginal people are targeted by organized crime and many Aboriginal youth are feeding organized crime groups in Alberta.[50]

In addition to racializing crime, these intelligence reports emphasize that racialized groups are predominantly involved in street-level crime, and it is on the streets that racial profiling largely occurs. It's enlightening to compare the treatment of Aboriginal, Italian, and Eastern European groups in the 2003 Annual Report of Criminal Intelligence Service Canada (CISC):[51]

> Aboriginal-based gangs are generally involved in street-level trafficking of marihuana, cocaine, crack cocaine and methamphetamine as well as other criminal activities....
>
> While Eastern European-based organized crime (EEOC) groups participate in most types of criminal activity, they are notable for their ability to plan and carry out sophisticated fraud schemes.... The most powerful Traditional (Italian-based) organized crime (TOC) groups continue to be based in Ontario and Quebec; however TOC groups either directly or indirectly exploit criminal activities across the country. TOC continues to increase their wealth and influence through criminal activities, such as illicit drug importation/distribution, money laundering, illegal gaming/bookmaking, and their subsequent investment of illicit profits in legitimate businesses.[52]

While these materials may not explicitly instruct officers to target racialized communities on the street, the implicit message is there. Indeed, CISC has felt the need to include the following disclaimer in its annual reports:

> References to organized criminal activity associated with particular ethnic-based organizations in this report are not meant to suggest that all members of that specific ethnic group are involved in organized crime or that the government of the country of origin or its authorized agencies permits or participates in illegal activities. These references allude to the illegal activities of particular criminal organizations, the majority of whose members share ethnic origins.[53]

This disclaimer arguably makes profiling even more likely. By suggesting that the link between race and crime does not tar all members of the group, this statement suggests that it will be appropriate to target individuals where race plus some other distinguishing factor such as age, gender, or clothing is present. However, as noted earlier, this is racial profiling because what is being targeted is appearance, not behaviour. In addition, on a practical level, it is difficult to understand how the official linking of crime with racialized groups is of any assistance to the day-to-day policing of our streets. While some internal tracking may be relevant to the establishment of undercover operations where it seems advisable to have an officer who shares a similar background to a known group of criminals, it's unclear how this information assists officers conducting routine street patrols unless they use it as part of a generalized profile.

This official racialization of street crime explains, in part, why Black police officers are just as likely as their White counterparts to engage in racial profiling and why there is no "armed insurrection," as Young puts it. For example, in *Singh*, a case involving an allegation of racial profiling against a Black police officer, the trial judge observed: "It seems that any person of any race could consciously or unconsciously believe that persons of a particular race, his own or others, have a propensity toward criminal activity and thus should be targeted for attention by the police."[54] While we do not have any data on this issue in Canada, the evidence from the United States confirms that African-Americans experience differential stops and searches "at the hands of white *and* black officers alike."[55] As David Harris, one of the leading racial-profiling scholars in the United States and author of *Profiles in Injustice: Why Racial Profiling Cannot Work*, has observed:

> If both black and white officers seem to use traffic stops and searches disproportionately against blacks and other minorities, this implies that profiling is about more than the racism of a few racist whites with badges. Rather it is an institutional problem, and an institutional practice.[56]

There is also an official document that invites racial profiling in the national security context. One week after the September 11, 2001, terrorist attacks, the Royal Canadian Mounted Police (RCMP) issued the following profile of the "adversary," to use their words, in a Criminal Intelligence Brief:

> *Law Enforcement Requirement to Combat Terrorism*
>
> The second phase is to develop a longer term strategy to deal with future potential attacks. This longer term strategy will have to take into account the type of adversary we are up against. By all accounts the hijackers of the four planes were men who lived in the United States for some time, did not act conspicuously, were well spoken, well dressed, educated and blended in well with the North American lifestyle. Similar subjects live in Canada and some have been identified.... These identified individuals travel internationally with ease, use the Internet and technology to their advantage, know how to exploit our social and legal situation and are involved in criminal activities. Indications from investigative leads in the past week have given us a glimpse that there are many more potential terrorists in Canada.[57]

By specifically identifying the adversary as the men who flew the planes, the profile implicitly includes their ethnic and religious characteristics. In addition, the profile is so general that it requires the reader to add these elements if it is to have any practical use at all.[58] When Superintendent Michel Cabana, the former command officer of Project AO Canada, an RCMP-led anti-terrorist probe that had a number of Ottawa Arab men, including Maher Arar, under surveillance,[59] testified at the Arar Inquiry, he confirmed that this document was an express invitation to use racial profiling.[60] And so, after September 11, the RCMP effectively warned all security officials that any young, educated, well dressed Arab or Muslim male living in Canada could be a terrorist and, therefore, must be investigated.

As a normative matter, most Canadians understand what is alleged when a claim of racial profiling is made and recognize that the practice is unjust and fundamentally wrong. Although there is no question that the policing of race is the product of both overt and systemic racism, we should not fear giving it a more precise identifying marker. Young appears concerned that "our choice of language"[61] has contributed to the resistance of the police to recognize the disparate treatment faced by racialized groups.[62] However, will labelling it as racist further the dialogue? Racial profiling is a term that focuses on the underlying conduct that gives rise to the differential treatment of racialized groups, rather than explicitly labelling an officer as a racist as the term "racist" does. It also focuses on institutional beliefs and norms, not on the individual officer.

To that extent, the phrase is consistent with the view of the Ontario Human Rights Commission's *Policy and Guidelines on Racism and Racial Discrimination* which states: "... except in the most obvious circumstances, such as where individuals clearly intend to engage in racist behaviour, it is preferable that actions rather than individuals be described as racist."[63] While the commission's position has come under attack as "soft" or as shifting responsibility away from the individual,[64] this approach may increase the likelihood of an open dialogue — something that is often missing when it comes to the issue of race and policing. For example, it allows reform-minded police officers like Kingston Police Chief

Bill Closs to undertake measures to address racism within his force and yet attempt to maintain morale and internal legitimacy by publicly stating that his officers are not racists. As he puts it: "I believe racial profiling exists. I believe biased policing exists. Because we're human, we all come into a police department with our own experiences and values and beliefs and I've learned that when police officers engage in racial profiling or biased policing, it can be intentional, unintentional or subconscious ... [but] I don't believe for a moment that I have racist officers."[65]

BEYOND DWB OR TWA

THE PROBLEM, OF COURSE, is that the practice is easier to define than apply. The depths of racial profiling extend beyond the archetypical cases of walking or driving while Black (DWB) or travelling while Arab (TWA). In defining racial profiling as I and others have, we attempt to distinguish between encounters based on stereotypes (caught by the definition) and stops based on reliable information or objectively suspicious behaviour that would lead a reasonable person to suspect that the individual is involved in criminal activity (not caught by the definition). What sometimes gets lost in the discussion of profiling is that stereotypes have some impact on the way officers interpret their environment.[66]

Psychologists call this reaction confirmatory bias.[67] It causes us to interpret behaviour within a preconceived set of expectations based on some identifiable characteristics of the actors involved. For example, there is nothing suspicious about being in an high-crime area, making eye contact, or talking on or possessing a cellphone or a pager, yet we routinely see the police testify that they relied on behaviour of this kind to justify stopping a racialized individual.[68] And so, even where an officer claims to be appropriately focusing on suspicious behaviour (the hallmark of good policing), it may be a racialized stereotype that is driving the apprehension of suspicion, and, where that happens, racial profiling has occurred. This sort of reaction suggests that what the police sometimes term an intuitive "sixth sense," or what one officer called his "Spidey" sense,[69] may often be racial profiling.

In the "war on terrorism," we have also seen innocent behaviour become suspicious because of guilt-by-association reasoning. As *New York Times* journalist Jeffrey Rosen pointed out:

> The evidence against most terrorism suspects arrested and prosecuted [in the United States] since Sept. 11 is circumstantial.... Critics have charged that this raises the constant danger of guilt by association or arrests based on innocent information taken out of context.... Almost all of the more than 1,200 citizens arrested based on circumstantial evidence after Sept. 11 turned out not to be terrorists.[70]

Rosen describes the ordeal of one Egyptian student named Abdallah Higazy. He was put in solitary confinement following the attack because FBI agents accused him of using a ground-to-air radio, found in his hotel room located near the World Trade Center, to transmit information to the terrorists. The charges were eventually withdrawn when another guest claimed ownership of the radio.[71]

In Canada, guilt-by-association reasoning appears to be one of the reasons that Maher Arar, a thirty-three-year-old Canadian father of two young children, was identified as a possible national security threat. On September 26, 2002, Arar planned to return home to Ottawa, where he worked as a computer technician, from a family vacation in Tunisia. He left early because of business. That night he was detained at JFK Airport in New York City. Apparently the Americans had him on an al-Qaeda "watch list."[72] Arar remained in New York until October 8, 2002, when he was flown to Jordan and then Damascus, Syria. According to Arar, he was placed in a cell about 1 metre wide and 2 metres long and brutally tortured until he confessed to having trained at a camp in Afghanistan.[73] On October 5, 2003, he was finally released and sent home, thanks largely to the efforts of his wife.[74] Since his return to Canada, he has steadfastly maintained that he has never been involved in terrorist activity.[75] Arar is not the only Canadian to be detained in a foreign country after September 11 and to claim to have been tortured.[76]

The interest in Arar appears to stem from his association with two of these other Canadians, Ahmad Abou El-Maati and Abdullah Almalki.[77] However, based on what we know, there does not appear to be any reason to believe that Arar's association with either of them was suspicious. Arar says that he hardly knew El-Maati, having "once bumped into Mr. El-Maati at a garage in Montreal." He had worked with Almalki's brother at high-tech firms in Ottawa and, because the two families had emigrated from Syria at about the same time, there was a casual relationship.[78] In addition, in 1997 Arar asked Almalki's brother to sign his lease, but he was unable to come and Abdullah came in his place. This lease was apparently shown to Arar by American officials when he was detained in New York before being flown to Syria.[79] Shirley Heafey, chair of the Commission for Public Complaints Against the RCMP, has used the Arar case to point out that "[t]he preventive nature of the *Anti-Terrorism Act* means the police must cast their net of suspicion widely. How they do it should concern us." She went on to observe: "We have heard ... that Mr. Arar came to the attention of the authorities because he had an apartment lease witnessed by another person who was under scrutiny. This is important because it means that a large number of people can get caught in the crosshairs of a preventive national security investigation."[80]

On February 4, 2004, an inquiry was called by then Deputy Prime Minister Anne McLellan.[81] Associate Chief Justice Dennis O'Connor of the Ontario Court of Appeal was appointed as commissioner. He was a natural choice, given his reputation for "speed and thoroughness, a man who is not intimidated by power, and man who has the common touch."[82] Three years earlier Justice O'Connor served as commissioner for the tainted-water Walkerton Inquiry. The fact-finding mission of the inquiry is to investigate Canada's role in Arar's being sent to and detained in Syria. In the summer of 2005 Justice O'Connor appointed Stephen Toope, a McGill law professor and current president of the Pierre Elliott

Trudeau Foundation, as a fact finder to investigate the treatment of Arar in Syria and the effects on him and his family. On October 27, 2005, the inquiry released a report from Professor Toope which concluded that Arar was, in fact, tortured while he was detained in Syria:

> When I compare information available from public sources with the cross-referenced testimony of Messrs. Almalki, Elmaati, and Nureddin, I conclude that the stories they tell are credible. I believe that they suffered severe physical and psychological trauma while in detention in Syria. Mr. Almalki was especially badly treated, and for an extended period. When I compare all of this information to the story told to me by Mr. Arar, I am convinced that his description of his treatment in Syria is accurate....
>
> I conclude that the treatment of Mr. Arar in Far Falestin constituted torture as understood in international law....
>
> ... The effects of that experience, and of consequent events and experiences in Canada, have been profoundly negative for Mr. Arar and his family. Although there have been few lasting physical effects, Mr. Arar's psychological state was seriously damaged and he remains fragile. His relationships with members of his immediate family have been significantly impaired. Economically, his family has been devastated.[83]

The inquiry also has a policy mission: to recommend an arm's-length review mechanism for the national security activities of the RCMP. We will return to the issue of accountability later in this book.

IT'S NOT JUST STOPS

RACIALIZED STEREOTYPES INFLUENCE NOT only who is stopped and questioned but also who is searched, arrested, subjected to police force, or ultimately detained in custody. In some cases the stereotype will lead the police to overreact because they have perceived the situation to be far more dangerous than it really is. We have seen this occur on a number of occasions in relation to the "war on terrorism," including the execution-style shooting of Jean Charles de Menezes, an innocent Brazilian man, in London following the July 7, 2005, subway bombings. Apparently Menezes was singled out because he lived in an apartment under surveillance and, according to the police, because he "had dark skin and Mongolian eyes."[84] Over the last few years we have seen two Canadian examples of overreaction in the war on terrorism which have the hallmarks of racial profiling.

PROJECT THREAD

In February 2003 Mohammad Khalid Jahangir applied for permanent residency status at the Canadian Embassy in Mexico City. The immigration officer reviewing his file became suspicious that this student had $40,000 in his bank account. She attempted to verify that he had attended the Ottawa Business College in Scarborough, Ontario. However, she hit a dead end and contacted the multijurisdictional Public Security and Anti-Terrorism Unit (PSAT).

The matter ultimately led to an investigation of the college and more than four hundred students linked to it. Apparently the school was being used fraudulently as a shell to assist foreign students in securing visas.[85] What led RCMP and Immigration Department investigators to think that as many as thirty-one South Asian men linked to the college were part of a terrorist cell? The following facts were provided in a document filed during the Immigration detention review hearings for those arrested in the sweeps of August 14, 2003: the men were of similar age; they had all, except for one, come from the Punjab province in Pakistan, a region the document claimed was "noted for Sunni extremism"; they resided in "clusters"; many were in the United States between May 2001 and January 2002; there were unexplained fires in their apartments; and there was an apparent interest in the Pickering nuclear power plant.[86]

With respect to the last allegation, one of the arrested men had been taking flying lessons that included a flight path over the power plant.[87] Two others had been questioned, in April 2002, after being seen outside the gates of the nuclear power plant in the early morning hours. They apparently wanted to go for a walk on the beach.[88] There were also vague allegations of an interest in the CN Tower and other buildings, including courts, airline schematics, indirect links to suspected terrorist groups, and access to materials that could be used to make explosives.[89]

While there was some documented behaviour that clearly warranted investigation, most notably the fires, flying lessons, and links to the Pickering plant, what occurred was a far cry from a fair and neutral investigation. Twenty-three men were swept up and arrested, even though only a few appeared to be linked to the suspicious behaviour.[90] They were all labelled terrorists, a "sleeper cell" for al-Qaeda.[91] And they were all subjected to preventative detention pursuant to new terrorism-related powers under the *Immigration and Refugee Protection Act*.[92]

Ultimately, the so-called terrorist link quickly evaporated, as none of the men were charged with terrorism offences.[93] What appears to have occurred was a rush to judgment based on nothing more than "slender threads."[94] Although an internal RCMP review of Project Thread concluded that the investigation had not been tainted by racial profiling,[95] a lingering suspicion remains that the fact that the men were Muslim and from Pakistan played a role in this rush to judgment. In commenting on the case, NDP leader Jack Layton noted:

> There is some serious explaining to do and a committee of Parliament should be taking this up.... If we don't nip this kind of activity in the bud, it simply swoops people up off the street with no good reason, leaves them with a tarnished reputation, traumatized and with major personal and family setbacks.[96]

The majority of the men have now been deported.

Taking Photos in the Montreal Subway

ON MAY 16, 2004, Shanake Seneviratne, a South Asian McGill University student, was taking photographs at a subway station in Montreal. He was doing research for three urban planning professors. He was spotted by two Montreal Transit officers, who questioned him and issued him a ticket for impeding the flow of traffic. The decision to question him was certainly reasonable in the circumstances. In light of the Madrid commuter train terrorist attacks two months earlier and the concern about "soft" targets such as transit systems, subway officials should have been watching for this kind of unusual behaviour, regardless of skin colour.[97] In addition, the police apparently had also recently received a threatening letter in relation to the subway.

But was what happened to Shanake reasonable, particularly after he had presumably provided them with an explanation that was easily verifiable? According to Shanake, the Montreal police arrived at the station, handcuffed him, and told him he was a threat to national security. He was driven to a northern operations centre, where he was handcuffed, photographed, interrogated, including information about his Sri Lankan background, and placed in a holding centre. An undercover RCMP officer was assisting the Montreal police. After six hours, he was eventually released.[98]

IT'S NOT JUST THE POLICE

WHILE THE FOCUS OF this book is on the use of racialized stereotypes in policing, manifestations of racial profiling have been documented in other contexts that employ measures related to security. These contexts include employment, retail stores or shopping malls, nightclubs, and schools.[99] It is important to think about the issue in other contexts because these instances make us aware of the pervasiveness and silence of the problem, the difficulty of detection, and the fact that the solution will not be found alone in police and law reform. Indeed, the more systemic the problem, the harder it will be to convince well-meaning individuals that a problem exists and to engender the necessary political and legal will for reform.

Shopping While Aboriginal

IN LATE NOVEMBER 2002 Roxanne Monkman, who is Aboriginal, was shopping for groceries at an Extra Foods store in Winnipeg with her young niece. When she got to the checkout counter, she was told by the cashier that she could not purchase a can of hair spray. Although the clerk did not provide any reason, she was likely thinking about proposed legislation that would permit the province to revoke a retail store's licence when they sold an intoxicating substance such as glue or solvents to anyone likely to use it as an intoxicant.[100] The problem, however, was that, other than her Aboriginality, there was no reason to believe that Monkman was about to use the hair spray for that purpose. The next day Monkman received an apology from the store's district manager, who said that the incident was "uncalled for" and "inappropriate." A store spokesperson told the media that it was "under pressure from the police department to handle the sale of these products carefully."[101]

Working While Muslim

MOHAMED ATTIAH WAS AN engineer at the Chalk River nuclear power plant near Ottawa. His contract was about to expire, but he had been told that he was going to be hired back. Less than two weeks after the terrorist attacks on September 11, Attiah was confronted in the parking lot of the plant by RCMP and CSIS officials. He was questioned for more than ninety minutes about, among other things, his religious beliefs and practices and whether he was a member of the Muslim Brotherhood—a group that merged with al-Qaeda in Afghanistan.[102] They also asked him about his association with the controversial imam Aly Hindy, who had worked with Attiah at Ontario Hydro in the 1980s.[103] When he returned to work, he discovered that his pass card did not operate and that he had been fired. The chief of security, who escorted him out of the building, told him he was a security risk. Attiah was eventually reinstated after filing a civil suit.[104]

Attending High School While Black

ON MAY 11, 2004, the Toronto District School Board's Task Force on Safe and Compassionate Schools issued a report calling for the repeal of Ontario's *Safe Schools Act*[105] or, alternatively, the collection of data on which students were being suspended or expelled.[106] The task force concluded that the Act's approach to school discipline, often referred to as a zero-tolerance policy, has had a disparate impact on minority students.[107] Six months earlier, the Ontario Human Rights Commission had come to a similar conclusion:

> [There is a] perception that children from ... [minority] groups may be stereotyped as "slow to learn" and aggressive, and so are considered to be the instigators of any conflict or problems at school. Behaviour that would likely be assumed to be harmless or just a "kid being a kid" if engaged by another child is seen as threatening if a racialized child is involved.
>
> Participants ... indicated that there may be assumptions drawn that children from their communities are involved in gang activities when they hang out with kids of the same background. And, another common concern was that when a racialized child is involved with an incident with a White child, his explanation is less likely to be believed and he is more likely to be punished or to be punished more severely.[108]

While stories of racial profiling were making headlines in the United States in the early to mid-1990s,[109] it would be almost a decade before the phenomenon became part of the mainstream discourse on policing in Canada. Chapter 2 documents the significant events and stories of the last four years that have served to expose the existence and nature of racial profiling in Canada. It is these stories that have placed profiling, at least momentarily, at the forefront of public discourse and that have revealed much of the harm caused by discriminatory policing.

Exposed

SINGLED OUT

THE CANADIAN MEDIA HAVE never been shy in talking about race. All too often, though, race talk in the media has not been positive. Rather, it has served only to perpetuate the many stereotypes surrounding race and crime.[1] By focusing on racialized suspects, identifying gangs by racial origin, and describing in sensational detail certain crimes involving racialized suspects, the media are one of the prime conveyors of the message that there is a link between race and crime. For example, in the summer of 2005, both the *Globe and Mail* and the *National Post* published two large-size photograph arrays of Toronto's twenty and ten "most-wanted" criminals.[2] The *National Post* published its story following the interim release of the Kingston Police study on racial profiling. The headline read, "The Truth About Racial Profiling." One of the commentaries pointed out that a majority of the most wanted were Black, in an apparent effort to convince readers that racial profiling is about disproportionate offending rates.[3]

PART ONE: UNDERSTANDING RACIAL PROFILING

This inflammatory exercise of journalistic prerogative failed to reflect on the fact that violent crimes make up a very small percentage of criminal activity and that the police are rarely thinking about the "most wanted" when they are patrolling the streets and conducting vehicle or pedestrian stops. Nor did the stories raise the possibility of systemic bias in the creation of the most-wanted lists. Indeed, federal prison data reveal just how misleading these lists and other statistically inaccurate stereotypes can be. In 2003, 69.8 percent of the offenders serving time in our federal prisons for sex, homicide, and robbery offences (i.e., the most dangerous offenders) were White. Blacks made up only 4.8 percent of homicide offenders, 5.1 percent of sex offenders, and 6.7 percent of robbery offenders.[4]

And so, other than the usual disclaimer that "of course, not all members of the community are criminals," which arguably serves to subtly reinforce the stereotype, the media often fail to reflect critically on issues surrounding race, crime, and policing. In 2002 one media outlet engaged in a critical look at systemic racism with a focus on the police. On October 19, 2002, readers of the *Toronto Star* woke up to a headline that read "Singled Out."[5] For the next week or so, the *Star* ran a series of articles which focused much-needed attention on the issue of racial profiling.[6] The newspaper explained that its purpose was to "to seek out the truth, to focus attention on practices and issues that need to be discussed and addressed.... [to] detail troubling facts surrounding minorities and police."[7]

The Toronto Star *Findings*

A LARGE PART OF the *Toronto Star* series focused on police data that had been obtained by the newspaper through a Freedom of Information request. Of particular interest were the traffic-stop statistics, as vehicle stops provide a low-visibility opportunity to investigate the driver and passengers for possible criminal activity. The data revealed that Blacks were disproportionately charged with "out of sight" traffic violations such as failing to update a driver's licence. Blacks constituted almost 34 percent of all drivers charged with such offences, even though they made up only about 8 percent of the city's population.[8] These statistics are entirely consistent with racial profiling, as it was clearly not behaviour that attracted the police investigation. In the criminal context, the *Star* also discovered differential treatment following an arrest. Blacks arrested for simple drug possession were more likely to be taken to the police station and detained, pending a bail hearing, than White suspects.[9] These data confirmed previous research.[10]

"Singled Out" also presented the lived experiences of many members of the Black community in Toronto.[11] As Toronto columnist Royson James pointed out in a column, "Ask your black colleague and he or she will share DWB stories.... They have the scars, mostly emotional but some physical ones as well, to prove it. They know that while a car symbolizes freedom to the young, it soon becomes a modern working reminder of enslavement."[12] The series included narratives about several incidents:

> I am a young black male. Recently I was sitting in my car with my girlfriend. There were other black males and females sitting on a nearby park bench having a meal. A police officer pulled up right in front of my car, high beams and all. The officer asked if I had any drugs or alcohol and do I partake of any such substances. When I said no, he took my driver's licence. When he realized that he had made a fool of himself, he then proceeded to the other black people. The white people in the park were invisible.[13]

> I'm black and have been pulled over 7 times in the past year. I have yet to receive a ticket. No speeding tickets, no lane violations, no sign infractions. I drive a 1995 Neon. Nothing fancy, but every time I'm pulled over, there's one that has just been reported stolen and I always fit the description, or it's just a routine stop. It seems that driving while black has become a crime.[14]

[I am a police officer.] About every six months, like clock-
work, I get pulled over just for being a black man driving.[15]

In one story, "Racism Was a Gun at His Head," David Mercury,
a former police officer, described his personal experiences with
racial profiling. In addition to repeated stops while off duty, Mercury had to endure a partner who referred to young Black men on
Yonge Street as "chimps."[16] Mercury also experienced one particularly traumatic incident. He was working as an undercover drug-
squad officer. He had just finished a successful arrest and was on
his way to the station to drop off the incriminating evidence. He
was speeding and caught the attention of two police who were
parked in a gas station. Before he knew it, he saw a .38-calibre
revolver aimed at his head. As he put it, "I don't normally swear,
but some expletives definitely came out of my mouth. Thank God
I was a cop and didn't panic and duck because they likely would
have assumed I was going for a weapon and started firing." While
the police may have been justified in stopping Mercury for speeding, he quite reasonably observed: "You can't convince me that
they pull over all speeders at gunpoint. They saw a black man in
a car going fast and they panicked." Mercury complained to Chief
Bill McCormick, but no action was taken.

The Backlash

DESPITE WINNING NUMEROUS AWARDS for outstanding journal-
ism,[17] "Singled Out" generated a tremendous backlash from the
police.[18] The police brass, the union, and members of the Police
Services Board all took the position that racial profiling was not
a problem.[19] The police also went on the offensive. Chief Fantino
hired Ed Harvey from the University of Toronto and prominent
criminal defence lawyer Alan Gold to review the *Star*'s interpretation of the police data.[20] Then, at a Toronto Police Services Board
meeting that had been advertised as an opportunity for the Black
community to express its profiling concerns, Gold and Harvey
proclaimed that the newspaper's conclusions were "bogus, bogus,

bogus" and based on "junk science."[21] The Toronto Police Association also launched an attack with an unprecedented \$2.7 billion
libel lawsuit filed against the *Toronto Star.* The basis for the civil action was, as association lawyer Tim Danson put it, for "[a]ccusing
the members of the Toronto Police Service of racism.... [W]earing
a uniform, for many, is now synonymous with racism and intoler-
ance."[22] The lawsuit was dismissed on summary judgment.[23]

The Lived Experiences of Black Police Officers

DURING THIS TURBULENT TIME, the public was unaware of
what Chief Fantino had learned from his Black officers on the
force. Fantino had asked four senior Black police officers, including Superintendent Keith Forde, now deputy chief of police, to
investigate how allegations of racial profiling were affecting Black
police officers. In October 2003 thirty-six Black (and two South
Asian) police officers met to discuss the issue. The officers agreed
that racial profiling was a problem and that "the stereotype that
black motorists in expensive cars and neighbourhoods receive extra attention was true."[24] One officer described how a colleague referred to Black citizens on bicycles as "chimps on bikes."[25] During
this informal focus-group session, the majority of officers reported
having experienced racial profiling first hand. Three officers reported that they had been stopped more than once in the course
of a week, while six officers reported having been stopped more
than twelve times in a year. Fantino was eventually informed of
the content of the meeting and, in a presentation to their fellow
officers, the senior Black officers began with the statement, "We
know racial profiling exists."[26]

The results of this meeting were publicly revealed following
an incident at a police gas pump on February 20, 2005. Inspector
David McLeod, a twenty-six-year veteran of the Toronto Police Service and one of the conveners of the focus group, was about to
fill his unmarked police vehicle at a gas pump at 42 Division in
Toronto. McLeod was in plain clothes. It was two o'clock on a Sun-

day afternoon. A more junior Asian officer was also at the pump. He approached McLeod, who was about to fill in the gas sign-out sheet, and demanded to see his identification. When McLeod asked whether he thought anyone would steal gas from a police station, the officer replied, "You never know."[27] He also indicated, in response to McLeod's question about whether he would have questioned him if he were White, that he would have asked for identification from anyone.[28] The officer believed that he was only following orders. Apparently, an order had been issued to "challenge or to ask people to identify themselves when they are on police property using police gas."[29] However, it was the middle of a Sunday afternoon. It would have taken a pretty brazen criminal to attempt to steal gas at that time with a police officer present. McLeod lodged a complaint that he had been racially profiled.

The complaint was informally resolved by Acting Deputy Chief Bill Blair, who had the officers directly address the issue at a meeting with other senior officers, including Keith Forde. The mediation appeared to work, as the junior officer broke down in tears when listening to McLeod's experiences with racism on the job. The meeting ended with a handshake. Blair later told the media he was satisfied that the incident was a misunderstanding.[30] Not long after, Blair was appointed Toronto's new police chief. Unlike his predecessor, Blair immediately admitted that racial profiling is a problem. As he put it: "I think racism and racial bias in policing is a problem. I do not deny the existence of racial profiling. As a matter of fact, if we deny its existence, how can we ever take the steps so it doesn't happen in our relationship with the public?"[31]

Paying the Price: The Ontario Human Rights
Commission's Racial Profiling Inquiry

ON DECEMBER 9, 2002, the Ontario Human Rights Commission announced it would conduct an inquiry into the effects of racial profiling. The *Toronto Star* series and the hostile police reaction that followed likely contributed to the commission's decision to investigate the harm caused by racial profiling. The commission received approximately 400 submissions about profiling.[32] One year later it released its report, entitled *Paying the Price: The Human Cost of Racial Profiling*.[33] In it, the commission began by recognizing that there is no longer any doubt that racial profiling is a real and serious problem in Ontario. It stated: "[P]revious inquiries have considered this and found that it does occur.... In addition to the various task forces, social scientists, criminologists and other academics have studied racial profiling ... these studies have consistently showed that law enforcement agents profile ... racial minorities."[34] Many of the commission's findings on the harm caused by racial profiling are documented throughout the book. This damage includes serious physical and psychological harm, the creation of a sense of injustice and mistrust of our institutions, alienation, and a diminished sense of citizenship.[35]

A TRIAL JUDGE'S FOUL ON A TORONTO RAPTOR

ON NOVEMBER 1, 1999, Dee Brown, a popular point guard for the Toronto Raptors, was driving home from a Halloween party in his brand new Ford Expedition on the Don Valley Parkway. Shortly after 12:45 A.M., Brown caught the attention of a police officer who was patrolling the area. He claimed that Brown's vehicle was speeding and had twice crossed the dividing lane. During the stop, the officer formed the opinion that Brown might be impaired and, when he failed a breathalyzer test, Brown was charged. At trial, Brown alleged that he was stopped because he was a young Black male driving an expensive vehicle. The trial judge disagreed. Brown appealed, and the case eventually found its way to the Ontario Court of Appeal.

As it would turn out, the landmark decision would be written by one of the longest-serving justices in the history of the Ontario Court of Appeal, Justice John Morden. It would be one of his last judgments. Justice Morden was first appointed to the Supreme Court of Ontario in 1973 at only thirty-nine years of age by Otto Lang, the federal minister of justice.[36] Five years later he was appointed to the Court of Appeal, where he remained until his retirement in 2003. He followed in the footsteps of his father, Ken Morden, who also served on the Court of Appeal. No one ever doubted that Justice Morden had the courage or the temperament to be an influential jurist. Indeed, on three occasions he refused to follow his father's judgments.[37] In Brown, Justice Morden began his judgment, much like the Ontario Human Rights Commission had begun its report, with a recognition that racial profiling is a social reality in Ontario.[38] He also recognized the systemic nature of profiling. As he put it: "The attitude underlying racial profiling is one that may be consciously or unconsciously held. That is, the police officer need not be an overt racist. His or her conduct may be based on subconscious racial stereotyping."[39]

At the appellate level, the case was less about whether Dee Brown had been profiled and more about whether the conduct of the trial judge during the trial would have led a reasonable member of the public to think he was biased. Justice Morden concluded that it did, as the trial had been marked by unwarranted interventions and statements that suggested an aversion to the racial-profiling allegation. What likely tipped the scales was the trial judge's suggestion to Brown in his reasons for sentence that "it would ... be nice if perhaps you might extend an apology to the officer because, I am satisfied, the allegations were completely unwarranted."[40] This request motivated Brown to appeal. As his lawyer, Steven Skurka, commented later: "I can't say that I ever would have received instructions from Dee Brown to pursue an appeal in the case if it wasn't for the request for an apology. That was the moment that ironically fed the momentum for the seminal judgment in Canada on racial profiling."[41]

Although no findings were made about whether Brown's allegations were true, the court noted that there was evidence capable of supporting such a finding.[42] Now living in Florida and his licence

prohibition already served, Brown decided not to go through another ordeal and to plead guilty.[43] *Brown* would not be the only case
where the intemperate conduct of a trial judge in a racial-profiling
case would be criticized by an appellate court. One year later the
Ontario Court of Appeal ordered a new trial in *R. v. Watson.*[44] As
the court observed: "We are satisfied ... that the combined effect of
the frequency and nature of the trial judge's interjections during
the conduct of the trial created the appearance of an unfair trial."[45]

KIRK JOHNSON'S HEAVYWEIGHT
FIGHT WITH THE HALIFAX POLICE

KIRK JOHNSON IS ONE of Canada's greatest heavyweight boxers
of all time. This standing, however, has not shielded him from
attracting unwarranted attention from the police. According to
Johnson, between 1993 and 1998 he was stopped by the Halifax
police twenty-eight times. He had had enough. In December 1998
he launched a formal complaint with the Nova Scotia Human
Rights Commission in relation to an incident that occurred earlier that year on Easter Sunday, when the police stopped, ticketed,
and towed his Texas-registered 1993 black Ford Mustang. Johnson was a passenger, with his long-time friend Earl Fraser in the
driver's seat. As Johnson put it in the complaint, "I feel that I was
pulled over and harassed ... because I am a black man."[46]

The hearing before a Board of Inquiry was chaired by Dalhousie
law professor Philip Girard. The officer accused of profiling offered what is now becoming a common defence in racial-profiling
allegations: "I couldn't see the race of the driver before I pulled
him over." In contrast to the officer's evidence, Fraser testified
that the officer had looked into their vehicle as he passed them
on the highway and then braked to let Fraser pass him. Johnson
provided a similar account at trial and in his police complaint not
long after the incident. As for why he pulled the car over, the officer testified that he was initially attracted to the vehicle because
it was a "nice sports car with tinted windows" and with a "Texas

licence." When the vehicle "seemed to be taking evasive action" (turning off the highway as he was following it and parking in a shopping plaza), he decided to stop it.[47]

The Board of Inquiry reserved its decision. Meanwhile, Johnson went back to work, trying to keep his No. 1 World Boxing Association contender status. On December 6, 2003, he fought Vitali Klitschko at Madison Square Garden in New York City for a shot at the heavyweight title. He lost in a second-round knockout that ended his chance to be the heavyweight champion of the world.[48] But two weeks later he received some personal good news. On December 22, 2003, the board concluded that Johnson was stopped, ticketed, and towed because he and Fraser were Black.[49] Professor Girard accepted Fraser's and Johnson's evidence that the officer had passed them, looked inside their vehicle, and seen that they were Black.[50] He was satisfied that the unusual driving of the officer, as described by Fraser, and his denial of seeing the vehicle's occupants, which he rejected, were sufficient to establish a *prima facie* case of discrimination. In human rights cases, once a *prima facie* case is made out, the burden falls on the other party—in this case, the officer and the Halifax Regional Police—to establish a justification for the differential treatment. While Girard concluded that there were some objectively legitimate reasons for following the car, he was satisfied that race had become an operative factor:

> [M]y finding that [the officer's] testimony on some key points was less than candid leads me to conclude that he has not succeeded in rebutting the *prima facie* case established by the complainant. I infer that once [the officer] was aware of the race of the occupants of the vehicle, this fact confirmed his suspicions that something was amiss. It was an operative element in his decision-making, although mixed in with other legitimate factors. I am not required to find whether this resulted from a conscious decision on his part or resulted from a subconscious stereotype. Either way it was still a violation of the Nova Scotia *Human Rights Act*.[51]

Johnson was awarded $10,000 in general damages, and, in addition, certain institutional remedies were also ordered. In particular, the Halifax Regional Police Service was required to hire two consultants to prepare a needs assessment of the service's "current policies and practices on anti-racism education and diversity training" and to propose an action plan for studying the impact of race on traffic stops.[52] One month after the board's decision, Johnson finally received an apology from the chief of police.[53] Perhaps encouraged by the actions taken by the Ontario and Nova Scotia human rights commissions, we are now seeing a greater willingness among victims to seek relief from their various provincial commissions. In Quebec, for example, one report suggests that there are between twenty and twenty-five racial-profiling cases currently before the Quebec Human Rights Commission.[54] Meanwhile, Johnson returned to the ring and, in July 2004, he beat Gilbert Martinez, winning with an eight-round technical knockout. He demonstrated his perseverance, fighting the last six rounds with a broken right hand.[55]

NEIL STONECHILD AND STARLIGHT TOURS

IN THE EARLY MORNING hours of November 25, 1990, seventeen-year-old Neil Stonechild, an accomplished wrestler and painter, took his last breath on a cold winter night in the outskirts of Saskatoon. The temperature had reached –28C, and Stonechild was partially clothed with only one shoe and a light jacket. He was found four days later with marks across his nose and wrist, the latter being consistent with the use of handcuffs.[56] Earlier that night, Jason Roy had seen him bleeding and screaming for help in a police cruiser. On February 20, 2003, Saskatchewan justice minister Eric Cline ordered an inquiry into his death. On September 16, 2004, Justice David Wright released his report, following a lengthy inquiry. He concluded that Stonechild, who was Aboriginal, had been in the custody of two Saskatoon police officers the night he had died, that Roy had seen him calling for help, and that there had been sufficient time for the officers to drive Stonechild out of town between two recorded dispatches they responded to that night.[57] Despite these findings, no criminal charges were laid against the officers. They were dismissed from the force after the release of Wright's report and have appealed that decision.[58]

On January 28, 2000, two police officers arrested Darrel Night, who is Aboriginal, for causing a disturbance. They drove him to a remote area on the outskirts of the City of Saskatoon and left him to walk back. It was 5:40 A.M., and the temperature was between −22 and −25C. Night was dressed in a lined denim jacket, shirt, blue jeans, and running shoes. He was without long underwear, gloves, hat, or scarf. After walking for 15 to 20 minutes, Night was able to make it to safety. Following a trial, the officers were convicted of forcible confinement.[59] On sentencing, the defence lawyers requested a traditional Aboriginal form of sentencing for the officers. As the trial judge mildly put it, "Notwithstanding that most of the community has been affected by allegations of racism and feelings of mistrust, the accused, in a somewhat surprising and ironical approach, now request a sentencing circle."[60] The trial judge refused to accede to the request and sentenced the officers to eight months' imprisonment.[61]

Within days of Night's ordeal, two Aboriginal men (Rodney Naistus and Lawrence Wegner) were found frozen to death in a southwest industrial area of Saskatoon near the Queen Elizabeth power station, not far from where Night testified he had been dumped.[62] Naistus was found on January 29, 1990, and Wegner on February 3, 2000.[63] Both men were missing items of clothing: Naistus, his shirt, and Wegner, his shoes.[64] An RCMP task-force investigation determined that no criminal charges were warranted. Two coroner's inquests were also unable to reach a conclusion about how Naistus and Wegner died other than that the cause of death was hypothermia.[65] However, the Wegner inquest had heard evidence from four witnesses that they had seen Wegner, or an Aboriginal man who looked like him, in the back of a police cruiser the night he died.[66]

These cases do not appear to be aberrations.[67] In Saskatchewan the practice of targeting Aboriginals and exiling them in the outskirts of town is known as "starlight tours."[68] In British Columbia the practice is known as "breaching."[69] In its 2001 report Amnesty International identified the practice of abandoning Aboriginals as a human rights concern for Canada.[70] At the Stonechild Inquiry, Justice Wright heard evidence that it was not uncommon for the police to "drop off" arrested individuals in so-called safe places. He also heard of three incidents of abandonment, including a 1976 case involving an Aboriginal woman.[71] In 2004 the CBC aired a documentary entitled *Two Worlds Colliding*, by Saskatoon Cree filmmaker Tasha Hubbard, which examined the "issue of police dropping troublemakers outside of the city instead of making an arrest."[72]

Since 1991, Aboriginal task forces, public inquiries, and commentators have concluded and recognized that Aboriginal communities are over-policed.[73] For example, quoting from Tim Quigley, a law professor at the University of Saskatchewan, the Task Force on the Criminal Justice System and Its Impact on the Indian and Metis People of Alberta noted: "Police in cities tend to patrol bars where Native people congregate, rather than private clubs frequented by businessmen. Remote Native communities, by comparison with largely White communities, tend to have more policing."[74] Similarly, the Manitoba Aboriginal Justice Inquiry observed:

> Complaints of over-policing focus on the perception that Aboriginal people are singled out for enforcement action and subjected to stereotyping by police forces. Many who appeared before us complained about being stopped on the street or on a country road and questioned about their activities.[75]

JUDICIAL FINDINGS OF RACIAL PROFILING IN TORONTO AND MONTREAL

In 2004 and 2005 two trial courts in Toronto and Montreal concluded that the police had improperly used race in stopping two young Black men. A few years earlier, Justice Brian Trafford had come to a similar conclusion in another Toronto case, and it is with this example that we begin our judicial history of successful racial-profiling cases. Justice Trafford is no stranger to confronting difficult questions of systemic racism and policing.[76] In 1993 he was the lead prosecutor in the prosecution of a White police officer charged with criminal negligence causing bodily harm and related offences in the shooting of Royan Bagnaut, a young Black male in downtown Toronto. On December 3, 1991, the officer was pursuing Bagnaut, who had purportedly snatched a woman's purse at knifepoint. The officer repeatedly fired at him, striking him in the arm and chest. He later claimed that he thought Bagnaut had a gun, though no gun was ever found. A hunting knife was, however, discovered in the lining of Bagnaut's jacket.[77]

At trial, one of the prosecutors on Trafford's team argued a motion to prevent the officer's defence lawyer from striking prospective jurors from the jury simply because of the colour of their skin. These challenges, known as peremptory challenges, allow defence lawyers to remove a prospective juror for any reason and without having to account for their decision.[78] The Crown argued that using peremptory challenges in a discriminatory fashion violated the right to equality guaranteed in section 15(1) of the *Charter*. The trial judge refused to restrict the defence's use of its challenges. Justice Bruce Hawkins held that "it is fanciful to suggest that in the selection of a jury ... [the accused] doffs his adversarial role and joins with the Crown in some sort of joint and concerted effort to empanel an independent and impartial tribunal."[79] At trial, the defence exercised seven of his allotted twelve challenges. Four of the seven challenges were used to exclude racialized jurors, including at least one Black juror, from the jury box. The jury that ultimately tried the case consisted of eleven White jurors and one Asian juror.[80] Like most police officers charged with using deadly force, the officer was acquitted.[81]

As a trial judge, Justice Trafford presided over the emotionally and racially charged "Just Desserts" trial in which three Black men were charged in the shooting death of Georgina Leimonis.[82] In that case, he held that the Crown (and defence) would not be permitted to use peremptory challenges in a discriminatory fashion.[83] Finally, Justice Trafford also heard the first level of appeal in the Dee Brown case and, like the Court of Appeal, concluded that the trial judge's conduct had risen to the level of apprehended bias.[84] It was no surprise, then, that with this track record he would become one of the first judges in Canada to make a finding of racial profiling.

In the early evening of November 19, 1998, Dwayne Peck and his friends were on their way to shop at the World of Shoes in the Eaton Centre in downtown Toronto. They had come from Brampton and parked nearby. They walked through O'Keefe Lane, located near the intersection of Dundas and Yonge streets. The laneway was under police surveillance because of the number of incidents of drug trafficking that apparently take place there. Peck was stopped, and the police discovered a large piece of crack cocaine. However, there was nothing objectively suspicious about his behaviour which warranted the police stop. Consequently, Justice Trafford was satisfied that he attracted the attention of the police simply because of "[s]tereotypical assumptions linking young black men and the illegal use of narcotics."[85] The officer had attempted to justify his decision to stop Peck based on what he claimed was suspicious behaviour, but Justice Trafford concluded that this evidence had been fabricated.[86] In excluding the evidence because of the officer's unconstitutional conduct, Justice Trafford held that "[t]he inherent worth and dignity of all people regardless of their race or ethnic origin must be respected by the police at all times during the investigation of even the most heinous crimes."[87]

In cases such as *Peck*, the police and others often point to the fact that contraband was found, as if to suggest that the officer's suspicions were warranted or, alternatively, that at least drugs or guns were removed from the street. These *ex post facto* justifications miss the bigger picture. Cases where police misconduct results in a drug seizure are isolated occurrences. If the police had no objective basis to stop Peck, they likely had no basis to stop many other young Black men they encountered. Accused like Peck are, in essence, the surrogate litigants for all the innocent individuals who either cannot afford to pursue civil remedies or who, as a result of experiencing racially biased policing, have lost faith in the ability of the system to adjudicate their claims fairly. As one lawyer observed after successfully convincing a court that her client had been racially profiled, "someone caught fleeing with drugs and scales in his possession might not be the most sympathetic victim of human rights abuse.... The other people who are profiled and tackled and searched and nothing is found on them don't go to court."[88]

Peck marked the second judicial finding of racial profiling in Canada. Four years earlier, in *R. v. Chung*, two Ontario Provincial Police officers in Sault Ste. Marie targeted the accused as a cigarette smuggler because he was Asian. As the trial judge concluded in his reasons, "[one of the officers] indicated unabashedly that Asians were a target group because they were suspected of being smugglers."[89] Since *Peck*, there have been four additional judicial or tribunal findings of racial profiling, bringing the total to six in Canada.[90] Two of these six cases included *Khan* (2004) and *Campbell* (2005).

Kevin Khan

KEVIN KHAN WAS A successful businessman. Although only twenty-six years old, he bought, refurbished, and sold condominium units when he was not teaching high school. He also had an interest in a hair salon. Just after noon on October 22, 2001, Khan picked up his 2000 Mercedes CLK320 from his brother, who had used it over the weekend. He had an appointment to meet with someone who was interested in purchasing one of his condominium units. When two police officers, who were on routine patrol, saw Khan in his Mercedes, they decided to run a Canadian Police Information Computer (CPIC) check on his licence plate. They allegedly did so because they found his conduct at an intersection "peculiar." This conduct included letting the officers proceed through, even though Khan had the right of way. The check revealed nothing out of the ordinary, but the officers decided to stop Khan because he was now allegedly driving in an erratic fashion. According to the officers, as they approached the vehicle, they saw Khan's right hand extended towards the glove box and his left hand trying to push what looked like a garbage bag under the driver's seat. They became concerned that he might have a gun, and one of the officers pulled him from the vehicle. As he did so, he detected a strong odour of cocaine. The officer looked inside the garbage bag and discovered a kilogram of cocaine with a street value of $100,000.

Khan testified to a very different version of events. After the stop, the officers approached his car and asked for his licence and registration, both of which he provided. They went back to the cruiser and returned, advising Khan that his licence was suspended. As Khan was using his cell phone to find someone to come and pick up his car, the officers were searching it. The next thing he knew, he was under arrest. Khan testified that he was unaware of the presence of drugs. Apparently his brother, who had used the car all weekend, had a drug-related criminal record. Forensic testing found none of Khan's fingerprints on the bags containing the drugs.

The trial judge, Justice Anne Molloy, was highly suspicious about the police officer's claim to being hit with a strong odour of cocaine. In order to test it, she had the bag of cocaine put on her dais at her feet. As she explained in her reasons, the odour "certainly did not come 'flying out' and it is difficult to believe that even the most sensitive of human noses would have smelled it to the extent described by [the officer]."[91] This observation no doubt played some small role in Justice Molloy's rejection of the officers' evidence. Based on the documentary evidence and her assessment of credibility, she concluded that Khan's testimony had the ring of truth. As she put it: "[T]he officers involved in this case fabricated significant aspects of their evidence.... Why did they single out Mr. Khan on Marlee Avenue[?] ... Because he was a young black male driving an expensive Mercedes.... Mr. Khan was targeted for this stop because of racial profiling."[92] With this finding, the Crown's case folded.

Justice Molloy went further than she had to because she felt that Khan was entitled to have his name cleared. She concluded that, based on his testimony, the absence of his fingerprints, and his brother's drug involvement, he did not know about the drugs in his car. Khan, who had to spend eleven days in custody before being released on bail, has launched a $3 million civil suit against the two officers and former police chief Julian Fantino.[93] Following this decision, drug charges were stayed in another 2001 incident involving Sheldon Jackson. Jackson, who was driving a BMW at the time he was stopped, alleged that he, too, had been racially profiled by the same two officers.[94]

Alexer Campbell

ON A SPRING NIGHT in 2004, Alexer Campbell caught the attention of two police officers as they were patrolling an area near downtown Montreal. He was a young Black male and, according to the officers, was leaning forward in a taxi as they drove by as if to avoid being seen. They found this behaviour suspicious. A few metres later, Campbell exited the taxi and walked quickly down the street, although he testified that he was walking normally. This turn of events confirmed the officers' suspicions that something was out of the ordinary, and they moved in to get a better look. At this point, one of the officers recognized Campbell from a previous arrest and remembered having been told that he had a curfew of 10 P.M. The officers claimed that only then did they see he was Black, a claim ultimately rejected by the trial judge. When one of the officers called out after him, he started to run. Eventually the officers caught up to him and arrested him for breach of recognizance. A search revealed a small quantity of marijuana. The police also later claimed to have found crack cocaine under the seat of their cruiser.

Campbell's trial judge was Justice Juanita Westmoreland-Traoré, one of only a handful of Black judges in Canada and the only Black judge in Quebec. Before her appointment to the bench in 1999, Justice Westmoreland-Traoré had a distinguished legal career. It included appointments as the president of the Quebec Council on Cultural Communities and Immigration, as Ontario's commissioner of employment equity, and as a commissioner with the Canadian Human Rights Commission.[95] She also served as dean of the Faculty of Law at the University of Windsor from July 1996 to April 1999.[96] In 2005 she was awarded the 2005 Touchstone Award by the Canadian Bar Association for her outstanding efforts in promoting equality in the profession.[97]

After conducting a thorough review of the racial-profiling phenomenon and the relevant jurisprudence, Justice Westmoreland-Traoré concluded that the officers had singled out Campbell that night because he was Black and likely fit their stereotypical profile of a drug dealer. As for his furtive action, she noted that "[i]n the context of a minority person, his reflex to move away from the police does not necessarily infer that he had committed an offence."[98] Campbell served to highlight the problem of racial profiling in Montreal. As Fo Niemi of the Centre for Research-Action on Race Relations has noted, his organization receives three complaints a week from young Black men, Latinos, South and Southeast Asians, as well as Muslims.[99]

* * *

THESE FIRST TWO CHAPTERS have explored the meaning and exposure of racial profiling and identified some of its manifesta-

tions in policing and other contexts. This overview was not difficult to compile. We seem to have reached a consensus in Canada
as to what profiling is, and, generally speaking, we agree that it is
wrong.[100] For example, there was a swift and almost uniform con-
demnation by the police chief, public officials, and commentators
alike of the suggestion by Toronto councillor Michael Thompson
in the summer of 2005 that the police should use racial profiling to help solve the problem of gun violence.[101] But that response
raises the question as to why there has not been the same reaction
to the persistent and compelling complaints from the affected
communities. Why are we not seeing racial profiling when it occurs and demanding that our elected officials take the appropriate
action? Why do we appear so willing to treat it as a problem of the
"bad apples" rather than as a systemic problem?

A number of possible explanations come to mind. There seems
to be a pervasive myth in Canada that racism is not a problem
and that, thanks in large part to our official ideology of multiculturalism, we are far more tolerant and colour-blind than our
neighbours to the south.[102] Indeed, in commenting on racism in
this country, Prime Minister Paul Martin once referred to those
who are responsible for it as "un-Canadian."[103] This myth is further perpetuated by our historical ignorance or amnesia. Selected
historical moments of Canadian tolerance become frozen in
time, allowing us to conveniently forget hundreds of years of racist practices throughout the country.[104] But, as we will see in the
next chapter, there is a long history of racial profiling in Canada.
There are also other powerful assumptions working to blind us
from what is really happening on our streets. Chapter 3 critically
evaluates these assumptions, which include arguments that differential police scrutiny is based not on racism but on criminal
profiling and differential offending rates.

Of course, it is possible that there is a lack of recognition and
of political and moral will to address the problem because there
is, simply, no systemic problem. However, to date, no one has ever
presented a single piece of evidence to suggest that this assertion

has any factual validity. Indeed, all the social science and experiential evidence we have supports just the opposite conclusion. As we will see later in the book, this evidence confirms not only that there is differential policing of Whites and Blacks in Canada's largest city, for example, but that it is based on skin colour, not criminal behaviour.

[3]

Adjusting Our Lens

IT WAS SHORTLY AFTER II P.M., on April 8, 1967, when the police were called to the Old Stope Hotel in Yellowknife. In the hotel lobby, they found Joseph Drybones, a forty-year-old trapper, passed out.[1] They arrested and charged him with "being an Indian" who was "unlawfully intoxicated off a reserve, contrary to s. 94(b) of the *Indian Act*."[2] This section of the Act singled out Aboriginals for disproportionate criminal justice surveillance. While it was, and still is, a provincial offence to be intoxicated in a public place in Canada,[3] section 94(b) made it an offence for Aboriginals to be intoxicated in any private location off the reserve, including their homes. Section 94 also imposed a more severe sentencing scheme than the provincial legislation outlawing public intoxication. Under the Northwest Territories Liquor Ordinance, the maximum term of imprisonment was thirty days. There was no minimum fine.[4] Section 94, in contrast, imposed a mandatory minimum fine of $10, and three months imprisonment could also be imposed.

Drybones, who did not speak English, initially pleaded guilty before a magistrate. He was ordered to pay the minimum fine of

$10 plus costs and, in case of default, sentenced to three days in jail. When reviewing a list of convictions from the lower court, Mary Driscoll, a legal secretary for Justice William G. Morrow of the Northwest Territorial Court, was concerned that Drybones had been convicted of an "off the reserve" offence at a time when there were no reserves in the Northwest Territories. When she pointed this discrepancy out to Justice Morrow, he appointed Bruce Purdy to file an appeal. Justice Morrow had, in his days as a lawyer, convinced another judge that it was impossible to convict in these circumstances.[5] His familiarity with the issue was only part of the twist of fate that would ultimately lead to one of the most important equality decisions ever handed down by the Supreme Court of Canada.

Justice Morrow was a jurist who was willing to take an active role in using the law to rectify injustices.[6] He was also particularly sensitive to the impact of the criminal justice system on Aboriginals. For example, in March 1975, when he delivered the George M. Duck Lecture, a prestigious annual lecture at the University of Windsor Law School, he talked about the unique challenges of sentencing Aboriginal offenders:

> I think that in the Northwest Territories, more than in any other part of Canada, I have a tougher problem than most trial judges, because I am dealing with more than just the normal sentencing problems. I am dealing perhaps with the clash of social cultures.... I think I have a heavier burden than most trial judges in an attempt to hit the proper sentence, so that the impact of the culture that is taking over ... from the south is not too harsh.[7]

Twenty-one years later, Parliament recognized the challenges that Justice Morrow spoke about and amended the *Criminal Code* to require trial judges to consider all reasonable alternatives to imprisonment and, in doing so, to pay particular attention to the circumstances of Aboriginal offenders.[8]

Justice Morrow allowed Drybones to change his plea to "not guilty" because he was not satisfied that Drybones had appreciated the consequences of his original guilty plea.[9] At the new trial, Purdy raised the "off the reserve" issue. However, he also argued that section 94(b) was discriminatory under section 1(b) of the *Canadian Bill of Rights*, which had been enacted by Parliament in 1960.[10] In his memoirs, Justice Morrow wrote that he was initially surprised with this alternative argument but that "[t]he more I examined it, the more I was intrigued with the ... argument.... In the end, I decided that the lack of reserve was of no consequence."[11] And so, upon reflection, he concluded that section 94(b) did indeed violate the equality guarantee in the *Bill of Rights* because of the differential treatment accorded Aboriginals.[12] In doing so, he refused to apply a precedent from the British Columbia Court of Appeal which had come to the opposite conclusion.[13]

The case eventually made its way to the Supreme Court of Canada. On November 20, 1969, the Court upheld Justice Morrow's decision by a vote of 6 to 3. Justice Ritchie, for the majority, rejected the argument that an individual's right to equality before the law is protected "so long as all the other members [of the claimant's group] are being discriminated against in the same way."[14] Instead, he held that "an individual is denied equality before the law if it is made an offence punishable at law, on account of his race, for him to do something which his fellow Canadians are free to do without having committed any offence or having been made subject to penalty."[15] In many respects, *Drybones* was Canada's symbolic *Brown v. Board of Education*, the United States Supreme Court decision that overruled "separate but equal" racial segregation in American schools.[16] In his concurring opinion in *Drybones*, Justice Hall further elaborated on the majority's recognition that separate is not equal:

> The social situations in *Brown v. Board of Education* and in the instant case are, of course, very different, but the basic philosophic concept is the same. The Canadian Bill of Rights

is not fulfilled if it merely equates Indians with Indians in terms of equality before the law, but can have validity and meaning only when ... it is seen to repudiate discrimination in every law of Canada by reason of race, national origin, colour, religion or sex in respect of the human rights and fundamental freedoms ... in whatever way that discrimination may manifest itself not only as between Indian and Indian but as between all Canadians whether Indian or non-Indian.[17]

THE HISTORICAL RACIALIZATION OF CRIME

DRYBONES REMINDS US THAT racial profiling has a long history in Canadian criminal law. One of the myths surrounding the practice is that it is a relatively recent phenomenon that emerged, as we will see, out of the criminal-profiling phenomenon and, in particular, after race was added to the profile of the drug courier in the "war on drugs."[18] This myth has helped to give investigative legitimacy to a discriminatory practice. However, racialized individuals have been constructed as criminals and in need of policing as long as organized police forces have been around.[19] The North-West Mounted Police, the predecessor to the Royal Canadian Mounted Police (RCMP), was used, for example, to further the colonization of Aboriginal peoples in this country:

The NWMP was used to seize resource-rich Metis land and transfer control and effective ownership to the federal government. This semi-military police force was created to control Metis resistence as well as potential native allies farther west who also revolted against the forcible take-over of their land by the Canadian government. The federal government feared a war waged by the Métis and natives against white settlers. The belief was that the NWMP would civilize the wild, barbaric, heathen Indians. The mission was violently and enthusiastically carried out by its racist officers.[20]

In one of the most thorough looks at historical discrimination in Canada's criminal justice system, sociologist Clayton Mosher discovered that, at the turn of the century, Asians were "portrayed as being disproportionately involved in drug and public-order crimes,"[21] while Blacks were described as "prone to involvement in drug and other public-order offences such as gambling and prostitution."[22] Blacks were also perceived to be "violent and more likely to be involved in more serious forms of crime than the Chinese, and thus posed a greater threat."[23] Consequently, one of the motivating factors behind the criminalization of opium in Canada in 1908,[24] cocaine and morphine in 1911,[25] and cannabis in 1923[26] was to enable the policing of these racialized communities by the RCMP.[27] Indeed, RCMP data from 1924 to 1936 reveal that Chinese made up 60 percent of narcotics arrest in Canada.[28]

In other historical incidents of racial profiling, crime and national security threats were linked to particular racialized groups. In 1942 one of the worst incidents of racial profiling occurred when Japanese living in Canada were classified as traitors and as security threats.[29] Approximately 22,000 men, women, and children of Japanese ancestry were designated as "enemy aliens" and uprooted from their homes in British Columbia.[30] The majority were forced to live in settlement camps in the interior regions of British Columbia, camps that some have argued had all the trappings of a "prison complex."[31] Others were exiled to the Prairies or placed in formal internment camps in Ontario. It was not until April 1, 1949, that the last restriction preventing Japanese Canadians from returning to the West Coast was removed.[32] By that time, however, approximately 4,000 had been forcibly deported.[33] While Italians and Germans also faced internment during this time, only a small minority were affected, as compared to an entire group of Japanese.[34] As political scientist Reg Whitaker of York University has written, "[t]he Canadian state, along with its allies, constructed a public image of the enemy which, in the case of Japan, relied far more on overt and crude racism than was ever employed against the white, albeit ideologically repugnant, fascist states of Europe."[35]

In the 1960s and 1970s the RCMP became concerned over the possibility that the Black Panther Party, a revolutionary American civil rights group, might bring violence to Nova Scotia. In response, the RCMP began to target and spy on the activities of Black civil rights leaders in Halifax. In 1994 Canada discovered what its national police had been doing. With the support of his bureau chief, Dean Beeby, Canadian Press Halifax reporter Alan Jeffers made an Access to Information request after hearing repeated stories from the Black community about RCMP surveillance. The initial request was refused, but Canadian Press got its story when Canada's information commissioner intervened.

The request produced a 2,000-page file on the Black community in Nova Scotia. One RCMP report, in reference to a Black settlement in Guysborough County, stated: "[T]he men work long enough to make money for another liquor binge," and "it may be borne in mind that Negro women are prolific child-bearers." Another report referred to the followers of the Black Panther movement in Halifax as "illiterate, semi-illiterate and hoodlums." A further report stated that "there are a few colored youths in this area who like to think of themselves as Black Panthers. This group, at the most 10 people, occasionally roll a drunk, etc. I suppose they feel it is more flattering to be referred to as Panthers than as thieves."[36] These racist statements reveal that race was the driving force behind the Nova Scotia surveillance.[37]

The spying on the Black community did not end in the 1970s. In 1989 the Toronto police began a probe of Black "activists" and so-called radical groups following a community protest over the shooting of Michael "Wade" Lawson, an unarmed Black teenager.[38] Lawson was shot and killed by two police officers on December 8, 1988. The officers fired six times at the car, hitting Lawson in the back of the head. Both officers were eventually acquitted.[39] Lawson's mother was one of eighteen individuals placed under investigation. The officer in charge of the probe, who is Black, offered the following justification: "[T]hese groups were unknown to police and we had a look to see ... whether or not they were supported by criminal activity.... Were they a threat to the community? Were these groups terrorist groups?"⁴⁰ In addition to the Urban Alliance on Race Relations, other groups investigated included the National Black Coalition of Canada, the Coalition of Concerned Community Groups, the Coalition of Visible Minority Women, the Anti-Apartheid Coalition of Toronto, and the National Council of Jamaicans.

What this historical snapshot reveals is that, when we think about why and to what extent certain racialized groups are subjected to over-policing, we need to acknowledge that this discrimination has always been the case.[41] As Charles Smith, equity adviser for the Canadian Bar Association, has pointed out, "Racialized law enforcement has been an extraordinarily important tool in preserving social power, and over the last 150 years police forces have been a central resource to social control."[42]

THE FALSE ASSUMPTIONS THAT FUEL THE POLICING OF RACE

IN ADDITION TO THE myth that racial profiling is a recent phenomenon, a number of other powerful assumptions fuel the increased surveillance of racialized individuals in Canada. These assumptions have given racial profiling its systemic character and have shielded many people from recognizing that what is occurring on our streets is not good and fair policing but, rather, the exercise of a discriminatory practice that causes significant harm. The first assumption is that heightened scrutiny of racialized individuals can be explained, generally speaking, because those targeted fit the profile of the usual offender (e.g., the drug courier). This criminal profile is one, the argument goes, which has been generated by the Criminal Intelligence Service Canada, for example, or one of its provincial counterparts (as discussed in chapter 1), and which sometimes includes race or ethnicity as one of a number of physical identifiers.[43] A second related assumption argues that differential offending rates explain differential enforcement. A third assumption holds that racial profiling is necessary to fight the war on terrorism. Those who advocate this position argue that, although a form of racial discrimination, it is, nevertheless, a reasonable one.[44] Do these assumptions stand up to closer scrutiny?

Race and Criminal Profiles

NORM GARDNER, THE FORMER chair of the Toronto Police Services Board, once observed that the "[p]olice deal with criminal profiling. From my perspective, if there is a description of individuals who have been involved in ... *certain types of crime*, you would look at those people who would be suspects."[45] Similarly, Thomas Gabor, a criminology professor at the University of Ottawa, asks in relation to what he calls "informed criminal profiling," "If most armed robbers or drug dealers in an area are of a certain ethnicity, should this knowledge be ignored?"[46]

What is criminal profiling? Criminal profiling is a method of investigation that many believe originated in the 1880s, when two British physicians, George Phillips and Thomas Bond, attempted to help the police track the infamous Jack the Ripper. It eventually became institutionalized in the United States in 1974, when the Federal Bureau of Investigations created its Behavioral Science Unit.[47] Over the last thirty years, policing has come to rely on behavioural sciences such as psychology or criminology in its effort to create a criminal profile of violent, usually serial, offenders. Criminal profiling has become sensationalized in such movies as *The Silence of the Lambs* and in television series such as *The Profiler.*

Generally speaking, criminal profiling consists of "the analysis of a crime scene and other details about a crime, in conjunction with the analyst's understanding of cases of a similar nature, for the purpose of inferring the motivation for the offence and producing a description of the type of person likely to be responsible for its commission."[48] On June 17, 2005, for example, the RCMP released the following profile of a serial killer who has killed at least twelve sex-trade workers in the Edmonton area.[49] It was created by the RCMP's Behavioural Sciences Branch in Ottawa in the hope that it would generate some leads:

- The person or persons responsible drives a truck, a van, or a sport utility vehicle as opposed to a car, and that he is comfortable driving in rural areas.
- The vehicle will be suitably maintained and likely has a significant amount of mileage. This does not necessarily mean that it is exceptionally clean but that it is a reliable vehicle. The vehicle may be used for work and outdoor activities such as hunting, fishing, or farming.
- [The person m]ay participate in outdoor activities such as hunting, fishing, camping, etc.
- There is likely a past or present connection to the areas south of Edmonton, perhaps Leduc, Camrose, New Sarepta, or the surrounding communities. He may have lived or worked in those areas, has family or friends in the area, or has used the area for recreational purposes.
- The person or persons responsible may have periodically cleaned the interior and exterior of his vehicle, perhaps at times that are unusual for this particular individual.[50]

Given the tactical and resource challenges facing the police in solving certain kinds of crimes, particularly those that are prevalent or difficult to solve, it is not surprising that we have seen a proliferation of criminal profiling. Profiles have been created for the usual arsonist,[51] smuggler,[52] drug courier,[53] drug importer,[54] and sex abuser.[55] It did not take long for race, ethnicity, or nationality to become part of the profile, particularly in the context of the drug courier profile.

In *R. v. Marin*,[56] the accused was detained at Pearson International Airport because he was of Romanian descent, returning from Marguerita Island. Three weeks earlier, Customs officers had intercepted cocaine smugglers of similar descent returning from

Venezuela. When they saw five Romanian names on the accused's flight, the individuals were placed on a "look-out" list. At secondary inspection, Marin also fit other so-called indicators of the importer profile (e.g., purchasing tickets in cash shortly before departure and talking quickly). Consequently, he was strip searched, asked to provide a urine sample, and compelled to have a bowel movement (known as a "bedpan vigil"). The vigil produced a number of cocaine pellets that he had swallowed. In upholding the targeting, Justice Belleghem held that "[t]he ethnic issue here is objective, it is not subjective. It is based on the experience of the Customs officials three weeks earlier."[57] *Marin* gives us an insight into what fuels profiling and, in particular, racial profiling—a belief that an objective assessment can be made about criminal or terrorist conduct from the conduct of others who share similar characteristics. The perception that this assessment is somehow objective also assists us in understanding why those who profile in this fashion do not think of themselves as doing anything improper.

Experience has taught us, however, that criminal profiles are inherently unreliable.[58] There are probably thousands, if not tens of thousands, of men in western Canada who fit the RCMP profile of the Edmonton killer. Guy Paul Morin, who was wrongfully convicted in the killing of Christine Jessop, was arrested following a profile prepared by the FBI Behavioral Science Unit. Ironically, as Justice Kaufman concluded in his report into the conviction, "though features of the profile did parallel Guy Paul Morin, it could not reasonably be said that the profile matched or even closely resembled Guy Paul Morin."[59] What this discrepancy reveals is the extent to which officers seize on those parts of the profile that correspond with pre-existing assumptions. At the time the profile was prepared, Morin was already a suspect. Nigel Hadgkiss, the assistant commissioner of the Australian Federal Police Force and an expert on police misconduct, testified at the inquiry that "this kind of methodology is as good as clairvoyance," and that "[a]s soon as you start stereotyping your suspect ... I feel your whole investigation is very much constrained."[60]

Other examples of profiles widely missing the mark include the profile of the 1995 Oklahoma bombing suspect as an "Arab terrorist," when in fact he was a White American (Timothy McVeigh); the 2002 profile of the Washington Beltway sniper as a White male (the snipers were both Black);[61] and the use of drug courier and importer profiles in Ontario. In *Calderon*, two Ontario Provincial Police officers were, in the early morning hours, patrolling a quiet stretch of the Trans-Canada Highway in Nipigon, Ontario. They stopped a white Lincoln Town car with British Columbia licence plates for travelling 10 kilometres over the speed limit. Using the drug courier profile they had been taught at a drug interdiction course, the officers decided to investigate the driver and passenger. That investigation led to the seizure of 22 pounds of marijuana. It was, however, the first time they had struck gold.[62] One of the officers said he had made between ten and twenty stops, and the other between fifty and one hundred stops, without any successful seizure.[63]

As a result of the number of false positives generated by the officers' use of profiling and the neutrality of the so-called indicators (e.g., the presence of fast food, duffel bags, a road map, cell phones, and pagers), the Ontario Court of Appeal held, in *Calderon*, that the police can no longer detain individuals simply because they fit a drug courier profile. As Justice John Laskin, for the majority, noted, "[g]iven the neutrality and apparent unreliability of these indicators, I fail to see how their presence could amount to reasonable grounds for detention."[64]

Although racial profiling was not raised in *Calderon* either at trial or on appeal,[65] one of the officers testified that his suspicions were triggered, in part, because the Lincoln Town car seemed too expensive "for what the driver and passenger looked like to me."[66] In his reasons for judgment on the *Charter* motion, the trial judge noted:

> Details of the meaning of this statement was not explored or explained in cross-examination. I cannot say whether Os-

borne was referring to the age of the defendants, their dress, grooming or their racial or ethnic origin. (The defendants appear to be in the mid to late twenties age bracket. Both have dark skins. My best guess is that they are East Indian or Middle East origin).

... There was no reflection of bias, discrimination or discourtesy during the investigation or after the arrest. The conduct and politeness of Osborne and the other officers was exemplary and inconsistent with bias or prejudice.[67]

The problem with the trial judge's reasoning is that it misconceives the scope of racial profiling. If we assume that skin colour did, in fact, play some role in the officers' decision to stop Calderon, then racial profiling was involved. Moreover, the way Calderon was treated is largely irrelevant on this issue since racial profiling can be unconscious. Because the issue was not explored at trial, Justice Laskin did not address the source of the stereotyping involved in the officer's statement, but he did properly hold that he was not going to rely on it in assessing whether there were grounds to detain the accused.[68]

In the context of importing drugs, data collected by the Canada Customs and Revenue Agency over a twenty-six-month period at the Toronto airport revealed an extraordinarily high number of false positives (those who were targeted because they fit the profile but who were, in fact, not in possession of any drugs). These individuals were compelled to sit in a room, known as the super loo, until they produced a bowel movement. In the 536 cases analyzed, the false positive rate at Terminal 1 was 75 percent. At Terminals 2 and 3, it was 79 percent and 83 percent, respectively.[69] Although the study did not provide information about the race or ethnicity of the travellers, it is reasonable to conclude that a significant number were Black, given the overrepresentation of Black women in our courts for importing offences and the targeting of flights from the Caribbean—both of which suggest that race is part of the importer profile.[70] For example, as noted in the 1998 Criminal Intelligence Service Canada's Annual Report:

Cocaine enters Canada concealed in footwear, toiletries, false bottomed suitcases and dissolved in liquor, among other methods. Couriers tend to be females in their early 20s to mid 30s, who smuggle cocaine into Canada aboard commercial flights from Caribbean countries, primarily Jamaica and Trinidad and Tobago.[71]

Moreover, as the Commission on Systemic Racism in the Ontario Criminal Justice System noted in its 1995 report: "[I]ntensive policing of airline travellers produces arrests of a ... disproportionate number of black female couriers."[72] The false positive rates from the Customs study reveal not only that the police are engaging in serious violations of individual rights but that they are also missing the real criminals because of the unreliability of the profile.[73]

Trying to shield the use of race under the rubric of criminal profiling does not remove its objectionable foundations. Since the essence of racial profiling is a reliance on appearance and stereotypes, as opposed to particularized and objectively criminal behaviour, all generalized criminal profiles that rely, in part, on race are properly characterized as manifestations of racial profiling. Even where a portion of the criminal profile relies, in part, on neutral or ambiguous behaviour such as nervousness, sweating, or purchasing airline tickets with cash or shortly before departure, as in the case of the drug-importer profile, the use of race as part of that profile is extremely dangerous, given the salience of race to our interpretation of human behaviour.

Race, Informed Statistical Generalizations, and Necessity

MARGARET WENTE, A COLUMNIST with the *Globe and Mail*, once wrote that "a disproportionate number of crimes are committed by young black men ... [A]nyone connected with the penal system will tell you who's in jail: lots of aboriginals and lots of blacks.... I think that the real problem here is crime, not systemic racism."[74] Wente is correct that some racialized groups are overrepresented in our prisons. For example, although Aboriginals made up approximately 3.3 percent of the population in 2000/2001, they represented 19 percent of provincial admissions and 17 percent of federal admissions.[75] These numbers become even more stark when we look at specific provinces. In 2000/2001, Aboriginals made up 76 percent of admissions in Saskatchewan, and 64 percent of admissions in Manitoba.[76] With respect to the Black community, the percentage of Black inmates in the federal system is three times higher than their percentage in the general population.[77] These numbers become even more troubling when we look at Ontario. The only provincial data that is available is for 1992/1993, and in that year the adult admission rate to prison for Black males was 6,976 per 100,000. The admission rates for White and Aboriginal males was 1,326 and 3,600, respectively.[78]

This kind of data is used to argue that while the over-policing of racialized communities may result in differential treatment, its roots lie not in race-based stereotypes but on informed statistical generalizations about offending rates.[79] In an effort to give legitimacy to this argument, some people analogize racial profiling to the use of personal characteristics by insurance companies, for example. In assessing risk for vehicle insurance, these companies rely on factors such as age and gender — a practice most of us accept as reasonable or at least as unobjectionable.[80] Outside the insurance context, our courts have addressed, under the equality provisions of the *Charter*, the legitimacy of law enforcement targeting based on statistical generalizations. In *Little Sisters Book and Art Emporium v. Canada*, a case involving the importing of gay and lesbian erotica, the Supreme Court of Canada recognized that, given limited resources, the state might be able to justify differential treatment as reasonable where it could demonstrate that the profile was an *accurate* one.[81] Justice Binnie, for the majority, held that "[t]argeting is not necessarily unconstitutional. The Customs Department is obliged to use its limited resources in the most cost-effective way. This might include targeting shipments that, on the basis of experience or other information, are more likely than others to contain prohibited goods."[82] In *Little Sisters*, the Court ultimately held that there was no evidence that gay and lesbian erotica is proportionately more likely to be obscene than heterosexual erotica.[83]

Having reached this conclusion, the Court did not address the additional issue of whether targeting based on an accurate profile would still be reasonable if the deleterious effects exceeded its purpose. This latter analysis would presumably have been required to sustain the reasonableness of statistically informed differential treatment under the reasonable limit section of the *Charter*.[84] Similarly, in the aftermath of September 11, in *R. v. Smith*, a case involving a racial profiling challenge to a charge of importing drugs, the trial court observed that while using race to ascribe criminality to an entire group was inappropriate and unconstitutional, there was a difference between that offensive use of race and circumstances where "there is solid evidence to link a group, defined in part by their race, to a legitimate state interest or concern."[85] Here we see a linkage between the statistical and the necessity assumptions.

Although this argument has a superficial appeal in explaining the over-policing phenomenon, there are many inherent dangers in relying on differential offending rates to justify targeting racialized individuals. Some of the data that has been relied upon as evidence of actual crime rates (arrest and incarceration rates) may itself be biased—the product of over-policing and the detection of crimes that would otherwise go undetected. In other words, the overrepresentation may be generated by what is known as the self-fulfilling prophecy:[86] if you focus all of your attention on one group, you will find a disproportionate amount of the activity you are searching for and thereby confirm the generalizations used to justify the initial targeting.[87] Suppose, for example, that Revenue Canada decided to focus all its attention on restaurant owners because of a belief that a significant percentage of income in this business was not reported. Assuming that the over-policing worked and a significant number of arrests were made, so that fraud among restaurant owners was fifty times higher than in other businesses, would we be prepared to say that this depiction of fraud rates in the country was accurate?

As this simple example illustrates, for most offences, particularly those without an identifiable victim, arrest rates are often more a reflection of the people the police focus on than a reliable indicator of offending rates. Indeed, as the Ontario Systemic Racism Commission observed: "Studies in Canada and elsewhere show, for example, that more than 90 percent of young men say they have committed criminal offences. This indicates that variations in offending rates by race or economic class are small. Variations in enforcement practices likely make the difference."[88] The overrepresentation is also likely linked to systemic racism in the exercise of discretion at other stages of the criminal justice process, including decisions made at the bail and sentencing stages.

Given the dangers of the self-fulfilling prophecy, is it safe to rely on this data to draw any reliable conclusions about differential offending rates or to guide social policy? It is here that the analogy to insurance rates and the use of other generalizations based on reliable actuarial evidence breaks down. We may, however, be able to generate a statistically accurate usual-offender profile that includes race or ethnicity where the frequency of the offence can be accurately determined and the identification of the assailants ascertained. Homicides, home invasions, robberies, kidnappings, and terrorist offences immediately come to mind. In this context, is there any room for a rational debate about the reasonableness of the practice? Let us look at this issue from the perspective of both the profilers and the profiled.

From a law-enforcement perspective, is it efficient, when resources are limited, to target an entire group to find a very small number of offenders? In other words, is racial profiling (and criminal profiling more generally) not inherently flawed because of the problem of over-inclusiveness, even where we have included other variables in the profile such as age, place of origin, citizenship, gender, and location? Or to put it in more colloquially, does it not inevitably lead the police on a search for the proverbial needle in a haystack? For example, in 2005, there were fifty-two gun homicides in Toronto.[89] The vast majority of the shooters appear to be Black.[90] How does knowing this fact assist the police when there are well over 143,000 Black males living in Toronto?[91]

Similarly, the recent terrorist attacks in the United States, Spain, and Britain were largely committed by Muslim men. But again, how does this information help security officials when there are hundreds of millions of Muslim men in the world? In the terrorism context, do we not also run into a problem of under-inclusiveness if we try to add other characteristics to the profile to reduce the problem of false positives? For example, many Muslims are White, others are Black. The terrorist profile is rapidly changing. The September 11 terrorists were Arab and from the Middle East. The London terrorists were South Asian and British citizens. Are we not at greater risk of a terrorist attack when we use profiling as part of our national security policy, as opposed to relying on suspicious behaviour and good intelligence?

From the perspective of the profiled as well as public and constitutional policy, how reasonable is the practice when we factor in the extensive damage visited on the innocent? Racial profiling causes tremendous psychological and physical harm. It is demeaning and it has a negative impact on the dignity of all members of racialized communities. It is the essence of discrimination.[92] Moreover, will it not perpetuate the very harm it seeks to address? To the extent that there are differential offending rates based on race, they are the product of the historical, social, and economic inequality that racialized communities disproportionately face.[93] Is it reasonable to rely on a policing practice that further perpetuates this inequality and may cause greater levels of offending in the future? We will return to many of these questions about cost and effectiveness later in the book. Having attempted to rebut, on a theoretical level, the commonly held assumptions that blind us from recognizing racial profiling when it occurs, chapter 4 provides the social science evidence which suggests that the police often target race in carrying out their duties.

Part Two

HOW PERVASIVE IS RACIAL PROFILING IN CANADA?

[4]

Social Science and Beyond

THE SOCIAL SCIENCE EVIDENCE

The Ontario Systemic Racism Commission

IN OCTOBER 1992 THE Ontario government established the Commission on Systemic Racism in the Ontario Criminal Justice System to "inquire into and make recommendations about the extent to which criminal justice practices, procedures and policies reflect systemic racism."[1] The impetus for the commission was a growing and vocal sense of frustration in the Black community about the colour of justice and, in particular, their vulnerability to police violence.[2] That frustration was expressed in civil disturbances in downtown Toronto in early May 1992.[3] The disturbances followed the acquittal by an all-White jury of two White police officers charged in the shooting death of Michael "Wade" Lawson;[4] the acquittal of four White police officers charged in the beating of Rodney King;[5] and the fatal police shooting of Raymond Lawrence.[6] After the disturbances, Premier Bob Rae retained Stephen Lewis, the former Ontario NDP leader and Canadian ambassador to the United Nations, to make recommendations to address race relations in Ontario. In his June 2002 report to the premier, Lewis stated:

> [W]hat we are dealing with, at root, and fundamentally, is anti-Black racism.... It is important, I believe, to acknowledge not only that racism is pervasive, but that at different times in different places, it violates certain minority communities more than others....
>
> ... There is a great deal of anger, anxiety, frustration and impatience amongst those with whom I talked.... Often during our discussions, there was a weary and bitter sense that I was engaged and they were engaged in yet another reporting charade. It was truly depressing....
>
> ... there was another emotion that was palpable, and it was fear. Mostly, of course, it was from members of the Black community, and in particular, mothers. The eight shootings over the last three years, and the sense, real or imagined, of unpredictable police encounters with Black youths have many families very frightened. I will admit to you that nothing left so indelible an impression on me as the expressions of apprehension and fear. I can't even begin to imagine it about my own children. Nor can you.[7]

Given this experience and the "horror stories" he heard, Lewis recommended that an inquiry be held to examine the criminal justice system. And so it was called. The co-chairs of the commission included Margaret Gittens, a community legal worker in Toronto, and Justice David Cole, a well-respected trial judge in Toronto.[8] In December 1995 the commission released its 445-page report, generally regarded as the most extensive examination of racism in policing in Canada.[9] Indeed, the following month, the report was discussed in the *New York Times* under the headline: "Canada's Justice System Faces Charges of Racism."[10]

To determine the existence (and extent) of differential policing in Toronto, the commission used researchers with York Univer-

sity's Institute for Social Research. In 1994 they conducted tele-
phone interviews in with 1,257 individuals who self-identified as
Black (417), Chinese (405), or White (435). They were satisfied that
this group made a representative sample of the population living in Metropolitan Toronto. The data revealed that 28 percent of
Black residents reported having been stopped in the previous two
years, compared to 18 percent of White residents. The discrepancy
further increased when the commission looked at multiple stops
and at stops of Black males:

- 17% of Black residents reported having been stopped on
  two or more occasions over the previous two years, as
  compared to only 8% of White residents; and
- 43% of Black male residents reported having been stopped
  by the Toronto police in the previous two years, as opposed to only 25% of White male residents.[11]

In Dee Brown's appeal, it was these findings that the Ontario Court
of Appeal relied on in taking judicial notice of the existence of racial profiling in Ontario. As Justice Morden, for the Court, held:

In the opening part of his submission before this court,
counsel for the appellant [Ministry of the Attorney General]
said that he did not challenge the fact that the phenomenon
of racial profiling by the police existed. This was a responsible position to take, because, as counsel said, this conclusion
is supported by significant social science research.

I quote from the Report of The Commission on Systemic
Racism in the Ontario Criminal Justice System ... at p. 358:

The Commission's findings suggest that racialized
characteristics, especially those of black people,
in combination with other factors, provoke police
suspicion, at least in Metro Toronto.[12]

Scot Wortley, one of the commission researchers and now a
criminology professor at the University of Toronto, conducted fur-

ther analysis on the 1994 commission data. After controlling for relevant factors such as age, gender, education, and income, he found that Blacks in Toronto were twice as likely as Whites to report experiencing a single police stop and four times more likely to report experiencing multiple stops over a two-year period.[13] Wortley was also able to demonstrate that having a university degree does not protect Blacks from the police, as the level of education actually increases the likelihood of being stopped. The reverse was true for Whites.[14]

Professor Wortley's name has become synonymous with racial-profiling research. He is one of the few social scientists in Canada to study systemic racism in the criminal justice system and, in particular, racial profiling. But why? Are lawsuits such as the defamation suit launched by the Toronto Police Association causing a chilling effect in the academy? In an interview with the *Kingston Whig-Standard*, Wortley offered some of his own thoughts on why there is a paucity of research: "[I]t's very frustrating to want to do research on this issue. It makes you realize how powerless researchers are and how powerless members of the community are.... I think a lot of the academic community ... doesn't want to deal with the police associations, doesn't want to deal with the public critique of their work in the newspaper." The lack of access to data and the mythology that race doesn't matter in Canada were additional reasons offered by Wortley. On the latter point, he noted: "We're very comfortable in Canada saying that race doesn't matter ... we're not the United States. We're the land of multiculturalism and the land of co-operation. We tend to be very emotionally upset when allegations of [racism] are made."[15]

The Toronto Youth Crime and Victimization Survey

IN 2000 A SURVEY involving a random sample of 3,393 Toronto high school students in both the Catholic and the public systems was conducted by Wortley and his University of Toronto colleague Julian Tanner. As they explain, "The school boards agreed to provide us with one class period (usually 75 minutes) for the students to complete the survey. After a brief introduction, in which the students were reminded of the confidential nature of the study, respondents were asked to complete a 32-page questionnaire."[16] The data revealed that 51 percent of Black youth reported having been stopped two or more times in the previous two years, compared to 23 percent of White youth. In addition, 23 percent of Black youth reported having been searched two or more times in the last two years, compared to 8 percent of White youth.[17]

Given the detailed questions contained in the survey, the researchers were able to control for those factors likely to attract police attention. These factors include involvement in criminal activity, gangs or other deviant behaviour, use of drugs, or alcohol, or otherwise engaging in public leisure activities likely to attract the attention of the police (riding in cars with friends, hanging out in malls, or activities such as attending house parties, nightclubs, or raves). They made this adjustment in order to respond to the argument that Blacks more frequently come into contact with the police because they are more likely to be "up to no good." Gender, age, social class, and neighbourhood (public housing projects) were also controlled for in order to determine what impact race alone has on police surveillance.

According to the data, Black youth who did not engage in activity that was likely to attract police attention were nevertheless four times more likely to report being stopped and six times more likely to report being searched within a two-year period than similarly situated White students.[18] The researchers also found that

34% of the black students who had not engaged in any type of criminal activity still reported that they had been stopped by the police on two or more occasions in the past two years, compared to only 4% of white students in the same behavioural category. Similarly, 23% of black students with no deviant behaviour reported that they had been searched by the police, compared to only 5% of whites who reported no deviance.[19]

In other words, the study was able to establish that being "good" does not shield Blacks from police surveillance. It provides compelling evidence to rebut the differential offending-rate explanation for differential treatment.[20] Indeed, it is arguably one of the most compelling studies confirming the existence of racial profiling in the world. Three years later, Scot Wortley became involved in another data-collection project, this time in Kingston, Ontario.

The Kingston Data-Collection Project

ON MARCH 16, 2001, the police received a 911 call from a frantic woman who said she feared for her life. A black Mercedes was near her house, and she thought that the man who had beaten her and left her for dead years earlier was inside. During the call, the woman exclaimed: "You know, I'm sure there's not a lot of black people running around in Mercedes in Kingston ... who dress like, like the hip-hop style, driving a $60,000 car."[21] But the woman was completely wrong. The car's occupants were not criminals but two brothers, Mark and Andrew Wallen. Mark was seventeen years old; Andrew twelve. There was also a young woman in the car. The Wallens were waiting for their father. When the police arrived, they surrounded the car with their guns drawn. One by one, the occupants were ordered out, told to get on their knees, handcuffed, and placed in the police cruiser. When Morais Wallen came out of the building, he was shocked to see his younger son on the ground with guns pointed at him.[22]

The officers would later be cleared of any wrongdoing, following an OPP investigation. Nevertheless, Chief Bill Close realized that the incident had served to ignite the perception within the Black community in Kingston that they were unfairly dealt with by the police. On March 24, 2003, Mark Wallen was again confronted by a Kingston police officer as he was walking down the street with a friend, even though they were doing nothing wrong. Yet again he faced down the barrel of a gun, this time for not taking his hands out of his pocket.[23] Chief Close quickly acted. He became the first chief in Canada to ban racial profiling, in May 2003.[24] Montreal would follow suit one year later.[25] Closs also proposed that Kingston become the first police force in Canada to collect data on those whom the police stop.[26] As he put it later: "This policy recognizes the extraordinary powers given to police officers and the absolute need for the fair application of justice to all.... It's about changing the way policing is done, about transparency and about accountability."[27]

Closs was subjected to intense criticism for his data-collection plan by the police association, his officers, and other police chiefs across Canada.[28] Some, like Tom Kaye, president of the Ontario Association of Chiefs of Police, even went so far as to suggest that data collection would "deter officers from stopping members of visible minorities, even if they are suspected of a crime."[29] Some officers also seem to have joined in an unofficial three-day job action in protest, where they refused to issue tickets.[30] It was reminiscent of the Toronto wildcat strike in the Drummond case. Chief Closs stood his ground, and, in July 2003, the Kingston Police Services Board unanimously approved his plan.[31] Ten months later Chief Closs became the first police chief to receive a special community award by ABLE (Association of Black Law Enforcers) in Canada for his "bold leadership and initiative in ensuring equity."[32]

For the next year (October 1, 2003, to September 30, 2004), police officers in Kingston, a city with a Black population of approximately 685 (according to the 2001 Census), would be required to fill out a form whenever they made a traffic or pedestrian stop (figure 4.1). Wortley was retained by Chief Closs to conduct the analysis of the data, and on May 26, 2005, the Kingston Police Force released the preliminary results of its year-long data collection project. The data revealed that Blacks were overrepresented in police stops. Chief Closs issued an emotional apology to the Black community in Kingston.[33] Not long thereafter, Mark Wallen was once again stopped by the police, this time while he was driving his girlfriend's car.[34] The final report was released on September 15, 2005. The general conclusion was that Blacks, and particularly

Figure 4.1

KINGSTON POLICE CONTACT CARD	ASSOCIATES: SUBMIT A CARD WITH SAME DATE/TIME FOR EACH SEE REVERSE FOR MORE INFO	1 of 1

CONTACT DATE	Zone	Badge No.
Year Month Day Time		

LOCATION

SURNAME	DATE OF BIRTH
	Year Month Day
GIVEN	

NICKNAME

ETHNICITY	□ E Asian	**DISPOSITION**
□ B White	□ F Aboriginal	□ A Arrest Made
□ C South	□ H Arab	□ B Warrant Arrest Made
Asian	□ L Latino	□ D Traffic Warning
□ D Black	□ Z Other	□ F Contact Card

REASON FOR STOP	□ G T.T.P.
□ 1 Bulletin / Suspect	□ N Completed No Report
Description Broadcast	□ O Warning (Other)
□ 3 H.T.A. Violation	□ P Property Seized (bike, vehicle,
□ 5 C.C.C. Violation	drugs, etc.)
□ 6 Drug Related Offence	□ R Searched Vehicle
□ 7 By-Law Infraction	□ S Searched Person(s)
□ 8 Citizen Generated	□ W Ticket issued (HTA, LLA, etc.)
□ 99 Other, i.e. LLA, Provincial Statute	

COMPLEXION			
□ A Fair	□ B Medium	□ C Ruddy	□ D Dark
□ E Freckled	□ F Pock Marked	□ G Acne	□ Z Other

ADDRESS □ N.F.A.

□ KINGSTON

CONTACT Nos.	Home Work	Mobile Pager Other (Specify)
SEX HEIGHT WEIGHT		EYES HAIR COLOUR/DESCRIPTION

□ GLASSES

VECHICLE		Licence Plate	Province
□ NONE	□ PEDESTRIAN	□ UNPLATED	□ ONT
□ OWNER	□ DRIVER		
□ PASSENGER	□ BICYCLE	COLOUR YEAR MAKE	
□ ASSOCIATED TO VEH		MODEL STYLE	

CONTACT TYPE	□ STREET CHECK	□ INFORMATION	
□ Charged	□ Bicycle	□ Soliciting	□ Rollerblade
□ Warned	□ Noise	□ Panhandling	□ Skateboard
□ Other	□ H.T.A.	□ Tresspass At	□ Other

young Black males, are overrepresented in police stops, compared to Whites.[35] In addition, the data revealed that 15 percent of the Black residents had been stopped during the project, compared to 5 percent of the White residents. This outcome virtually mirrors the findings of the Ontario Systemic Racism Commission in Toronto.

What inferences can be drawn from the Kingston results? First, we must consider the benchmark that was used in the study. A benchmark is "the standard against which stops by police are measured.... It is the appropriate fixed point for comparison to determine if too few, too many, or a roughly proportionate number of individuals from a given minority are being stopped."[36] It is an integral part of the calculation of the "odds ratio," the statistic used to tell us the degree to which an event will occur in a given population. In the context of racial-profiling research, the odds ratio is "calculated by dividing the % of all police stops involving a particular racial group with their % representation in the benchmark population."[37] An odds ratio of greater than two has been interpreted to mean that there is "serious evidence that racially biased policing may exist."[38] In the Kingston study, for example, the odds ratio (using census data as the benchmark) tells us that Blacks were three times more likely to be stopped than Whites, while Black pedestrians were 3.67 times more likely to be stopped than White pedestrians.[39]

Benchmarking is a contentious issue in data collection because the benchmark chosen can obviously have an impact on the odds ratio.[40] For example, the most commonly used benchmark is census data—comparing the number of stops in a given group with their numbers in the general population.[41] This method has been criticized because it does not necessarily capture who is at risk, assuming no racial bias, for being stopped in a particular location. For example, with respect to vehicle stops, Black drivers may be stopped more frequently because they are committing a disproportionately higher number of traffic violations or because there are a proportionally greater number of Black drivers in a particular area that is being monitored by the police. Indeed, one of the criticisms of the Kingston project by Ron Melchers, a criminology professor at the University of Ottawa, was that a census benchmark was used.[42]

However, as Wortley points out, there is a difference between adjusted and unadjusted census benchmarking, and Melchers does not appear to distinguish between the two in his criticism. Adjusted census data involves controlling for those relevant factors that have an impact on the size of the group likely to be stopped. These factors could include gender, age, residency, or car ownership. Adjusted census benchmarking was used in the Kingston study and, interestingly, the odds ratio reported earlier stayed the same or actually increased.[43] In support of the reliability of an adjusted census benchmark, Wortley relied on a treatise by the American Police Executive Research Forum which devotes an entire chapter to using this benchmark.[44] The Kingston study also looked at stop outcomes, and they enable us to determine whether the overrepresentation in stops can be explained by differential offending rates. The answer is that it cannot, because Whites were more likely to be ticketed than Blacks, while Blacks were only slightly more likely to be arrested or charged than Whites following the stop.[45] Finally, given the relatively small size of the Black community in Kingston, it was important to be able to determine whether the overrepresentation could be explained by repeated stops of a small number of individuals.[46] In the Kingston study, the contact card information included the person's name, address, and date of birth. This detail enabled Wortley to create a data set that counted individuals only once—and the odds ratio was three for Blacks.[47] No matter how you look at the Kingston data, then, the overrepresentation of Blacks in police stops remains present.

BEYOND SOCIAL SCIENCE

THE SOCIAL SCIENCE EVIDENCE reveals a serious problem of racial profiling in parts of Ontario. But how pervasive is it in the rest of Canada? To what extent are Aboriginals over-policed in the West or Asians in British Columbia? These are all questions that social scientists across Canada need to address. While we clearly need more national data collection to get an exact handle on the scope of the problem, we can, for the moment, move beyond social science to get some appreciation of its scope. If we look at what fuels racial profiling, there is every reason to believe that it has become pervasive in police forces across Canada. So far in the book, we have looked at the prevalence of systemic racism and stereotyping in Canada (chapter 1) and the false assumptions that differential treatment is the product of criminal profiling or differential offending rates (chapter 3). Both of these factors play a significant role in perpetuating racial profiling. The remainder of this chapter and the next three chapters will look at the other pieces of the puzzle. They include the nature of modern-day policing, the commonality of experience in the United States and England, and the racialization of crime in law enforcement's efforts to fight drugs, gangs, and terrorists.

Proactive Policing

POLICING TODAY, AS IT has been for some time, is heavily influenced by proactive or problem-solving policing, as opposed to reactive policing, especially in the "wars" on drugs, gangs, and terrorism.[48] When the police are out patrolling our streets, they are maintaining order and looking for those who may be "up-to-no-good" and involved in criminality. This form of policing relies heavily on intuition, or what police officers affectionately call their "sixth sense." As one officer put it, "I have the unique ability to distinguish between a law-abiding person and an up-to-no-good person."[49] Proactive policing is the breeding ground for racial profiling, because it enables and masks the use of race as a basis of suspect selection. It is a form of highly discretionary and low-visibility policing.[50] The methodology of proactive policing include heightened presence and surveillance,[51] pretext vehicle and pedestrian stops,[52] street sweeps,[53] and random virtue testing.[54] All these forms of proactive policing use targeting as their modus operandi.

In Montreal, for example, the police announced in 2004 that they were cracking down on what they called "incivilities" and created twenty-six new categories of acts that disturb the peace or harm the use of public spaces.[55] Racialized individuals appear to be the primary targets of these "incivilities," which are highly discretionary. According to Fo Nieme, "'uncivil' conduct is so broadly defined — anything from prostitution to spitting, loitering, or making noise — that police can target just about anyone for the slightest infraction."[56] Niemi reports that the Centre for Research-Action on Race Relations (CRARR) has received a number of complaints from Black, Latino, and South Asian youth who are being ticketed for "uncivil" conduct. Montreal has also seen allegations of racial profiling by the police, transit officials, and housing authorities.[57]

The Commonality of Experience

ONE RELIABLE INDICATOR OF the existence of a social phenomenon is whether it is replicated in different places and times, or what I call the "commonality of experience." The Ontario experience does not stand alone. In 2004 Amnesty International published a report entitled *Threat and Humiliation: Racial Profiling, Domestic Security and Human Rights in the United States*. In it, Amnesty documented that an estimated 32 million Americans have been victimized by racial profiling and that a further 87 million are at risk.[58] In England, Blacks are eight times more likely to be stopped and searched by the police than are Whites.[59] In 2004, stops and searches of Asians under Britain's anti-terrorism powers rose by 300 percent.[60] And these numbers will continue to rise, as British authorities have all but admitted they are targeting Muslims for stops and searches, particularly after the subway bombings of July 7, 2005.[61] This commonality of experience has largely gone unnoticed in the racial-profiling debate, in large part because the experience the police and others rely upon (e.g., the assumption that over-policing is the result of differential offending rates) is far more consistent with our belief that discrimination is not a problem in Canada. However, as this and the other empirical data presented in this book reveal, it is the common lived experiences of racialized individuals that is truly in accord with social reality. As Keith Norton, the former commissioner of the Ontario Human Rights Commission, once observed, "[a]n entire community cannot have the same impression (of racial profiling) and ... all [be] deluded."[62]

Context and the Current Racialization of Crime

FINALLY, IN ORDER TO appreciate the scope of the problem of racial profiling, we need to examine the different contexts within which profiling flourishes. History has taught us that marginalized groups are particularly vulnerable to discriminatory law-enforcement targeting in times of moral panic about the prevalence of crime or the imminence of a terrorist or enemy attack.[63] The discriminatory treatment of 22,000 Japanese in Canada during the Second World War is a prime example.[64] Current moral panics include the "war on drugs," the "war on gangs," and the "war on terrorism." These law enforcement initiatives, like all wars, rely on coercive, heavy-handed tactics and panic. The next three chapters reveal that each war has officially identified its target and that targeting has become sanctioned, if not explicitly, then certainly by implication.

Some wars engender profiling by creating panic. For example, it would appear that the panic created by the current war on terrorism, and to a lesser extent the war on gangs, is its most lethal weapon. Panic can often serve to lull people into a state of suspended judgment, where civil liberties can be sacrificed and discriminatory treatment justified as reasonable because they are deemed necessary.[65] This attitude is no more evident than in London and Toronto, where recent terrorist and gang violence have left many in fear and in search of protection. According to a poll conducted after the British bombings, an overwhelming majority of Canadians were more concerned with implementing security measures than with civil liberties: 72 percent indicated that they favoured installing video cameras in public places, while an even greater percentage (81 percent) wanted those who publicly support terrorism to be jailed or deported.[66] Although participants were not specifically polled on the issue of racial profiling, it would appear, based on these numbers, that profiling would find tremendous support among the general public. Indeed, earlier polls had found a significant number (49 percent) in favour of profiling to fight terrorism.[67] Later in the book, we will examine why racial profiling will not make us safe from terrorist (or gang) violence and how the collateral damage far outweighs any benefit to law enforcement. Chapter 5 looks at one of the oldest law enforcement battles in Canada, the war on drugs. It was a war, as we saw earlier in the book, that was born out of racism. That legacy continues.

The War on Drugs

IN THE MID-1980S CANADA decided to follow the lead of the United States and, in particular, the Drug Enforcement Agency (DEA) and intensified its domestic efforts to stem the tide of drug use. "Just say no" became the slogan of a "war" that would see heightened drug interdiction both on our streets and at ports of entry and transit. The weapon of choice became, as we saw earlier, the creation of a profile of the drug courier. That profile ultimately became fixated on race, when authorities began to focus on low-income neighbourhoods that were predominantly racialized.[1] Suddenly, Blacks became overrepresented in drug arrests in Canada and the United States. These numbers then confirmed the legitimacy of the profile in the eyes of law enforcement, and the surveillance of these communities became even more intense. Aggressive front-line crime control would be supported through heavy reliance on lengthy periods of imprisonment, regardless of personal circumstances.[2]

How successful has this war been?[3] Many have now acknowledged the futility of focusing law enforcement on low-level suppliers and couriers. In its report, the Ontario Systemic Racism

Commission, for example, concluded that "effective drug policies emphasize treatment and prevention of abuse…. Without a local demand for drugs, street trading would disappear and small-scale couriers would not be recruited."[4] The war also does not appear to have made a dent on the "hard" drugs. The vast majority of drug arrests are for marijuana offences,[5] a drug that 44 percent of Canadians have admitted smoking.[6] But most troubling is the collateral damage felt by racialized groups. The war on drugs, for example, has had a devastating impact on the Black community, particularly in Ontario.

A "WAR ON BLACKS"

ON THE ISSUE OF race, policing, and drugs, the Ontario Systemic Racism Commission concluded, "It is clear from our findings that in Ontario … one effect of the 'war on drugs,' intended or not, has been the increase in imprisonment of black people."[7] And this increase, it concluded, is the product of "the intensive policing of low income areas in which black people live."[8] The most compelling evidence of this impact of the war on drugs can be seen by examining the Metropolitan Toronto prison admission data from 1986 and 1992, as it was during these years that the war took to the streets of Toronto.[9] In 1986/87, 131 Blacks were admitted to Toronto prisons for drug trafficking offences, constituting 25 percent of the total trafficking admissions.[10] Although a relatively small number, Blacks were still overrepresented in admissions, given that they made up only 3.7 percent of the Toronto population.[11] In 1992/93 the numbers dramatically increased, and Black admissions stood at 1,656. This number constituted 60 percent of the total trafficking admissions,[12] or approximately fourteen times the percentage of Blacks in the Toronto population.[13]

In the span of a few years, we witnessed a 1,164 percent increase in Black admissions in Toronto, compared to a 151 percent increase for White admissions.[14] Considering that the Black population in Toronto grew by 31 percent during this period, the increase can be explained only by either a sudden exodus from the drug trade by Whites or a massive surveillance, looking for drug traffickers, of the Black community.[15] There is simply no evidence of the former, and the more likely cause is a shifting focus of police surveillance. As the Ontario Systemic Racism Commission concluded: "The particular strategies selected in the so-called 'war on drugs' account for much of the growth of racial inequality in prison admissions between 1986/7 and 1992/3."[16] As noted earlier in the book, if the police devote their resources and their focus to detecting a particular offence, which is prevalent in society, among a particular community, they are likely going to find what they are looking for.

Other data support the conclusion that this dramatic increase in arrest statistics was the product of disproportionate policing. In their 2000 high school survey, Wortley and Tanner discovered a much higher drug-use rate among White students.[17] This finding is consistent with the conclusion of the Ontario Systemic Racism Commission that "[n]o evidence shows that black people are more likely to use drugs than others or that they are overrepresented among those who profit most from drug use."[18] It is also consistent with American data concerning crack and powder cocaine use. In the United States, 71.3 percent of crack cocaine and 81 percent of powder cocaine users are White. African-Americans make up only 17.7 percent of crack cocaine and 7.7 percent of powder cocaine users.[19] Drug-use patterns, then, cannot explain why Blacks constitute the majority of prison admissions for drug offences.

What about trafficking patterns? Interviews of drug users suggest that their dealers are from similar racial and ethnic backgrounds.[20] Logic confirms this trend. Most middle-class Whites, for example, are not likely to go to housing projects in the early morning hours to get their fix. Empirical data also confirms it. In Canada, Blacks make up only 8.9 percent of drug offenders in our federal institutions, where most of the serious traffickers and importers are imprisoned.[21] Moreover, in the United States, an emerging body of data known as "hit rate" data (the likelihood of finding drugs on a traffic stop), which the police are now required to collect, reveals that the police are as likely, and many times more likely, to find drugs when they stop White drivers.[22] These statistics have had a significant impact in the United States in exposing the fallacy of the stereotype of the Black drug dealer. A *New York Times* commentary written by a prominent race law professor and a statistician, for instance, observed that "[t]hose who defend the police argue that racial and ethnic disparities reflect not discrimination but higher rates of offenses among minorities.... But the racial profiling studies uniformly show that this widely shared assumption is false."[23] The hit-rate data also reveal that the police are wasting valuable limited resources in targeting racialized individuals.

The incarceration, use, and trafficking data presented here all support the proposition that, beginning in the late 1980s and early 1990s, young Black men were targeted in Toronto as the usual drug offenders. This targeting had an immediate impact, as Blacks suddenly became overrepresented in Ontario prisons. This now visible face of drug crime likely fuelled more profiling in Toronto and other cities in Canada. The wrath of the war on drugs has also been felt by other racialized communities across Canada.

TRAVELLING WHILE SOUTHEAST ASIAN

ON AUGUST 29, 1999, four RCMP officers and their drug-sniffing dog were waiting at the Calgary bus station for two buses that were arriving from Vancouver. Although there was no evidence that drugs were being transported on the buses, the officers had been trained that Vancouver is a known supplier of drugs to Calgary. Of the more than 130 passengers on both buses, the officers decided to focus on only two, Trung Kien Lam and Hanh Thi Dinh. They did not disembark immediately, and the officers found this suspicious. Lam and Dinh explained that they had lost a ring. The loss was confirmed by another passenger, who was still on the bus and who was able to locate it. As Lam and Dinh walked by the police dog with their luggage, he gave no indication that he smelled drugs.

The officers nevertheless continued with their investigation. Eventually they found more than 6 kilograms of marijuana in Dinh's bags, which had been put in a locker. At trial, the judge concluded that there were no reasonable grounds for the detention or search and, under the *Canadian Charter of Rights and Freedoms*, he excluded the evidence.[24] On appeal, Justice Conrad, for the Alberta Court of Appeal, upheld the decision of the trial judge. She also observed that "the trial judge was understandably left to wonder if the respondents were not a target of racial profiling. When the officers stopped [them], virtually nothing indicated they possessed drugs." The court further observed that since "[t]he trial judge ultimately concluded, however, that they were not so profiled [it did not need to] review the correctness of that finding given his conclusion that no articulable grounds existed for targeting them."[25]

OPERATION PIPELINE AND THE RACIALIZATION OF DRUG TRAFFICKING

THE OFFICERS IN *Lam* were part of Operation Pipeline/Convoy/Jetway (OPCJ) of the RCMP, a training program for drug courier interception on the streets (Operation Pipeline) and at ports of entry such as airports and bus and train stations (Operations Convoy/Jetway).[26] This training is advertised to "enhance ... police officers' observational, conversational and investigative skills, heightening their ability to detect the abnormal activity of travellers, and take action."[27] OPCJ has now been used to train police officers across Canada, including officers with Canada Customs, the Ontario Provincial Police, and police forces in Toronto, Montreal, Calgary, Winnipeg, and Vancouver.[28] According to the RCMP, 5 percent of OPCJ trained officers use it on a daily basis.[29]

In addition to *Lam*, many of the other reported cases involving challenges to OPCJ stops and searches concern Southeast Asians.[30] Is this outcome a coincidence? In answering this question, it is instructive to consider the origins of Operation Pipeline/Convoy/ Jetway. In 1986 the DEA in the United States launched a drug interdiction program called Operation Pipeline. Pipeline's methodology included using pretext traffic stops to provide the police with an opportunity to investigate and secure the driver's consent to search the vehicle. Many believe that an integral part of the methodology included the use of a "racially biased drug courier profile" to determine which vehicles to stop and search.[31] While DEA officials have publicly stated that the use of race plays no role in Pipeline training,[32] the sheer number of complaints against Pipeline-trained officers in the United States tends to confirm that race plays a role in the Pipeline profile.[33] Moreover, some of the training materials used with Pipeline encourage the targeting of racialized motorists.[34] For example, in a video produced by the New Mexico State Police on how to identify potential drug couriers on the highway, all the mock traffic stops have drivers with Hispanic names.[35] In another training video, the police are told that Jamaicans control various parts of the drug trade. A "picture shows a black man in informal dress and dread locks. The image then changes, showing a similar black man wearing a business suit with short hair. The voice admonishes trainees that they should not be fooled; these drug dealers can look like anything at all."[36]

Operation Pipeline was imported into Canada by Corporal Rob Ruiters of the RCMP, after he learned about it at a lecture on drug smuggling in Minnesota. The program continues to share intelligence and training with drug interdiction agencies in the United States. In 2002, for example, Pipeline officers went down to Georgia and watched drug interdiction techniques used in that state. The sharing of intelligence and operational methods is part of this joint effort. In an interview, Ruiters has indicated that "[w]e're equally interested in learning about the Trooper's role in state homeland security."[37] Is race or ethnicity a relevant indicator under this RCMP program? Like his DEA counterparts, Ruiters has denied that OPCJ uses racial profiling.[38] Lawyers have been unable to access the training materials used by Ruiters in order to test this claim because they are protected by privilege.[39] Such use may, however, be a reasonable inference, given the links between OPJC and its American counterpart and the number of reported OPJC cases involving racialized accused.

In addition, certain intelligence materials likely influence policing under OPCJ. These materials invite the use of race as part of a drug courier profile. For example, the 1998 Annual Report by the voice of Canada's criminal intelligence community—the Criminal Intelligence Service Canada (CISC)—contains a section on Asian-based Organized Crime and states:

> Vietnamese gangs, made up of both ethnic and Chinese Vietnamese ... control much of the street level drug trade in Vancouver.... More than half the targets of the Calgary Police Service Drug Undercover Street (DUST) team are Asian criminals. There is every indication that these individuals are actively expanding their share of the local drug trafficking scene.[40]

CISC's 2004 Annual Report further states that "in Alberta, AOC [Asian-based Organized Crime] groups dominate the majority of street-level cocaine trafficking in urban centres and control a significant portion of marijuana grow operations in southern Alberta.... Across the country, Vietnamese-based groups remain extensively involved in multiple residential marijuana grow operations."[41]

In its first report in 1997, CISC linked street trafficking, the place where most policing in the war on drugs takes place, with racialized groups:

> Criminal elements within various Caribbean immigrant communities are still involved in street level cocaine sales. In Western Canada the involvement of Asian-based crime groups in cocaine trafficking is increasing. Iranians, Roma-

nians, Lebanese, Jamaican, Korean and South Americans are increasingly involved in the importation and trafficking of cocaine while Chinese, Vietnamese and Laotians are stepping up their connections at all levels of cocaine trafficking. Vietnamese traffickers from Alberta control the distribution of cocaine in the Northwest Territories.[42]

OTHER CISC REPORTS HAVE linked drug trafficking to Southeast Asian groups (heroin),[43] South American and Caribbean groups (cocaine),[44] Aboriginal groups (marijuana, cocaine and crack),[45] and Asian groups (ecstasy, methamphetamine, and cocaine).[46] As noted in chapter 1, this official link between race and drug trafficking throws into question the assumption that there are no official training materials in Canada that encourage racial profiling. These reports, which are produced each year, contain similar statements. Consequently, it is reasonable to assume that they influence who is most likely to attract police attention. The next case illustrates this point.

Driving While Lebanese

ON JUNE 1, 2003, the police stopped a 1993 BMW in Edmonton for driving with improper tinted windows. Khaled Safadi was sitting in the passenger seat. A police officer saw that he was Lebanese and that there were cell phones in the car. He also saw that Safadi had something in his mouth. The officer thought it might be cocaine and ordered Safadi to spit it out.[47] A search incident to Safadi's arrest revealed a gun concealed at his waist. Safadi challenged the constitutionality of his detention and search. He argued that there were no reasonable grounds to conclude that he was a drug dealer. The trial judge agreed and concluded that the officer had used a seat-belt infraction as a pretext to conduct a drug investigation, based on the fact that Safadi was Lebanese and that there were cell phones in the car.[48] The evidence was excluded, and the charges against Safadi were stayed.

If, as the trial judge had found, the officer used race in deciding to investigate Safadi, we might wonder why he did so. The answer may lie in the 2002–2003 Annual Report of the Criminal Intelligence Service Alberta, which contained the following section:

> *Middle East–Based Organized Crime*
>
> Several groups are known to be active in drug trafficking and money laundering.... The activities of these groups will continue to be monitored."[49]

This same report links drug trafficking and other organized crime to Asian, South Asian, Aboriginal, and Jamaican groups.[50]

Chapters 6 and 7 continue to explore the "racialization" of crime and, in particular, gang and terrorist violence. They also attempt to document the collateral damage caused by profiling, and why racial profiling will not protect Canadians from these manifestations of violence.

[6]

The War on Gangs

THE FEAR OF GANG and gun violence appears to be the heightened face of fear in Canada.[1] So, when police officials speak about
crime, they often highlight the havoc wreaked by gangs, or, as
some have called them, "urban terrorists."[2] And, as in the war on
drugs, a number of powerful institutions have linked race and
gang affiliation.

The Federal Government On the federal government's Public
Safety and Emergency Preparedness website, browsers can find
the following statement about street gangs in Canada:

> Street gangs are a relatively new phenomenon in Canada,
> but their activities can have wide-ranging effects on the
> communities in which they operate. Street gangs are often
> based on ethnic origin, *including Asian and Aboriginal-based
> gangs*.... Street gangs are often regarded as a youth problem,
> but this is not always the case.[3]

This passage is troubling. Has our government qualified ethnic
origin in the same way as age? The statement about ethnicity is
presented as a fact: "they *are* often based" on ethnic origin. The

reference about youth is to a myth or stereotype that the website seeks to displace: "Street gangs are often *regarded* as a youth problem, but this is not always the case." In other words, this passage tells the reader not to assume that all gangs are youth gangs but to bear in mind that gangs are often ethnically based.

The Police The police have also racialized street gangs. In 1999 the Toronto Police Association placed a poster in the Yonge/Bloor subway station in Toronto showing a group of five Latino young men. A provincial election was looming, and the poster asked voters to "help fight crime by electing candidates who are prepared to take on the drug pushers, the pimps and rapists." It also had a caption that read: "There's only one thing that these guys fear. Your vote." The poster remained at the station for three weeks until it was finally removed.[4] It provides some evidence of the degree to which stereotyping occurs within the police. This was, after all, a public display. Similarly, a 2002 Canadian Police Survey on Youth Gangs, commissioned by the federal solicitor general, linked gang activity with Aboriginal and Asian groups in western Canada and with Black groups in Ontario, Quebec, and Nova Scotia.[5]

Criminal Intelligence Service Canada (CISC) In its 2004 Annual Report, CISC identified the scope of street-gang activity by linking it to particular racialized groups.[6] For example, it stated:

> In Alberta, Saskatchewan and Manitoba ... Aboriginal-based street gangs are generally involved in opportunistic, spontaneous and disorganized street-level criminal activities. ...
> In Quebec, the main street gangs are Caribbean-based, though other ethnic-based groups are increasingly emerging.[7]

As we saw in chapter 5, the annual reports from CISC over the period 1997–2005 have linked drug and violent crime to Asian and other racialized gangs.

The Media The media further perpetuates these stereotypes. For example, the results of the 2002 police survey were reported in a

National Post article entitled "Toronto and Its Gangs."[8] In "New Kind of Gang Brings Terror to Streets," *Calgary Herald* readers were told by police experts that there is a problem with Vietnamese and Chinese gangs in Calgary, Latino and Black gangs in Toronto, and Indo-Canadian gangs in Vancouver.[9] Other headlines over the last few years have read "Police Target Indo-Canadian Gang Violence";[10] "Local Task Force Links 2,300 Natives to Gangs in Edmonton";[11] "Assault Possibly Linked to Sri Lanken Gangs";[12] "Chinese Gang Member Was Ring's CEO";[13] "Vietnamese Gang Wars Escalate";[14] "Asian Gangs Deemed Biggest Threat";[15] and "Police Identify Gangs as 'Latino.'"[16]

This official racialization of gangs has served to further place racialized groups at the margins of our society and at risk for increased surveillance. As we saw from the data presented in chapter 2, the vast majority of serious violent offences in this country are committed by Whites. And yet, as one *Toronto Star* reader put it in a letter: "Never, despite the brutality and violence of the crime, have I ever seen a single headline or subtitle about 'white on white' violence. ... Seems only appropriate to attach a race label on violence when it involves black people."[17] Turning the gang problem into a race issue has and will continue to transform stereotypes into reasonable assumptions. Consider, for example, the current practice of tracking Aboriginal gangs in Manitoba.

TRACKING ABORIGINAL GANGS IN MANITOBA

HAVING IDENTIFIED ABORIGINAL MEMBERSHIP in certain street gangs such as the "Indian Posse," "Ruthless Posse," and "Manitoba Warriors," a number of Winnipeg police officers appear to be routinely conducting spot checks based on nothing more than a person's Aboriginality and, sometimes, clothing. In *R. v. B.(K.)*, for example, a police officer with the Winnipeg Police Service Gang Unit testified that he spot checks five to twenty suspected gang members a day.[18] Based on this testimony, the trial judge concluded: "[I]t appears that such checks were a regular practice of at least some members of the Winnipeg Police Service."[19] In this case, K.B., who is Aboriginal, was stopped and searched because he was wearing red and was in the presence of a "known" gang member. The search revealed a pocket knife. On appeal, the Manitoba Court of Appeal upheld the trial judge's decision that the police did not have reasonable grounds to detain K.B., and it concluded that he had been the victim of "guilt by association" reasoning.[20]

WHY RACIAL PROFILING WILL NOT SOLVE THE GANG PROBLEM

THERE IS NO QUESTION that gang violence requires attention.[21] However, the answer does not lie with the aggressive policing of race on our streets as some, such as Michael Thompson, a Black Toronto city councillor, have suggested.[22] While it makes sense to have increased police presence in areas identified as "hot spots,"[23] there is a difference between increased police presence as part of a community-oriented and -directed initiative and the indiscriminate stopping and searching of racialized residents — which is what racial profiling is all about.[24] Is it fair to focus on an entire community in order to apprehend a very small number of offenders? Is it just, as a politically expedient means of dealing with a complex problem, to make communities feel they are under the constant eye of the police?[25]

In *R. v. Ferdinand*, two police officers testified about a community policing initiative in Humbermede, an identified high-crime area in the west end of Toronto (adjacent to the Jane-Finch corridor).[26] This neighbourhood has a significant racialized population.[27] As part of their proactive policing, the officers testified that they stop and fill out contact, or "208," cards with fifteen to forty-five individuals per shift.[28] These "208" cards contain information about the individual, and they are inputted into a police computer for monitoring purposes. As Justice Harry LaForme,

Canada's first Aboriginal appellate judge, observed, before being eleveated to the Ontario Court of Appeal, "[t]his kind of daily tracking of the whereabouts of persons — including many innocent law-abiding persons — has an aspect to it that reminds me of former government regimes that I am certain all of us would prefer not to replicate."[29]

Conducting mass stops and searches of racialized residents in certain designated neighbourhoods in Toronto (or elsewhere) will, in fact, make the problem worse. To be conducting countless numbers of stops of racialized youth, when the overwhelmingly majority of those stopped will not be a gang member or in possession of a gun, is an inefficient and unreliable use of resources. For example, a recent study suggests that 8 percent of Black youth are involved in criminal gang activity. The study also showed that while Black youth were overrepresented in gangs (4 percent of White youth reported gang membership), Whites still make up more gang members than any other racialized group (36 percent).[30] From a policing perspective, gang violence will be deterred or solved only in conjunction with good intelligence and tips from the community. In a speech to the National Black Police Association meeting in Toronto in August 2005, George Rhoden, a high-ranking member of Scotland Yard, made the same point: "If there is an influx of officers into the community, what they have to be careful about is the hyped tension around those who might be carrying guns. Officers may stop people who they think are committing a crime, but that should be intelligence-led. There needs to be intervention and enforcement, but not an abuse of their powers."[31]

One of the problems with intelligence gathering is that, in large cities like Toronto, Montreal, and Calgary, witnesses and others with relevant information, particularly in relation to gang shootings, often remain silent. This reluctance to come forward is partly due to the deep mistrust between racialized communities and the police, a gulf that is only perpetuated by racial profiling.[32]

Consider, for example, two statements made by respondents to the Ontario Human Rights Commission's racial profiling inquiry:

> Profiling does nothing but create distrust and resentment when it is done. This in turn causes a negative backlash in the community. This is part of the reason that the police force gets very little cooperation when dealing with the Black community.

> People are afraid to talk to the police in the Black community. ... There are good cops, but the bad ones make us mistrustful of all police. It makes it hard for them to solve crime.[33]

This mistrust has an impact not only on intelligence gathering but also on the efficacy of community policing efforts.

But perhaps, most significantly, there is reason to believe that racial profiling may, in addition to social and economic inequality, be a contributing cause of gun and gang violence. For example, there seems to be a link between the war on drugs in Toronto and the growth of gang activity, including youth gangs. With its use of a drug courier profile and intensive policing of poor and racialized communities, the war on drugs and racial profiling have created a one-way ticket to jail for many young Black men in Toronto. The limited education and employment opportunities that existed for them before prison because of systemic racism become even scarcer upon release.[34] Is it really a surprise that many of them turn to informal structures where they find self-worth, respect, community, and a means of earning a living?[35] Policing race instead of criminal behaviour is simply going to perpetuate this cycle. But it is not just racial profiling on the street that is contributing to the problem. The application of the *Safe Schools Act* in our high schools has had a disproportionate impact on Black students. When students are expelled and cannot find work, trouble is not far ahead. It is not a Black problem but one of human nature.

There is another link between racial profiling and gun violence. When you have done nothing wrong, it is an alienating, humiliating, and frightening experience to be confronted by the police on the street.[36] It confirms that race matters in Canada and that, regardless of what you do or whom you become, you will always be perceived by the police and society as the "usual suspect" or "up-to-no-good."[37] That is, in part, why racial profiling engenders a sense of anger, injustice, and a lack of respect for the state, including law enforcement and, most notably, the rule of law.[38] This sense of despair is only heightened when the police and others deny that profiling is a systemic problem and when our courts and politicians refuse to act. With despair and alienation comes conflict.[39] Moreover, the stigmatizing of a community, by treating crime and violence as a race issue, makes an impact on its psychological well-being and sense of self-worth. Racial profiling brings "fear, anxiety, intimidation, and feelings of helplessness and hopelessness. ... suicidal thoughts, depression and drug abuse."[40] It sends "a message to the person that he or she is less worthy of consideration and respect as a human being."[41] This, in turn, can lead to a general devaluing of human dignity and, ultimately, the sanctity of life.

For a small number of individuals, particularly those who have faced the brutality of prison, the damage becomes manifested in serious deviance and violence. As the Ontario Human Rights Commission discovered in its investigation into the effects of profiling, "[s]ome [respondents] even indicated that they felt that incidents of racial profiling would affect people's willingness to comply with the law."[42] And "[m]any participants noted that the psychological impact of racial profiling on their children has led to anti-social behaviour.... Several parents commented that one of their main fears was that racial profiling will lead their children, especially their sons, to view themselves as troublemakers and that this, in turn, will result in behaving badly."[43] This idea is not new. Criminological theories such as defiance theory[44] and

"forced criminality"[45] recognize that there is a link between perceived unfairness, bias, mistrust, and criminal offending.[46]

The problem of gangs and gun violence is clearly a complex
one requiring systemic solutions. It is not as simple as putting
more police on the streets to aggressively stop and search racialized youth or increasing the sentences for those convicted.[47] That
will only make things worse, without getting at the root of the
problem.[48] On the law enforcement side, gun control, both do-
mestically and as a border issue, remain an important part of the
solution.[49] On a more local level, Toronto's current mayor, David
Miller, put together a Panel on Community Safety in the spring
of 2004. The panel was "commissioned to bring forward public
policy recommendations and neighbourhood action plans to address gun-related violence, particularly among youth."[50] It is made
up of politicians, school board officials, members of the judiciary
(the panel is headed by Chief Justice Roy McMurtry of the Ontario Court of Appeal), community members, media, and rep-
resentatives from labour and business.[51] The mayor's vision and
plan to tackle youth violence is holistic, aimed at attacking the
root causes of crime — including racism, poverty, unemployment,
and despair.[52] The nine-point plan is focused on prevention rather
than enforcement. Miller tells the story of hearing a young person
at a public meeting say, "It's easier to get a gun than a job," as a
"wake-up" call for him and the city. His plan calls for more jobs
and recreation programs for youth, particularly in "at-risk" neighbourhoods.[53] It's an important step in the right direction.[54]

[7]

The War on Terrorism

On November 7, 2001, the United States president, George W. Bush, spoke to the nation about the need to stop terrorist financing. He announced that he had named sixty-two individuals and organizations that were, in his words, "quartermasters of terror." The next morning Liban Hussein, a thirty-one-year-old Somali-Canadian, discovered that both he and his money-transfer company, Barakaat North America, which had offices in Dorchester, Massachusetts, and Ottawa, had been listed by Bush on a terrorist financing list.[1] The Canadian government and the United Nations Security Council immediately followed suit. One month earlier Canada had adopted the *United Nations Suppression of Terrorism Regulations*, which created a Canadian list of entities and individuals with suspected terrorist ties and made it an offence to engage in financial transactions with listed targets.[2]

With civil war destroying the existing Somali banking system, money transfer companies, or hawalas, provide an important means for family members to send money back to Somalia.[3] Suddenly it was a crime to do business with Hussein, his bank account was frozen, he was charged, and he was subjected to extradition proceedings. The Americans wanted him for operating a business in the United States without a licence — a regulatory offence.[4] His brother, who worked as a clerk at the Dorchester location, was also listed and arrested in the United States. Hussein was released on bail when the government failed to produce any evidence of his involvement in money laundering or terrorist activity.[5] He remained in a state of limbo and fear for more than six months. On June 3, 2002, the Canadian government admitted that there had been a mistake and that Hussein would not be extradited. As the government conceded, "We've concluded he ought not to be on the list ... [t]here was no evidence he was connected to any terrorist activities. ... We relied on information from our partners."[6] Within six weeks, Hussein's name was removed from all terrorist lists.[7] Almost two years after he was wrongly listed, Hussein received compensation from the Canadian government.[8] Hussein's brother did not fare as well, however, because he was convicted of the licence offence and sentenced to eighteen months' imprisonment.[9]

The Liberal government served public notice of its intent to join the post–September 11 "war on terrorism" largely by introducing Bill C-36, otherwise known as the *Anti-Terrorism Act*, on October 15, 2001.[10] In explaining the purpose behind the bill, the minister of justice, Anne McLellan, stated that "[t]he horrific events of September 11 remind us that we must continue to work with other nations to confront terrorism and ensure that the full force of Canadian law is brought to bear against those who support, plan and carry out acts of terror — we will cut off their money, find them and punish them."[11] During the consultation phase, Irwin Cotler, who was then a member of parliament, and two University of Toronto law professors (Sujit Choudhry and Kent Roach) recommended that the bill include a ban on racial profiling or an anti-discrimination clause similar to section 4(b) of the *Emergencies Act*.[12] This suggestion was rejected by the drafters, leading observers to conclude that the government believed that some form of ethnic, religious, or country-of-origin profiling would be necessary to fight this war. Bill C-36 came into force on December 18, 2001, after just two months of debate.[13]

Canada has rarely seen the kind of damage caused by terrorist activity. It last felt the effects of a deadly and catastrophic terrorist act on June 23, 1985, when Air India flight 182 was blown up by a suitcase bomb near Ireland after taking off from Montreal.[14] Nevertheless, our government has repeatedly warned the public that Canada is not immune from an attack from al-Qaeda.[15] Canadians seem to agree. A poll taken after the London bombings revealed that 62 percent of Canadians believe that there will be an attack in this country in the next few years.[16]

THE PROFILE AND THE PROFILED

As we saw in chapter 1, one week after the September 11, 2001, terrorist attacks, the RCMP issued the following terrorist profile:

> By all accounts the hijackers of the four planes were men who lived in the United States for some time, did not act conspicuously, were well spoken, well dressed, educated and blended in well with the North American lifestyle. Similar subjects live in Canada and some have been identified. ... These identified individuals travel internationally with ease, use the Internet and technology to their advantage, know how to exploit our social and legal situation and are involved in criminal activities. Indications from investigative leads in the past week have given us a glimpse that there are many more potential terrorists in Canada.

By specifically identifying the adversary as the men who flew the planes, the profile implicitly includes their ethnic and religious characteristics. At the Arar Inquiry, Superintendent Michel Cabana of the RCMP confirmed that this document was an express invitation to use racial profiling.[17]

History appears to have confirmed that the document's invitation to use this profile in policing has occurred.[18] Since September

11, there have been numerous reports of the targeting of members of the Muslim and Arab communities in Canada.[19] Those on the front line urging the government to act, such as Senator Mobina Jaffer and Riad Saloojee, executive director of the Canadian Council on American-Islamic Relations (CAIR-CAN), have all recounted their own personal experiences with profiling.[20] Apparently CAIR-CAN was receiving so many reports that it ultimately decided to issue more than 30,000 copies of the guide, *Know Your Rights*. In describing the guide's purpose, Saloojee noted that "[w]e've been encouraging people to speak to CSIS and the RCMP because they should have nothing to hide, but we've also been telling them to do so with a lawyer present so that the questions are not intrusive, offensive or sort of witchhunt-type."[21]

Being on a No-Fly List

SHAHID MAHMOUD, A TORONTO architect and political cartoonist, has never been afraid to let his art speak its mind. In protest of the Iraq war, he drew a picture of Uncle Sam giving birth to Osama bin Laden and of George W. Bush reading a world atlas upside down. The picture, along with others in a collection Mahmoud called "Enduring Operation Freedom" (a spoof on Bush's Operation Enduring Freedom), was to appear in a show at the McMaster Museum of Art in Hamilton, Ontario, in January 2004. Mahmoud's participation in the exhibition was suddenly cancelled, when the curator told Mahmoud: "I don't think this is the proper political climate to be doing this in Hamilton right now." The curator later denied that the work's content was the reason for the cancellation.[22]

Shortly after his exhibit was cancelled, Mahmoud was at the Vancouver airport with his wife, planning to fly to Victoria to attend a friend's wedding. When they got to the counter to purchase tickets for flight AC-8087, he claims that he was told by an Air Canada employee that he had been flagged and would not be permitted on the plane. The Mahmouds eventually took the ferry.

The incident suggests that there is an unofficial Canadian "no-fly" list, despite official denials.[23] In any event, that issue is now moot, given that, on August 5, 2005, Transport Minister Jean Lapierre announced that the federal government intends to implement a no-fly list by 2006. It is to be part of a program called "Passenger Protect," designed to keep individuals who pose "an immediate threat to aviation security" off Canadian flights.[24] While the minister has vowed that ethnic origin or race will not be used as a criteria for inclusion, a no-fly list is a recipe for profiling, as there is virtually unlimited discretion and no accountability.[25] What kind of vetting, for example, will the minister do to determine whether a person he has been told is a threat by domestic or foreign security agencies has not been profiled? What standard will the minister apply to determine who is a threat? Who will be reviewing the minister's decision to include a name on the list? What process will be put in place to review that decision? After the Hussein and Arar incidents, these kinds of "lists" are of grave concern to the Muslim and Arab communities. As the Ontario Human Rights Commission found in its racial-profiling inquiry, "[a] common concern in this community is of facing increased deprivations of liberty in future or that persons' names may end up on 'lists' which will result in loss of privacy, further incidents of questioning, or worse."[26]

Security Visits

A 2004 SURVEY FROM CAIR-CAN involving 467 respondents suggests troubling levels of racial profiling in the Arab and Muslim communities outside the traditional airport/border context.[27] The study reveals that 8 percent of respondents reported being visited at home or at work and questioned, and in some cases threatened, by security officials.[28] Of those contacted, 54 percent were young Arab males, even though only 35 percent of the respondents were Arab.[29] Many believe that the numbers are much higher. As Saloojee has pointed out, some Muslims and Arabs are reluctant to come forward to report state misconduct, in part because silence was the norm in the countries where they were born. Others are naturally reluctant to report being targeted for fear of being publicly labelled a terrorist.[30] Perhaps a more accurate indication of the degree of profiling comes from the statistic that 43 percent of respondents knew of someone who had been targeted.[31]

THE COLLATERAL DAMAGE

THE WAR ON TERRORISM in Canada has created tremendous psychological and, in some cases, physical harm for Arabs, Muslims, South Asians, and others perceived to fall within the profile. Even those not directly affected are harmed by living under a constant fear that it will soon happen to them. Entire communities have been stigmatized. Islamophobia, defined as "stereotypes, bias or acts of hostility towards individual Muslims or followers of Islam in general," has grown to very troubling levels.[32] In one survey, 56 percent of Canadian Muslim respondents reported experiencing anti-Muslim incidents on at least one occasion in the year after September 11, with 33 percent of those incidents involving verbal abuse and a further 18 percent involving racial profiling. Other manifestations of hate crimes, such as attacks on Mosques and Islamic centres, have also been reported.[33] According to a 2003 statement by the Canadian Islamic Congress, Canada has witnessed a 1,600 percent increase in hate crimes since September 11.[34]

There are also some manifestations of reactionary justice. We have witnessed largely secret hearings for five Muslim non-citizens who have been in preventative detention without charge, in one case for more than six years, pursuant to security certificates issued at the discretion of the minister of immigration and citizenship and the minister of public safety and emergency preparedness.[35] The 2004 CAIR-CAN survey suggests that security officials are resorting to heavy-handed tactics to secure intelligence. These tactics include inadequate identification, discouraging legal representation, visiting Arab and Muslims at work, aggressive and threatening behaviour (including threats of preventative arrest under the *Anti-Terrorism Act* for not cooperating), and intimidating requests to become an informant.[36]

OFFICIAL DENIAL

DESPITE THE GROWING EVIDENCE and the RCMP profile, the government has consistently maintained that there is no racial profiling in Canada.[37] We are, however, beginning to see some cracks in this official position. A draft report prepared by the Department of Justice was obtained by the *Globe and Mail* in February 2005. It suggests that racial profiling is of "genuine concern" and requires further investigation, as it is a "high-profile and pressing issue."[38] The denial is likely the result of a misunderstanding about what profiling is all about. Perhaps the government thinks that profiling occurs only when a prohibited ground (e.g., ethnicity or country of origin) is the sole reason for the investigation. It is not profiling, it might argue, if agents detained a young male from Algeria who is a nuclear engineer because the focus is also on age, gender, and occupation. Or perhaps the government does not even equate the RCMP profile with racial profiling because it does not explicitly refer to ethnicity or religion or because it includes other features. However, because the Algerian example and the RCMP profile both focus on status, and not specific behaviour, they represent examples of classic racial profiling.

Alternatively, perhaps officials at the Ministry of Public Safety and Emergency Preparedness believe that this form of ethnicity plus profiling (where ethnicity or religion is only one part of the profile) is necessary to protect us. Since September 11 there has been no shortage of newspaper editorials, commentaries, and academic writing arguing in favour of using some form of racial profiling in screening and security investigations.[39] For example, Jonathan Kay of the *National Post* has said: "[W]e should not pretend that an effective fight against terrorism can be waged in a truly colour-blind fashion ... The fact is, those who plot the annihilation of our civilization are of one religion and, almost without exception, one race."[40] These views appear to be shared by 49 percent of Canadians.[41] But will racial profiling protect us from the next catastrophic terrorist attack?

WHY RACIAL PROFILING WILL NOT PROTECT US FROM THE NEXT ACT OF TERRORISM

IN FEBRUARY 1999 AHMED RESSAM, a twenty-two-year-old Algerian who had been in Canada since 1994 seeking political asylum, returned from a terrorist training camp in Afghanistan. For the next few months he used what he had learned in Afghanistan and planned and prepared for a terrorist attack on Los Angeles Airport (LAX) on December 31, 1999.[42] On December 14, 1999, Ressam left his Victoria motel with his rented Chrysler sedan. It was packed with 50 kilograms of explosives and bomb-making materials. He was headed to a ferry that would take him to Port Angeles in Washington State. At the Victoria Port, Ressam was able to pass scrutiny by the U.S. Immigration and Naturalization Service because he had earlier obtained a genuine Canadian passport under the name Benni Antoine Noris.[43] His journey of terror had begun.

Once at Port Angeles, Ressam waited until all the other vehicles had exited the ferry, thinking that would make him less likely to attract suspicion. However, he was ill, having acquired malaria while in Afghanistan, and visibly showing it.[44] When he presented himself to a U.S. Customs official, he was sweating, fumbling, and appeared nervous. He also appeared hesitant to answer her questions about his itinerary in the United States. The Customs official referred him to secondary inspection. As he was being further questioned and his car examined, he became scared and fled, but he was quickly apprehended and arrested.

In 2001 Ressam, now dubbed the "millennium bomber," was convicted on nine counts of explosives and terrorist conspiracy charges and, on July 27, 2005, he was sentenced to twenty-two years of imprisonment.[45] His sentence would have been much longer had he not assisted the American authorities. He had not only testified at the trial of one of his accomplices but had provided information about more than one hundred suspected terrorists operating around the world.[46] In sentencing Ressam, U.S. District Court judge John Coughenour went out of his way to use the case as a symbol of how open justice can work, even in the terrorism era. As he put it, "[w]e did not need to use a secret military tribunal, or detain the defendant indefinitely as an enemy combatant or deny him the right to counsel."[47]

Was Ressam profiled by American authorities? It is hard to say. There are conflicting reports about whether border officials were even on alert for a possible terrorist threat. According to Richard Clarke, the White House's trusted adviser on counter terrorism and author of *Against All Enemies*, an alert about Bin Laden attacks on Americans worldwide had been issued. However, at the September 11 Commission hearings, National Security Advisor Condoleezza Rice testified that, at that time, customs officials "weren't actually on alert."[48] It would appear, therefore, that the Customs agent more likely thought Ressam was a possible drug importer than a terrorist threat. There were objective signs to support her suspicion that something was amiss and, of course, Ressam fled when the officers started to investigate him and his vehicle. This sequence suggests that it was behaviour, and not racial profiling, that successfully prevented the attack. But let's assume, for the moment, that Ressam had been racially profiled: Does that mean that profiling would work to prevent a catastrophic event?

The lessons of history, common sense, and practice all teach us that racial profiling will not protect us against terrorism.[49] Let us start with history. After the bombing of Pearl Habor in 1941, the American and Canadian governments resorted to racial profiling in its most extreme form. Many Japanese Canadians and Americans living on the west coast were forced to move to internment camps. We now realize that this reaction was an unjust and unacceptable response that did not make us any safer. In the late 1960s we saw the use of profiling at American airports following an epidemic of airline highjackings (primarily of U.S. planes headed to Cuba). The profiling did not work. By 1973 the FAA abandoned its use of profiling and, instead, had airports across North America implement metal detectors and x-ray machines. By 1976 there was a 90 percent reduction in highjackings.[50]

As a matter of common sense, there are two reasons why racial profiling will not protect us from future terrorist attacks. The effectiveness of any form of profiling depends on an accurate profile of the suspect. The profile of the terrorist tells us very little.[51] Names can be changed, accents can be hidden, and, for that matter, many Arabs and Muslims do not look the part. For example, many followers of Islam are Black; others are White. Many Arabs are Christian. The London subway bombings on July 7, 2005, came from citizens, not foreign nationals.[52] Moreover, the size of target is enormous. With respect to the Muslim community, there are approximately 580,000 Muslims in Canada;[53] between 1 and 3 million Muslims in the United States;[54] and 1.5 billion in the world. Moreover, fifty-four countries in the world have significant Muslim populations.[55]

It is easy to play Monday morning quarterback and point to the fact that Ressam fit the profile. But that was yesterday, and the profile appears to be constantly changing. The terrorist attacks have all been well planned, and the terrorists are likely acutely aware of the use of racial profiling. Indeed, it would appear that they are conscripting individuals who will evade it at key locations such as the airport, border, or train station. Even before September 11, Jack Roche, a White British-born Australian, met Osama bin Laden at a training camp in Afghanistan and was told to recruit White Australians. Roche would later become the first Australian convicted under its anti-terrorism legislation for his involvement in an al-Qaeda plot to bomb the Israeli Embassy in Canberra.[56] Three months after September 11, Richard Reid, a British citizen of Jamaican ancestry, attempted to blow up American Airlines flight 63 from Paris to Miami with a bomb in his shoe.[57]

Similarly, John Walker Lindh, a White American, and David Hicks, a White Australian, fought for al-Qaeda in Afghanistan, and they would have been prime candidates to carry out terrorist acts in the United States or Australia had they not been caught.[58] And finally, on May 8, 2002, Jose Padilla, a Hispanic American and the so-called dirty bomber, was arrested at Chicago's O'Hare Airport. Authorities claimed he was on his way to contaminate an American city with a radiological bomb. No such bomb was found. Padilla was declared an enemy combatant and remains in custody in the United States.[59] Attempts to beat the profile have been tried by others seeking to perpetrate terrorist acts. For example, in 1986 a Palestinian man put a bomb in the suitcase of his pregnant and unaware girlfriend. Fortunately, it was detected when the woman's routine answers to questions alerted airport security.[60] These examples show why it is so dangerous to rely on past events like September 11 or the arrest of Ressam in trying to figure out whom to target to avert a future attack. Perhaps that is why the British were caught off guard on July 7, 2005 when they were attacked by their own citizens.

Racial profiling is not only unreliable but highly inefficient, because the profile is so over-inclusive. It will, therefore, impede law-enforcement efforts. The targeting of thousands of individuals on the street or at the airport, based on race, religion, or place of origin, is not an efficient use of limited resources. It is also a gross violation of human rights and dignity. Officials will be spending so much time and effort targeting and monitoring Arab and Muslim groups that there will be little time for real investigation. After four years of post–September 11 racial profiling at our borders, there is no evidence that it has had any impact on the war. More significant, the use of racial profiling will have only a negative impact on intelligence gathering. One of the best sources of intelligence on terrorism connected to the Arab-Muslim world will come from these communities. However, such sources are not likely to come forward with information if our governments implicitly sanction the use of racial profiling or if the police harass members of these communities, as they appear to be doing, in the hope that someone will agree to act as informant.[61]

What will protect us from future attacks? Real investigation, like all good policing, must focus on intelligence gathering and on suspicious behaviour, because it is behaviour, not appearance, that will identify future terrorists. Before September 11, this suspicious behaviour included travelling with expired visas, the cash purchase of a first-class one-way ticket, and learning to fly without also learning how to land. We have now learned that the attacks may have been prevented not by the use of racial profiling but by a coordinated sharing of intelligence data and vigorous pursuit of viable leads.[62] The key to national security policy will be the efficient use of limited resources, better and coordinated intelligence gathering, and stronger security measures at the border, airports, and other vulnerable targets.[63] Racial profiling will threaten rather than enhance the very effectiveness of these measures.

Returning to the Ressam case, an external review of CSIS's handling of the case by the Security Intelligence Review Committee (SIRC) concluded that there was no lack of vigilance in pursuing Ressam in Canada:

> Having reviewed all the relevant documentation from the time of Ressam's arrival in Canada in February 1994 through to March 2001, the Committee concluded that the Service did not possess information that would have forewarned it specifically of Ressam's planned terrorist operations, and that Ressam's ability to escape detection after his return to Canada in 1999 could not be attributed to a lack of vigilance on the part of the Service.[64]

There is evidence, however, that a better coordinated intelligence effort would have led to his arrest long before he crossed the Canadian border that mid-December day in 1999.

The French had warned CSIS about Ressam's terrorist-related activities.[65] By 1996 French intelligence was aware that he and six other Montreal men were selling fake passports to enable individuals to go to Afghanistan and train at terrorist camps.[66] And yet he remained at large in Canada, living in an apartment building in Montreal that served as the headquarters of the Armed Islamic Group (GIA), a terrorist cell linked to Osama bin Laden.[67] CSIS had him under surveillance for two years: it was aware that he had gone to train in Afghanistan and that he had returned to Canada, although it claimed to have lost track of him at this time and were unaware of his alias.[68] In April 1999 the French requested that search warrants be executed in Montreal in connection with the GIA terrorist cell, but it took Canada six months to process the request. Leaving national security coordination aside for a moment, there appeared to be little reason for Immigration to have not acted sooner in deporting Ressam. As the September 11 Commission Report pointed out:

> [After he made a claim for political asylum, he] was released pending a hearing which he failed to attend. His political asylum claim was denied. He was arrested again, released again, and given another hearing. Again, he did not show. He was arrested four times for thievery, usually from tourists, but was neither jailed nor deported.[69]

Part Three

MOVING FORWARD

Litigating Cases

HAVING IDENTIFIED THE SCOPE and nature of the problem of
racial profiling in Canada, this third part of the book examines
how courts and government can better respond to address the
problem. The response must ensure not only that victims have
access to a meaningful remedy but that sufficient safeguards are
put in place to deter police and security officials from using this
destructive and unreliable policing tool. This chapter explores the
challenges and potential strategies that can be used by civil and
criminal lawyers in litigating racial-profiling cases in our courts.
While criminal cases are the most likely place where profiling
claims will be litigated, given that the accused's liberty is often
at stake, we may begin to see more civil actions. To date, only a
handful of civil racial-profiling lawsuits have been reported in the
newspapers or law reports.[1]

In one of these cases, Rasim Karela, who is Muslim, and his neighbour, Kerry Bevis, sued ATV (a local CTV affiliate in the Maritimes) for defamation, and two RCMP officers for arbitrary arrest and detention.[2] Four days after the attacks on September 11, the RCMP received a tip that the two men, one of whom was identified as "a man of Middle-Eastern descent," appeared "suspicious" and were travelling to Halifax by ferry. It is not clear what was suspicious other than the fact that Karela had a dark complexion. Apparently, rumours were flying around the East Coast that some of the terrorists had arrived in the United States on a ferry from Halifax.[3] Some time after they got off the ferry, the two men were arrested at gunpoint and told that the arrest was in connection with the terrorist bombings in New York. After travelling a short distance, the men were released when the police realized they had made a mistake.[4] The arrests were caught on tape and broadcast in the Maritime provinces. ATV had received notice that the police were following two men possibly connected to the New York attacks.[5] Bevis and Karela won their lawsuit: they were each awarded a paltry sum of $1,500 by a jury for false arrest, and Karela received an additional $15,000 in relation to his action against the television station. The jury did not award Bevis damages for the broadcast because they must have felt he was not identified by it.[6]

Civil suits are important because they can bring about more systemic changes than in criminal cases, where the accused is most often concerned about being acquitted. In the United States, racial-profiling lawsuits, including class actions, have been effective in forcing police departments to take measures to address the problem: for example, instituting a data-collection program; getting video cameras in police cruisers; and ensuring equity in hiring, promoting, and training.[7] Class actions can also serve, to some extent, to shield the public exposure of the litigant. That is important in the terrorism context, where, as we have seen, individuals are understandably reluctant to come forward and complain that they have been unfairly singled out by security officials.

With the emergence of contingency fees in Ontario, more lawyers may now be prepared to entertain racial-profiling lawsuits.
Lawsuits could be further stimulated if courts were prepared to
forgo the usual awarding of costs to the winning party out of a
recognition that profiling cases are hard to prove and that the police have deep pockets, allowing them to retain senior lawyers and
to delay proceedings. This approach was taken in *Peart v. Peel (Regional Municipality) Police Services Board*, one of the first racial-
profiling civil actions in Canada. The plaintiffs, two Black men,
lost the action, and the defendants sought $160,000 in costs. In
refusing to order costs, Justice Lane held:

> I have no doubt that an order for costs against them would
> act as a significant deterrent to others who may have grounds
> for believing that they have been the target of racial profil-
> ing. I am reluctant to create such a deterrent. It is not in the
> interests of justice to erect barriers to access to the courts
> in light of the strong public interest in stamping out racial
> discrimination in all its forms.[8]

Some people may be concerned that not awarding costs will encourage frivolous litigation. However, there is simply no evidence
that this will occur. The problem is that there are not enough
lawsuits, not that there are too many. Moreover, lawyers have an
ethical obligation not to pursue frivolous claims, and civil claims
can be screened for merit before trial on what is called a motion
for summary judgment. If anything, it is the police who have too
often resorted to civil actions in an effort to silence criticisms.[9]
Consider, for example, the $2.7 billion lawsuit filed by the Toronto
Police Association against the *Toronto Star* for libel, one that was
ultimately dismissed on summary judgment.[10] Or the defamation
lawsuit filed by a Halifax police officer against Halifax lawyers
Anne Derrick, whose clients have included Donald Marshall Jr.
and Dr. Henry Morgentaler, and Burnley "Rocky" Jones, a criminal defence lawyer who was one of the victims of the RCMP spying
campaign highlighted earlier in this book.

Derrick and Jones were acting for three high school girls, all of whom were Black and who had been strip searched at their school by a female police officer in 1995. The officer was investigating the girls in relation to a $10 theft. The students intended to file a police complaint, and Derrick and Jones agreed to assist them for free. In a press conference, the lawyers discussed systemic racism within the Halifax Police Department and suggested that, if the girls had been White and affluent, they would not have been searched in this manner. The officer sued the lawyers and succeeded at trial, where she was awarded approximately $345,000 in damages ($240,000 for damaged reputation and $105,000 in legal costs). The verdict was overturned on appeal.[11] A majority of the Nova Scotia Court of Appeal held that Derrick and Jones had acted ethically and appropriately in speaking out against the injustice that had occurred in the case and that they were, therefore, immune from prosecution under what is known in legal terms as the doctrine of "qualified privilege."[12] The *Police Act* complaint was resolved informally with an acknowledgment that the officer had violated the girls' constitutional rights.[13] On September 2, 2005, Anne Derrick was appointed to the Nova Scotia Provincial Court.

In addition to examining how lawyers can strategically attempt to make a case of racial profiling, this chapter examines what law reform measures should be implemented by our courts. The Supreme Court of Canada's decision in *R. v. Golden*, a case involving a strip search of a young Black man at a Subway restaurant in downtown Toronto, should serve as an important stimulus for developing new constitutional standards. Following his arrest, Golden was taken to the basement's stairwell landing by two officers. Golden resisted when one of the officers looked down his pants and tried to stick his hand down Golden's underwear. Golden was then brought back into the restaurant, where his pants and underwear were lowered as he was bent over a bench. One of the officers attempted to remove a plastic baggie from his buttocks. At some point, Golden defecated. The officer asked the clerk who was still in the store to get a pair of gloves. He retrieved the gloves used to clean the washroom. The officer put on the gloves and was able, finally, to remove the baggie from Golden's buttocks. At this point, Golden was face-down on the ground, with one officer holding his feet and another near his head. The baggie contained approximately 10.1 grams of crack cocaine. All this activity had occurred in a public space, even though the police station was a two-minute drive away. It was "tantamount to a public lynching," as Donald McLeod, counsel for the intervener African Canadian Legal Clinic, emphatically stated in oral argument in the Supreme Court.[14] In its judgment finding that the strip search was unconstitutional, a majority of the Supreme Court recognized that racialized groups in Canada are over-policed and that constitutional standards need to be developed to address this situation.[15] Before examining how to construct a racial-profiling case, we will review a case that reveals one of the challenges that lies ahead.

THE BITTER LESSON OF R.D.S.

"ROCKY" JONES CAME TO national prominence in 1997 when he argued *R. v. S.(R.D.)*, one of the most important race cases ever argued in the Supreme Court of Canada.[16] Although the case was about an allegation of judicial bias, it was, in many respects, a case about racial profiling. On an early fall day in 1993, two Halifax police officers were on patrol when they received word that other officers were in pursuit of a stolen van. The occupants were described as "non-white youth." When the two officers got to the "designated" area, a predominantly Black neighbourhood, they saw two Black youths running across the street. One of the officers decided to detain and arrest N.R., one of the youths he saw running.

R.D.S., who was fifteen years old, happened to be in the area visiting his grandmother. On his way home on his bicycle, he saw a crowd and heard that his cousin had been arrested. When he got to the scene, he saw N.R. in handcuffs. He asked him what was going on and whether he should tell his mother. According

to R.D.S., the officer told him to "shut up, shut up, or you'll be under arrest too." When he continued to ask his cousin if he should
call his mother, the officer arrested him and put both of them
in a choke hold, one of the most dangerous uses of police force.
R.D.S. had difficulty breathing and speaking. The officer's version of events was different. He testified that R.D.S. had run into
his legs with his bicycle, yelled and pushed him. He decided to
arrest R.D.S. for a number of offences, including unlawful assault, unlawful assault with the intention of preventing the arrest
of N.R., and unlawfully resisting him in the lawful execution of
his duty. He did, however, admit to placing both boys in a "neck
restraint."

The trial judge was Justice Corrine Sparks, the only Black judge
in Nova Scotia at the time.[17] Justice Sparks was appointed to the
Family Court bench in 1987, becoming the first African Canadian
female to serve on the judiciary. In 1993 she was appointed to the
Canadian Bar Association's Gender Equality Task Force and completed a study on women of colour in the legal profession. Justice
Sparks has also been a leading proponent of judicial education
and, in particular, social context education, and she lectures on
issues of racial and gender discrimination at a new judges training program offered by the Canadian Association of Provincial
Court Judges.[18]

Justice Sparks acquitted R.D.S. of all charges. She accepted his
version of events and provided reasons for finding him to be a
credible witness. At the end of her oral reasons, she responded to
a question the Crown had asked in closing submissions — Why
would the officer lie? It was an unfair question for the Crown to
ask, as it implied that police officers always tell the truth. It also
placed an impossible burden on the accused to delve into the officer's mind at the time of the arrest. Moreover, in a criminal case,
an accused has only to raise a reasonable doubt, not to prove that
the central Crown witness is lying. Consequently, Justice Sparks
did not have to address this question. Nevertheless, she decided to
offer the Crown an explanation. Here is how she responded:

The Crown says, well, why would the officer say the events occurred the way in which he has relayed them to the Court this morning. I am not saying that the Constable has misled the court, although police officers have been known to do that in the past. I am not saying that the officer overreacted, but certainly police officers do overreact particularly when dealing with non-white groups. That to me indicates a state of mind right there that is questionable. I believe that probably the situation in this particular case is the case of a young police officer who overreacted. I do accept the evidence of [R.D.S.] that he was told to shut up or he would be under arrest. It seems to be in keeping with the prevalent attitude of the day. At any rate, based upon my comments and based upon all of the evidence before the court I have no other choice but to acquit.[19]

The Crown immediately appealed the case. It alleged that Justice Sparks's reasons revealed that she was racially biased against the police.[20] Imagine what was going through Rocky Jones's mind, who had himself been victimized by police overreaction and racist stereotyping, when he received the Crown's notice of appeal. It was an extraordinary allegation to make. In cases where a White judge's conduct is challenged, the claim is rarely one of actual bias but instead possible bias, or, in legal terms, a reasonable apprehension of bias.[21] Justice Sparks must have been deeply troubled by the allegation of bias, reminding her of the days when she grew up in a racially segregated community and attended a racially segregated school in Nova Scotia. The allegation reveals that the colour of justice in Canada has an impact on all participants in the criminal justice system.

At the first two levels of appeal, the acquittal was set aside and a new trial ordered. The courts concluded that Justice Sparks's comments would raise in the minds of "reasonable right-minded" individuals the possibility that the trial judge's "impartiality might reasonably be questioned."[22] This was the first time that a

Canadian court had found "racially grounded bias, either real or apprehended."[23] The acquittal was restored on a further appeal to the Supreme Court of Canada. Six of the nine justices ultimately agreed that there was no apprehended bias, although two of the six indicated that the comments had come close to the line because of the absence of any evidence linking the social context generalizations highlighted by Justice Sparks (systemic racism in the Halifax Police department) to the particular facts of the case.[24] Chief Justice Lamer and Justices Major and Sopinka dissented and ordered a new trial because they were of the view that the trial judge had stereotyped the officer.[25]

In *S.(R.D.)* the Supreme Court did, however, recognize the troubled history of racism in the Halifax police force. For example, Justice Cory (with Justice Iacobucci concurring) observed that this history "suggests that there is a reasonable possibility that the actions taken by the police in their relations with visible minorities demonstrate both prejudice and discrimination."[26] He also acknowledged, based on the sociological material filed by the parties on appeal, that "in some cases, racism may have been exhibited by police officers in arresting young black males."[27]

The problem was that, despite this recognition, Justice Cory was of the view, shared by a majority of the Court, that "there was *no* evidence before Judge Sparks that would suggest that anti-black bias influenced *this particular police officer's reactions*."[28] And so he wrote that, "although it may be incontrovertible that there is a history of racial tension between police officers and visible minorities, there was no evidence to link that generalization to the actions [of the police officer]."[29] But was the majority correct that there was, in fact, no evidence to link the officer's overreaction with systemic racism? Was the majority looking only for direct evidence? Looking at the case circumstantially, what other reasonable explanation could there have been for an armed officer to feel so threatened by two young boys, one of whom was handcuffed, that he had to place them both in choke or neck holds? Why was R.D.S. overcharged for such a minor incident? As we saw in the

Introduction, overcharging is one of the manifestations of systemic racism. In her supplementary reasons given after the appeal was launched, and which were not, for that reason, considered by the Supreme Court, Justice Sparks held:

> On cross-examination by defence counsel the police officer admitted that his police department routinely refers to African-Canadian persons, at least back in October 1993, the date of these alleged offences, as "non-white." At this point in his *viva voce* evidence, the officer became ruffled; and in my view became tense. The line of questioning by defence counsel was that this labelling of "non-white" was a pejorative categorization of African-Canadians.... Generally, the court observed that this witness appeared nervous when he commenced giving evidence. It was not unnoticed by the Court that this may have been due to the racial configuration in the court which consisted of the accused, the defence counsel, the court reporter and the judge all being of African-Canadian ancestry ...
>
> ... the Court notes that the police officer is a full bodied man while the young person is slight and slender and was probably lighter in weight when the incident occurred as the incident happened over one year ago. The Court questioned the necessity of choke-holding a young person of such a slight and slender build. Also, in my mind, was the fact that, from other proceedings, it is not routine for a police officer to place a 15 year old youngster in a choke-hold.[30]

The bitter lesson of *S.(R.D.)* is that, even with an evidentiary record, courts will be reluctant to draw the inference of racial profiling. Perhaps this hesitation will change as we move forward. Can we take anything positive from the decision? Does the majority's conclusion mean that the social context evidence of racial profiling, judicially noted in the Dee Brown case, cannot be used by triers of fact in assessing credibility? In a subsequent case, Justice Doherty of the Ontario Court of Appeal recognized that, in interpreting

evidence, triers of fact can indeed use social context evidence as a
lens to assist them in deciding what inferences to draw:

> *R. v. S.(R.D.)* draws a distinction between findings of fact
> based exclusively on personal judicial experience and judi-
> cial perceptions of applicable social context, and findings of
> fact based on evidence viewed through the lens of personal
> judicial experience and social context. The latter is proper;
> the former is not.[31]

PUTTING TOGETHER A CIRCUMSTANTIAL CASE

Vehicle Stops

FOR CIVIL OR CRIMINAL lawyers representing victims of DWB,
it will be a challenge to prove that race played a role in the officers' decisions to conduct the vehicle stop, given that officers can
simply shield their true motives by claiming that the vehicle was
speeding or that they simply wanted to check to ensure that the
driver had a valid licence. Direct evidence from the officers that
they relied on race is not likely to be forthcoming. Moreover, most
police officers do not even realize that their decisions are affected
by racialized stereotypes.[32] Consequently, lawyers are going to
have to be creative in establishing a circumstantial case of racial
profiling. Being creative requires, in part, an understanding of
policing methodology.

The exposure of racial profiling in the United States has been
linked to the use of pretext vehicle stops, particularly as an investigative tool in the "war on drugs."[33] Indeed, as Chief Bill Closs of
the Kingston Police once observed, "40 percent of all drug arrests
begin as a traffic stop."[34] Officer Bob Vogel of the Florida Highway
Patrol, one of the masterminds behind the creation of the drug
courier profile ultimately adopted by Operation Pipeline, discovered, after years of patrolling I-95 in Florida, that pretext vehicle
stops were an effective way of seizing an opportunity to look for

his profile "indicators."[35] Vogel's discovery is hardly surprising. Vehicle stops provide the police with a low-visibility opportunity to question the driver, conduct a visual surveillance of the interior of the vehicle (including with a flashlight at night), and, if lucky, obtain permission to search the vehicle. Moreover, there are so many minor traffic violations that most drivers likely commit one or two at any given time, and, in *R. v. Ladouceur*,[36] a decision we will examine in more detail later, the Supreme Court of Canada held that the police can randomly stop a vehicle without the need for any belief that the driver has committed a traffic violation.

While the police have tremendous discretion in carrying out vehicle stops, pretext vehicle stops are unconstitutional in Canada. In *Brown v. Durham Regional Police Force*,[37] a case involving the targeting of motorcycle gangs on a highway in eastern Ontario, the Ontario Court of Appeal held that section 9 of the *Charter* (i.e., the right to be free from arbitrary detention) is violated when the police use their traffic-stop powers as a pretext for a criminal investigation,[38] or where the police conduct a traffic stop with a coextensive improper purpose such as the targeting of racialized groups.[39] The Court of Appeal ultimately held that the targeting of members, friends, or associates of the Paradise Riders and similar organizations, in the circumstances of that case, was not arbitrary, as it was related, in part, to valid highway traffic concerns.

In coming to the conclusion that pretext stops are unconstitutional, the Ontario Court of Appeal did not follow the lead of the United States Supreme Court in *Whren v. United States*, where Justice Scalia, for the Court, refused to invalidate racially motivated traffic stops under the Fourth Amendment of the American Constitution, the one that protects against unreasonable searches and seizures.[40] Given the nature and extent of the racial-profiling phenomenon, a court should be satisfied of the existence of racial profiling where it has concluded that a vehicle stop of a racialized driver was a pretext for a criminal investigation. As Justice Morden observed, for the Court, in *Brown*:

The respondent submits that where the evidence shows that the circumstances relating to a detention correspond to the phenomenon of racial profiling and provide a basis for the court to infer that the police officer is lying about why he or she singled out the accused person for attention, the record is then capable of supporting a finding that the stop was based on racial profiling. I accept that this is a way in which racial profiling could be proven.[41]

In thinking about whether a stop was a pretext, the relevant question will be whether the officer acted in accordance with standard procedure for a traffic stop. In other words, taking into account all the circumstances, would a reasonable officer, in the shoes of the officer making the stop, have made the stop to pursue the alleged traffic violation or inquiry?[42]

In answering this question, there are a number of relevant factors that should be considered:

The nature of the police officers' work Most traffic stops are conducted by officers assigned to traffic duty or constables engaged in routine street patrol. It would be highly unusual for a narcotics officer, detective, or an officer in an unmarked car to conduct a routine traffic stop. In one case, for example, two officers from Toronto's Emergency Task Force, an elite division of the force, claimed to have stopped the accused's vehicle to enforce a minor traffic violation.[43]

The alleged traffic violation Given that all drivers commit traffic violations when they drive, whether it be driving a few kilometres over the speed limit, failing to signal, or failing to come to a complete stop at a stop sign, close scrutiny should be given to the alleged violation. Is it really reasonable to expect the police to stop and caution everyone who, for example, is driving quickly, as was the case in *Richards*[44] and *R. v. Martin*,[45] or because the rear passenger might not be wearing a seatbelt, as was the case in *R. v. Singh?*[46]

Whether the officers had to go out of their way to conduct the stop In a number of traffic cases, the police were driving in the opposite direction when they purportedly noticed some improper driving and thus had to make a U-turn to stop the vehicle, as occurred in *Richards*,[47] *Singh*,[48] and *R. v. McIntosh*.[49] That would appear to be highly unusual behaviour for relatively minor traffic infractions.

The nature of the call to the dispatcher It is not uncommon for the police to call dispatch to give notice of the pending vehicle stop. If a call is made and no reason is given for the stop, that would be suspicious, as it suggests the officer is hiding the true reason for the stop or has not yet realized a need to fabricate a reason. Similarly, a call for back-up made before the stop of the vehicle, as occurred in *Richards*, is far more consistent with a criminal investigation than a traffic stop.[50]

A computer check It is not uncommon for the police to conduct a computer check on the vehicle and the driver's licence as part of a routine traffic stop. However, the timing and scope of the check can provide some evidence of the officers' intent. In most cases, the computer check is conducted after the officer has obtained the name or licence from the driver. It would be unusual, therefore, for a computer check to be conducted before speaking to the driver.[51] It would be particularly suspicious if the computer check was conducted before the officer even pulled the vehicle over, in circumstances where the officer claimed the driver was speeding or otherwise driving in a hazardous manner. Generally speaking, pre-stop computer checks are more consistent with a criminal investigation, to see, for example, if the car is stolen. Finally, it would be suggestive of a criminal investigation if the criminal record or immigration status sections of the Canadian Police Information Centre (CPIC) database were checked during the stop, as occurred in *R . v. Davis*.[52]

The length of time it took for the motorist to be stopped When officers see a traffic violation, it's reasonable to expect that they will immediately stop the vehicle and issue a ticket or warning.

Where the stop occurs at some later time and place, we can reasonably infer that the officers are conducting criminal surveillance of the driver or occupants and are using the traffic violation to further that investigation. In *Richards*, for example, the officer waited fifteen minutes before making the stop.

The nature of the questioning When officers conduct routine traffic stops, they normally ask drivers questions about their licence, registration, and insurance status. It would be inconsistent with a routine stop if the officers' first questions were more of an investigatory nature — for example, What are doing in this neighbourhood? Where did you get this car?[53] Are you on bail?

An investigation of the passengers It is inconsistent with the purpose of a random vehicle stop for officers to ask for identification from the passengers, as occurred in *R. v. Safadi*[54] and *Martin*. It would be even more unusual for officers to conduct a computer check on the passengers.

The officer's notes Police officers who, for example, conduct a race-based stop and make the notation "stopped suspicious vehicle" may later realize, or be told, that the reason for the stop will not pass constitutional muster. They may then turn around and alter, add, or, in an extreme case, prepare a second set of notes with a "legitimate" reason for the stop, as was alleged in *Brown*.[55]

The issuance of a traffic ticket If officers claimed that drivers had violated some traffic law but then did not issue traffic tickets, those circumstances would be suspicious. As the appeal court judge held in *Davis*, "[t]he fact that no charge was laid in relation to turning right on a red light, and the reason given for not doing so, that the officer 'basically forgot,' cause this court some concern."[56]

Other relevant circumstances surrounding stops are those that tend to reveal stereotypical assumptions.[57] For example, a "red flag" is raised where a vehicle stop of a racialized individual takes place in a "high crime area," a predominantly White and affluent neighbourhood, or where the car is expensive, as in *R. v. Khan* (a Mercedes)[58] or *Safadi* (a BMW). Finally, given that Operation Pipeline is being taught in Canada, it will be relevant to determine if the officer has received formal or informal training in Pipeline methodology.

Criminal Investigative Detentions

IN 2003 THE SUPREME Court of Canada was called upon to decide whether the detention of Philip Mann, an Aboriginal man, in downtown Winnipeg was consistent with section 9 of the *Charter*.[59] The police were investigating a reported break and enter but did not have reasonable and probable grounds to believe that Mann was involved. The question before the Court was whether there is a power to detain on a lower standard of belief—namely, reasonable suspicion. Some hoped that the Supreme Court would reject the existence of such a power, or declare it unconstitutional, because of the problems of discriminatory policing.[60] Reasonable suspicion is such a low standard that it invites the use of experience and intuition, which can easily be distorted by unconscious racism. Some might say that the deck was stacked, however, because, by the time this issue finally reached the Supreme Court, almost every appellate court had, over the last decade, recognized such a power.[61] Indeed, *R. v. Simpson*,[62] the decision that first recognized a power of investigative detention in 1993, has been one of the most cited criminal law decisions.[63]

In *R. v. Mann*, the Supreme Court recognized a constitutional common law investigative power to both detain and search short of arrest. Justice Iacobucci, for the majority, held that the police must have reasonable grounds to suspect (i.e., reasonable suspicion) that the individual is implicated in criminal activity. He further held that "where a police officer has reasonable grounds to believe that his or her safety or that of others is at risk, the officer may engage in a protective pat-down search of the detained person."[64] The majority did, however, set out some important general limitations on the exercise of the power.

First, it recognized that reasonable suspicion is only part of the threshold test and that courts still have to consider the overall reasonableness of the decision to detain. This consideration opens the door for courts to read in additional rules. Second, the majority limited the power to the investigation of identified crimes and suspects. According to Justice Iacobucci, there must be a "clear nexus between the individual to be detained and a *recent or on-going criminal offence.*"[65] In other words, the power is largely a reactive one. Where the police are investigating future harm such as terrorist activity, for example, the threshold is higher. In *Durham Regional Police*, the Ontario Court of Appeal held that for future crimes involving serious breaches of the peace, an investigative detention can occur only where "the police ... have reasonable grounds for believing that the anticipated conduct, be it a breach of the peace or the commission of an indictable offence, will likely occur if the person is not detained."[66] Finally, Justice Iacobucci recognized that "[t]he presence of an individual in a so-called high crime area is relevant only so far as it reflects his or her proximity to a particular crime. The high crime nature of a neighbourhood is not by itself a basis for detaining individuals."[67]

In accordance with *Mann*, when called upon to justify conducting a criminal investigative detention, the police will have to point to behaviour that is objectively suspicious. Here the challenge for counsel litigating the constitutionality of the detention will be to convince the trial judge that the behaviour was not inherently suspicious and became so only because the officer was interpreting it through a stereotypical lens. Some of the behaviour of racialized individuals that frequently appears to be triggering suspicion includes

- driving an expensive vehicle (the "he couldn't afford this unless he were a drug dealer" stereotype);[68]
- being out late at night (the "he must be up-to-no-good" stereotype);[69]
- two or more men in a car or walking down the street wearing distinctive clothing (the "they must be a gang" stereotype);[70]

- walking in a wealthy neighbourhood (the "out of place" stereotype);
- standing on the street corner or present in an area purportedly known for drug trafficking or other crime (the "this must be a drug deal" stereotype);[71]
- talking on a cell phone in a high-crime area (the "he must be a drug dealer" stereotype);[72] and
- furtive or evasive action such as failing to make eye contact or quickly leaving the scene of an approaching officer (the "he must have something to hide" stereotype).[73]

In all seventeen cases cited at notes 68 to 73, the trial judges concluded that there were no reasonable grounds to conduct a criminal investigative detention of the racialized accused and that, therefore, section 9 of the *Charter* had been violated. Other than *Peck, Khan,* and *Campbell,* the courts did not go on in the other cases to explicitly conclude that racial profiling was involved, likely because the issue was not raised by counsel. In fact, in some of the cases, race or ethnicity are not even mentioned.[74] In future cases, where racial profiling is raised in cases like these, courts should be prepared to make a finding of racial profiling. If it is determined that it was not objectively reasonable suspicious behaviour which drew the officer's attention, then the only reasonable conclusion was that it was race or racialized stereotypes.

ENSURING CULTURAL COMPETENCE

ONE OF THE MAJOR challenges for racial-profiling litigation is the reluctance of defence lawyers to raise issues of race. This reluctance likely stems from a concern about judicial hostility (such as that displayed by the trial judge in Dee Brown's case), a lack of comfort in talking about race, or a lack of cultural competence. Cultural incompetence is, in part, the failure to appreciate the significance of a client's background to the legal claim being advanced.[75] Given the prevalence of systemic racism, it should not be a surprise that many defence lawyers are operating under the same stereotypical view of the world as police officers and thus do not recognize the possibility that their client's stop was the product of a stereotypical exercise of discretion.

In the summer of 2004 the Canadian Bar Association (CBA) passed a Resolution entitled "Racial Profiling and Law Enforcement."[76] In addition to defining the practice and calling on governments to pass legislation that includes measures to document and prohibit it, the Resolution imposes an obligation on the CBA and the Judicial Council (the governing body for all judges) to educate its constituents. It particular, the Resolution mandates that the CBA

2. develop and provide education for members of the legal profession at the national and branch levels on racial profiling and its legal implications;

3. prepare information materials on court cases and research to identify the impact of racial profiling and actions undertaken to eliminate it; and

4. call on judicial councils to educate their members about racial profiling.[77]

In one of its first efforts to comply with this cultural competence obligation, the CBA has created a racial-profiling link on its website which provides lawyers with background material to assist them in litigating profiling cases.[78]

RECONSTRUCTED CHARTER STANDARDS

ONE WAY TO STIMULATE the use of litigation as a tool in the fight against racial profiling and to ensure that profiling cases are fairly adjudicated is for our courts (and indeed Parliament) to develop enhanced constitutional standards that reflect an understanding of the nature and scope of the problem as well as the difficulty of proof. Racial-profiling cases are litigated under section 9 of our *Charter*, which protects individuals from being arbitrarily detained. As noted in chapter 1, courts have, generally speaking, recognized that the use of race or racialized stereotypes in deciding to detain an individual is a discriminatory and, therefore, an arbitrary exercise of discretion. The right to equal protection of the law is also entrenched in the *Charter* under section 15(1), and it is important not to think about *Charter* rights in isolation. Our equality jurisprudence under section 15(1) can be used when thinking about reconstructed section 9 standards. Given the nature of the context (racially biased policing), our understanding of equality should be guided by critical race theory. Critical race theory consists of a number of organizing principles,[79] including

- "racial inequality and discrimination are deep-seated aspects of the Canadian legal system that cannot be easily erased ...;"
- "historical racism of Canadian society and the Canadian legal system is not just a relic but has ongoing resonance for contemporary law.... For example, a person of colour may decline to identify or plead a race issue in a case because a lawyer has advised him or her not to raise 'the race card' for fear that the judge might react negatively ...;"
- "being black is not the problem, nor is race. The problem is racialization, which is not a biological phenomenon but a sociological one. Racialization means a series of assumptions and pervasive social practices that express, enforce and reinforce damaging stereotypes on persons of colour ...;"
- "whiteness is seen as part of the problem, to the extent that those who are identified as white are not only not discriminated against but are actually over privileged.... In short, despite moves towards formal equality ... the law is still 'used to protect the interests of white people' ...;"
- "colour-blindness and racelessness is part of the problem. Because the social impact of racialization is pervasive, ignoring it at law leads to a formal equality that entrenches inequality ..."[80]

Carol Aylward, a law professor at Dalhousie Law School and the author of Canada's first major work on critical race theory, points out that this theory not only seeks to deconstruct legal rules using

these organizing principles but, of equal importance, seeks to engage in a form of reconstruction which recognizes the transforma-
tive power of the law.[81] Reconstruction, in part, seeks to take the
law and use it to enhance equality by ensuring that it is conceived of
and applied so as not to impose disproportionate burdens on racialized communities. In its Resolution, Racial Equality in the Legal
Profession, the CBA stated that critical race theory is "a valuable stra-
tegic framework to use in working towards the elimination of racial
discrimination in law and in society."[82] This goal clearly places an
ethical obligation on all lawyers to ensure that they are culturally
competent and familiar with critical race theory and praxis.[83]

Using section 15(1) equality principles and critical race theory
in the determination and application of *Charter* standards is not
without precedent. In *R. v. Mills*,[84] the Supreme Court of Canada
struggled with where to set the boundaries on the section 7 right
to make full answer and defence in the context of the production
of third-party records in sexual assault cases. The Court applied
an equality-oriented approach. Chief Justice McLachlin and Justice Iacobucci, for the majority, held:

> Equality concerns must also inform the contextual circum-
> stances in which the rights of full answer and defence and
> privacy will come into play. In this respect, an appreciation
> of the myths and stereotypes in the context of sexual vio-
> lence is essential to delineate properly the boundaries of full
> answer and defence.[85]

Similarly, in *Golden*, the Supreme Court applied a critical race
analysis when determining the scope of the common law power
of the police to strip search individuals following their arrest. Justices Iacobucci and Arbour, for the majority, held:

> [W]e believe it is important to note the submissions of the
> ACLC and the ALST that African-Canadians and Aboriginal
> people are over represented in the criminal justice system
> and are therefore likely to represent a disproportionate num-

ber of those who are arrested by police and subjected to personal searches, including strip searches .... As a result, it is
necessary to develop an appropriate framework governing
strip searches in order to prevent unnecessary and unjustified strip searches before they occur.[86]

By recognizing equality and critical race issues in the interpretation of section 9, courts will become more alive and sensitive to the concerns of racialized groups. In this context, a prime
concern is ridding law enforcement of stereotypical thinking and
disparate treatment based on race, ethnicity, or religion. In order
to ensure that this concern is voiced in the interpretation and application of section 9, we need to recognize that police stops of
racialized individuals are all too frequent and intrusive, that they
have imposed disproportionate burdens on racialized communities, and that racial profiling has led to distorted and unreliable
policing. In this last part of the chapter, I want to explore three
reconstructed *Charter* standards that attempt to give expression to
the social reality of racial profiling.

Abolish the Random Vehicle-Stop Power

ONLY TEN DAYS AFTER the proclamation of the *Charter*, two Ottawa police officers decided to randomly stop Gerald Ladouceur
to see if he had a valid driver's licence. The officers had no reason
to believe that there was anything amiss about Ladouceur or his
vehicle.[87] As it turned out, Ladouceur's licence had, in fact, been
suspended.[88] The issue before the Supreme Court of Canada was
whether the police have a constitutionally valid power to *randomly*
stop a vehicle to check its fitness or to ensure that its paperwork is
in order—in other words, to stop a vehicle without the slightest
suspicion that something is amiss. While all nine Supreme Court
justices agreed that the legislative power to make random and suspicionless traffic stops constitutes an arbitrary exercise of discretion
under section 9 of the *Charter*, the justices split 5 to 4 on whether
the violation was reasonable under section 1 of the *Charter*.[89]

Justice Cory, for the majority, concluded that a random stop power was necessary to enable the police to control the "depressing picture of the killing and maiming that results from the operation of motor vehicles on the streets and highways of the nation."[90] He did attempt to place one limit on this wide-reaching power by suggesting that the police would not be permitted to take advantage of the detention to conduct unreasonable searches or seizures.[91] The dissenting opinion expressed grave concerns about the potential for abuse because of the lack of an objective standard to guide the police in deciding which drivers to stop. Justice Sopinka, for minority, put it this way:

> [T]he roving random stop would permit any individual officer to stop any vehicle, at any time, at any place. The decision may be based on any whim. Individual officers will have different reasons. Some may tend to stop younger drivers, others older cars, and so on. *Indeed, as pointed out by Tarnopolsky J.A., racial considerations may be a factor too.* My colleague states that, in such circumstances, a *Charter* violation may be made out. If, however, no reason need be given nor is necessary, how will we ever know? The officer need only say "I stopped the vehicle because I have the right to stop it for no reason. I am seeking unlicensed drivers."[92]

A similar concern was expressed by Justice LaForest, in his dissenting opinion, in *R. v. Belnavis*, a post-*Ladouceur* case involving two racialized accused:

> The vagueness of the standard also has grave implications for equality in the application of the law. As I noted in *Landry* ... such vague discretion "is unlikely to be used as much against the economically favoured or powerful as against the disadvantaged" .... *It does not prove but certainly does not detract from this thesis that the appellants in the present case are both members of a visible minority.*[93]

By upholding the random stop power, *Ladouceur* has given the police an implicit licence to engage in racial profiling by means of pretext stops. As Justice Sopinka observed, we will rarely know if "racial considerations" play a role because officers can insulate the true reason for the stop by claiming that they are just checking for a valid licence. The decision may, however, actually contain the seeds of its own demise. When discussing the proportionality prong of the reasonable limit test, Justice Cory held:

> Finally, it must be shown that the routine check does not so severely trench upon the s. 9 right so as to outweigh the legislative objective. The concern at this stage is the perceived potential for abuse of this power by law enforcement officials. In my opinion, these fears are unfounded.[94]

At the time that *Ladouceur* was decided, there was very little empirical evidence of racial profiling. This evidence now exists, and it establishes that the power to stop vehicles randomly is being abused by the police. The Supreme Court should, therefore, overrule *Ladouceur* as soon as it is given the opportunity and impose a reasonable-and-probable cause requirement in its place. In other words, the police should be able to stop a motor vehicle only where they have probable cause to believe that a traffic infraction has occurred. This restriction will not be a panacea, however, given the ease with which officers can fabricate an allegation of speeding or the simple fact that, if the police look hard enough, they will likely find some basis for a traffic violation. As has been observed, "[n]o one can drive for even a few blocks without committing a minor violation—speeding, failing to signal or make a complete stop, touching a lane or center lane, or driving with a defective piece of vehicle equipment."[95] Indeed, in the United States, where there is a probable-cause requirement for traffic stops, there remains a problem of racially biased traffic stops.[96] Therefore, additional safeguards need to be put in place.

Impose a Burden on the State to Prove That Race Was Not a Factor in Exercise of Discretion

ONE OF THE PROBLEMS with the ability of current (and proposed) section 9 standards to control racially motivated police encounters (especially traffic stops) is the issue of proof. Under the *Charter*, it is the individual who has the burden of proving whatever violation is alleged. However, in the context of allegations of racism, it is difficult to prove a discriminatory conscious or unconscious intent. Police officers are adept at ensuring that their notes and testimony conform to expected standards of conduct. In many cases, the officers may not even be aware that race played a factor in the stop. In other cases, the officer may fabricate evidence in order to disguise the true reason for the stop. Moreover, experience suggests that lawyers are often reluctant to raise the issue, and the judiciary is reticent about making findings of racial profiling.

Singh[97] reveals just how difficult it will be to establish racial profiling, particularly if trial judges are unwilling to scrutinize an officer's evidence with the suspicion that is often required. In *Singh*, a Black police officer was travelling in the opposite direction from a vehicle with three young racialized men. It was late at night in an area of Brampton, Ontario, with a high incident of criminal activity. The officer made a U-turn and started to follow the vehicle. The officer testified that he would have made the U-turn in any event as he had reached the outer limit of his patrol. He testified that he became suspicious because he thought a passenger in the back seat was not wearing his seatbelt. The officer agreed it was possible that he pulled up alongside the vehicle to have a look at the occupants. Following a licence-plate check and a call to dispatch, which was, in effect, a call for back-up, the officer stopped the vehicle. A search of the vehicle produced drugs and two firearms.

Given that the stop had many of the hallmarks of a pretext stop, there was a strong inference that the vehicle had attracted the suspicion of the officer because of the skin colour of its occupants.

There was a U-turn that allowed the officer to follow the vehicle. But most telling was the officer's reason for investigating the vehicle. How many reasonable officers decide to stop a car because of a concern that the back-seat passengers may not be wearing their seatbelts? Looking into the vehicle as the officer drove by the vehicle was evidence, as the trial judge seemed to agree, consistent with racial profiling. Notwithstanding this suspicious conduct, the trial judge concluded that no racial profiling was involved in the stop. The trial judge's decision was upheld on appeal.[98]

In light of the systemic nature of the problem and the difficulty of proof, consideration should be given to placing an onus on the state to prove, in all section 9 cases, that race or racialized stereotypes did not play a role in the officer's exercise of discretion. This shifting-of-the-onus approach resembles, in many ways, the current challenge-for-cause process employed in jury selection, where evidence of widespread racism is now deemed to rebut the common law presumption that all prospective jurors are unbiased and requiring all jurors to be pre-screened under section 638(1)(b) of the *Criminal Code* in cases involving racialized accused.[99] In *Parks*, one of the first cases in Canada to apply a critical race perspective to legal rules, Justice Doherty explained why he was, in effect, giving all Black accused the presumptive right to challenge prospective jurors:

> Racism, and in particular anti-black racism is part of our community's psyche. A significant segment of our community holds overtly racist views. A much larger segment subconsciously operates on the basis of negative racial stereotypes. Furthermore, our institutions, including the criminal justice system, reflect and perpetuate those negative stereotypes. These elements combine to infect our society as a whole with the evil of racism. Blacks are among the primary victims of that evil.[100]

In the context of vehicle stops, for example, this burden is not so onerous that it would lead to the unjust stigmatization of police officers who had, in fact, done nothing wrong. The burden would simply require the state to prove, on a balance of probabilities, that the officer's conduct was entirely consistent with a routine traffic stop. In the context of criminal or terrorist investigative detentions (on the street, in vehicles, or at the airport), the state would simply have to establish that there was objectively suspicious behaviour that warranted investigation. The state could go a long way in meeting its burden if it could establish that the detachment or division where the officer works has taken steps to document incidents of racial profiling by keeping track of those whom the officers or security officials stop.

In addition to being necessary and not onerous, a reverse onus is consistent with precedent and policy. We are beginning to see courts place a burden on the Crown in section 9 cases. In *R. v. Ferdinand*, an investigative detention case, Justice LaForme placed the burden on the Crown to establish that the detention was not arbitrary.[101] In *R. v. McKennon*, Justice Casey Hill, one of Canada's leading criminal law jurists, shifted the burden to the Crown in a random vehicle stop.[102] As Justice Hill held:

> I tend to the view that in a traffic stop case the discharge of proof regarding compliance with the Constitution and with the individual s. 9 *Charter* right should generally be upon the government. This is so where the alleged arbitrariness arises from a submitted absence of reasonable and probable grounds for the detention, especially in the context of an assertion of ulterior motivation for the detention. Vehicle stops are frequently based on subjective assessments of vehicle or driver impropriety without real or lasting evidence of an officer's impression. In traffic stops there is in effect a warrantless seizure of the vehicle and its occupants, permitting additional warrantless visual and olfactory searches and seizures in circumstances where the existence of the lawful grounds for the vehicle stop reside with the police. Unlike

detention effected by a warrant of arrest, there is no judicial authorization of vehicle stops.[103]

Similarly, in other contexts, our courts have imposed a number of shifting burdens in the *Charter* context, the most notable being in section 8, which protects all individuals from unreasonable searches and seizures. Pursuant to that section, where a search or seizure is conducted without a warrant, the burden shifts to the state to establish that the search was authorized by law, that the law is reasonable, and that the search was conducted in a reasonable manner.[104] As a matter of policy, the Crown is "functionally responsible for the maintenance of the administration of justice."[105] Since the police are part of the administration of justice, the Crown should be held accountable for systemic police misconduct such as racial profiling. Moreover, the Crown has access to far more information that could shed light on the intent of the police officer than does an accused person. And finally, given the evils of racial profiling, any doubt about the issue should result in an invalidation of the stop.

Taking Race into Account in the Meaning of Detention

THE KEY TO THE application of section 9 of the *Charter* lies in its triggering mechanism: detention. The Supreme Court of Canada has defined "detention" under section 9 in the same manner as it has under section 10, which ensures that everyone detained is informed of his or her right to speak to a lawyer. So, for example, a detention is said to arise under both sections where there is a deprivation of liberty by physical restraint, or criminal liability arising from the failure to comply with a police demand or direction, or a state of psychological compulsion arises in the form of a reasonable perception of suspension of freedom of choice.[106] All random vehicle stops are deemed to be a detention under section 9. The same is not true for criminal investigative stops that do not take place in a vehicle. In these cases, the trial judge still has to apply the threefold test noted above to determine whether, in all the circumstances, the stop amounted to a detention.[107] Unfortunately, our courts have too often been quick to deem street encounters as simply stops rather than detentions.[108] Testimony from the police officers that they requested the individual "to come over," asked "Where are you guys headed?" or "What's your name?" or said "We want to speak to you," too often gets characterized as a simple request rather than a demand. Indeed, perhaps the most disappointing part of the Supreme Court of Canada's decision in *Mann*, which recognized an investigative detention power, was its gloss over this important issue. Without any considered discussion of the relevant academic commentary or reference to social context, Justice Iacobucci simply stated that "the police cannot be said to 'detain', within the meaning of ss. 9 and 10 of the *Charter*, every suspect they stop for purposes of identification, or even interview."[109] This narrow approach to detention is problematic because it serves to further insulate race-based stops from judicial review.

I have previously argued that, to address the problem of racial profiling, there should be a different approach to detention under section 9 from that applied in the context of section 10.[110] Under this approach, all street-level criminal investigations would be deemed a detention. Unless the Supreme Court rethinks its approach in *Mann*, this argument is no longer viable. However, there is still room to argue under *Mann* and the "psychological detention" branch of the test that the relevant social context of racial profiling and police violence is relevant to the issue of whether the individual was detained when stopped by the police. The case of *Griffiths* is an example of the application of this critical race approach.[111]

In *Griffiths* the police approached a street corner in Toronto they claimed was an area known for drug trafficking. A group of Black men standing on the corner dispersed as the police approached. The police called out to the accused and said something to the effect of "Hey you, come over here." The accused testified that, given the history of police brutality towards young Black men in the city, he felt he had no choice but to comply. Based on the accused's testimony and the evidence of systemic racism, the trial judge was satisfied that the accused had been detained by the police. In reaching this conclusion, he likely asked himself: Can it really be said that it is reasonable to expect that a young Black man in Toronto would feel free to refuse an officer's request to "come over" or to "stop"? Similarly, in *R. v. Pinto*, Justice Hill observed that "the experience and perspective of visible minorities respecting the police often serves to inform their beliefs about the realistic existence of free choice in dealing with the police."[112]

THE LIMITS OF LITIGATION

A HOLISTIC APPROACH WILL be required to end racial profiling. Litigation is only one part of the solution. As a practical matter, there is little judicial review of discriminatory exercises of discretion. The *Charter* is generally invoked only where contraband is found as a result of the stop, because it is in these cases that the victim has a strong motive to litigate. In the vast majority of random stops, however, the police do not find any contraband. As Justice LaForest observed in *Belnavis*, "The courts have little 'feel' for what ... [unconstitutional misconduct by the police] means to persons who have committed no wrong or any idea of the number of such people who may be harassed by the overly zealous elements in any police force."[113] In these latter cases, there are a number of reasons why the victims do not get their day in court. Many cannot afford a lawyer.[114] Damage awards are likely to be relatively small, as we saw in the *Karela* case. One of the effects of profiling is an engendering of distrust of the justice system. And, finally, litigation can serve to further marginalize individuals, given the adversarial and public nature of the process, thereby deterring claims from individuals who do not want the public exposure or other aspects of their private lives revealed.

Litigation remains, however, an important strategy because, in addition to the systemic remedies identified earlier in this chapter, it may stimulate institutional reform. The lack of any institutional response to the findings of so many inquiries set up to look at systemic racism, such as the Ontario Commission on Systemic Racism, suggests that reform of issues affecting vulnerable and disenfranchised groups will occur only if state actors are "prodded" by the judiciary.[115] Chapter 10 will examine some of the institutional reforms that are necessary to end racial profiling. Before doing that, we need to turn our attention to the oft-ignored issue of race-based suspect descriptions. Is using race as part of a suspect's description also a form of racial profiling? Why has this issue largely been ignored in the dialogue? What are the dangers inherent in this practice? What constitutional standards can be created to protect against the misuse of race in this context? These questions are explored in the next chapter.

Rethinking the Use of Race in Suspect Descriptions

NARRATIVES OF ABUSE

The "Hurricane"

IN 1999 NORMAN JEWISON's film, *The Hurricane*, enjoyed tremendous box-office success, garnering a number of Golden Globe and Academy Award nominations. The movie chronicled the wrongful conviction and journey of Rubin "Hurricane" Carter. In the fall of 1966 Carter was arrested in the shooting of four individuals in the Lafayette Bar & Grill in Patterson, New Jersey. Three of the victims died. The fourth survived but was partially blinded. Carter, who was thirty years old at the time, was an accomplished professional boxer who was a contender for the middleweight crown.[1] He was convicted and sentenced to life imprisonment on June 29, 1967. Carter served nineteen years in a New Jersey prison before he was finally released on November 7, 1985.[2] In setting aside his convictions, Judge H. Lee Sarokin concluded that Carter had been the victim of racial profiling by the prosecutor and, ultimately, the jury:

The extensive record clearly demonstrates that petitioner's convictions were predicated upon an appeal to racism rather than reason.... In essence, the prosecution was permitted to argue to the jury that the defendants who were black were motivated to murder total strangers solely because they were white.

... For the state to contend that an accused has a motive to commit murder solely because of his membership in a racial group is an argument which should never be permitted to sway a jury or provide the basis of a conviction.[3]

In February 1988 the charges against Carter were dismissed. A week later, Carter came to live in Woodbridge, Ontario, with the group of Canadians, including his wife, who were instrumental in his legal victory.[4] However, his experience with the colour of justice was not over.

On April 11, 1996, Carter was enjoying dinner with his friends at a restaurant in Toronto. After dinner, he went to get his car in the parking lot. Suddenly, four unmarked cruisers surrounded him. The police were looking for a drug suspect described as Black, "thirty-ish," without glasses, and wearing a brown and white jacket. Other than the fact that he was Black and wearing a similarly coloured jacket, Carter looked nothing like the suspect. He was in his sixties and wearing glasses. Carter was handcuffed, arrested, and put in the back of the police cruiser. As one of the officers put it, "It was a drug buy in a dark area and he resembled the suspect."[5] Carter was understandably shaken by the incident and, as he put it, "It was like a nightmare ... the last time I was told I was under arrest I didn't see the light of day for 20 years."[6]

J.J. Harper

ON APRIL 13, 1988, the Manitoba government called the Aboriginal Justice Inquiry of Manitoba to examine the circumstances surrounding the deaths of two Aboriginals in Manitoba: the police shooting of John Joseph (J.J.) Harper in 1988 and the killing of Helen Betty Osborne in 1971. The inquiry was given a broad mandate to study all components of the justice system in Manitoba, including policing and the courts and whether Aboriginals are treated differently by the justice system. Two commissioners were appointed, Associate Chief Justice A.C. Hamilton and Associate Chief Judge C. Murray Sinclair, one of the few Aboriginal judges in this country.[7]

In the early morning of March 9, 1988, J.J. Harper was shot and killed by a Winnipeg police officer for no other reason than that he was an Aboriginal man walking down the street.[8] Harper was a member of the Wasagamack Indian Band. He was executive director of the Island Lake Tribal Council and a leader in Manitoba's Aboriginal community. Harper and his wife had three children.[9] The deadly encounter began when the officer decided to stop and question Harper, even after learning that the suspect he and his partner were pursuing in relation to a stolen vehicle had been arrested. Apparently, he wanted to make sure that the right suspect had been arrested. The problem was that other than being Aboriginal, Harper did not resemble the description of the suspect. As the Manitoba Aboriginal Justice Inquiry concluded:

> It was obvious that Harper didn't fit major elements of the description of the suspect. [The officers] described the man whom they had seen fleeing from the stolen car as a "native male, 22 years of age, wearing dark clothing." Harper was a native male wearing dark clothing, but he was 37 years of age, considerably heavier than [the suspect] and of much stockier build. [The suspect] had outrun the police, while Harper was walking and apparently not breathing heavily.[10]

The officer would later testify that he became even more suspicious when Harper refused to identify himself and walked away.[11] As he walked away, the officer grabbed Harper's arm. Harper responded by shoving the officer, who then pulled Harper on top of him. Within seconds, Harper was dead.

Although the inquiry was unable to conclude what happened once the men were on the ground, the commissioners were satis-

fied that, contrary to the officer's claim, "Harper never had any
significant control over [his] revolver."[12] They were also satisfied
that race was the reason that Harper was stopped by the officer:

> We believe that he decided to stop and question Harper sim-
> ply because Harper was a male Aboriginal person in his
> path. We are unable to find any other reasonable explanation
> for his being stopped. We do not accept [the officer's] expla-
> nation. It was clearly a retroactive attempt to justify stopping
> Harper. We believe that [he] had no basis to connect him to
> any crime in the area and that his refusal or unwillingness
> to permit Harper to pass freely was ... racially motivated.
>
> ... Racial stereotyping motivated the conduct of [the of-
> ficer]. He stopped a "native" person walking peaceably along
> a sidewalk merely because the suspect he was seeking was
> native. This then leads to the conclusion that race was a
> major contributing factor in the death of J.J. Harper. Race
> was one of the facts included in the description broadcast
> of the car-theft suspect for whom the police were looking.
> If Harper had not been a native person, [the officer] would
> have ignored him.[13]

The officer was never charged criminally and did not lose his job.[14]

Marcellus François

ON JULY 3, 1991, the Montreal police were trying to locate two
suspects in an attempted murder investigation. One of the suspects, Kirt Haywood, was described as Black, 6 feet tall, 160
pounds, and with Rastafarian-style braids down to his knees.[15]
Marcellus François, who was twenty-four years old, was mistaken for Haywood as he left an apartment building the police
had under surveillance because they believed this was a location
the suspects frequented. The officers were using a photocopy of
a faxed colour mug shot to help identify the suspects.[16] François,
however, looked nothing like Haywood. He was short-haired, 5

feet 7 inches tall, and 130 pounds. François got into a red Pontiac Bonneville with three other Black individuals.[17] The surveillance officers radioed for the SWAT team and began to tail the vehicle with François in it. The officers referred to the occupants over the police radio as "niggers" and "darkies."[18] They also stated: "There's a possibility he's one of the guys we're looking for" and "they appear to be nervous, they're looking everywhere."[19]

Once they arrived, the SWAT team was able to box in the vehicle. Shortly thereafter, one of the officers fired through the car's windshield. The bullet struck François in the head, and he died a few days later. The officer, who was actually familiar with Haywood, having arrested him on an earlier occasion, stated that he did not look at François's face.[20] According to the officer's account, François did not respond to his shouts of "Police!" "Don't move!" and "Freeze!" and he moved his hands in a way that appeared to be reaching for a gun.[21] No gun was found in the car.[22] In addition, there was conflicting police evidence as to whether anything had been said before the shot was fired, leading to doubt about the officer's version of events.[23] Following the shooting, another officer ordered the arrest and detention of the remaining occupants in the car, two of whom were women, even though he now knew that a terrible mistake had occurred.[24] The officer who shot François was not criminally charged and, like Harper's killer, did not lose his job.[25] The officer who ordered the arrest of the vehicle's occupants was suspended without pay for ten days.[26]

* * *

HARPER AND FRANÇOIS ARE not the only unarmed racialized individuals in Canada who have been shot by the police. For example, Gabriella Pedicelli, the author of *When Police Kill: Police Use of Force in Montreal and Toronto*,[27] the most widely cited book on police shootings in Canada, was able to confirm that, between 1987 and 1993, two other unarmed men were shot by the police in Montreal (Anthony Griffin)[28] and Toronto (Wade Lawson).[29] They were both Black.[30] On September 6, 1995, an Ontario Provincial Police (OPP) officer shot and killed Dudley George, an unarmed Aboriginal man, during a confrontation at Ipperwash Provincial Park.[31] Members of the Stoney Point Band had moved to the park and the adjacent Camp Ipperwash (an old military base). They claimed that the land was theirs pursuant to a treaty. They also wanted to preserve a burial ground inside the park.[32] George was shot after members of the band drove a school bus and car towards the OPP officers in an attempt to rescue a protestor they believed was being beaten by the police. As the vehicles retreated, after successfully dispersing the officers, the sound of gunfire was heard. The officer testified that his actions had nothing to do with the bus or the car. Rather, he thought that George was armed with a rifle. The trial judge rejected this latter claim. He concluded that not only was George not armed but that the officer knew he was not armed and had concocted his evidence about seeing a rifle and muzzle flash. The officer was convicted of criminal negligence causing death.[33] Notwithstanding these findings, the trial judge permitted him to serve his sentence in the community.[34] George's cousin, Warren Anthony George, was convicted of criminal negligence causing bodily harm. He drove the car that followed the school bus, and the car had hit a number of officers. Warren George went to jail for six months.[35] On June 18, 1998, the federal government signed an agreement returning Camp Ipperwash to the Kettle and Stony Point Band.[36] On November 12, 2003, the Ipperwash Inquiry was established, with Justice Sidney Linden appointed as Commissioner.

Tracking the race of the victims of police shootings in Canada is very difficult, given that official data is not available. One study, conducted by Scot Wortley, was able, using media reports, to identify thirty-four police shootings in Ontario from 1978 to 2000. The victims broke down as follows: nineteen (56%) were Black; ten (29%) were White, and five (16%) involved other racialized victims. Of the twenty-three victims who were killed, thirteen (57%) were Black.[37] In Montreal, eight Black and Hispanic men were shot and killed by the police between 1987 and 1993, compared to only three White men.[38] Aboriginals have also been vulnerable to police shootings, as revealed by both the *Harper* and the *George* cases. Race and racialized stereotypes are implicated in many of these police shootings because it causes the officers to overreact or misinterpret behaviour. That is certainly what occurred in the *François, Harper,* and *George* cases.[39] We also saw another example of overreaction in London following July 7, when the police repeatedly shot an innocent Brazilian man in the head on the subway because they thought he was a terrorist bomber.[40]

Devon Murray

ON JULY 24, 2002, a police officer reviewed a Crime Analyst Report before leaving a police station in Toronto to go out on patrol. In the report was a photograph of Joseph Coker, an African-American male, who was wanted on a warrant for failing to appear in court. Coker's last-known address was within the area that the officer was responsible for patrolling.[41] This area had been "designated a crime management initiative with a high gang presence, drug dealing and prostitution."[42] The officer saw Devon Murray, a Black man, walking down the street. He had a "dark coloured bandanna tied in a knot on his head and [was] wearing loose baggy clothing."[43] The officer typically associated this style of clothing with gang members. He later testified that Murray failed to make eye contact and "quickly looked away."[44] Based on a single glance, the officer also thought that Murray looked like Coker, and he decided to approach and question him while still in his cruiser.[45]

After talking to Murray, the officer realized that he was not Coker. Nevertheless, he got out of his cruiser and ordered Murray to identify himself. Murray was understandably upset at having been detained without cause and was letting the officer know it. When some neighbours came out of their house, Murray was arrested for causing a disturbance. During the arrest, the officer assaulted Murray. In addition, his pepper spray "accidentally" discharged and spilled on Murray's jacket. The arrest left Murray with a fractured cheekbone. The officer was charged and ultimately convicted of assault causing bodily harm. However, in her reasons for conviction, the trial judge did not conclude that the officer had misused race in his initial reason for approaching Murray:

> [The officer's] attention was drawn to Mr. Murray, because Mr. Murray from a distance resembled the African-American Mr. Coker, who was wanted on a bench warrant. It was reasonable under the circumstances for [the officer] to approach him. I am not satisfied that there was racial profiling in this case.[46]

Although the trial judge found otherwise, a troubling inference of racial profiling is left by the evidence. Why, for example, did the officer continue to investigate Murray once he had determined that he was not Coker? On sentencing, the officer was given a conditional discharge and placed on probation for one year.[47]

THE TRADITIONAL VIEW OF RACE AND SUSPECT DESCRIPTIONS

THE ISSUE OF RACE and suspect descriptions has received little critical attention, with most definitions of racial profiling excluding suspect descriptions from the prohibition.[48] In *Paying the Price,* for example, the Ontario Human Rights Commission noted that it is not racial profiling where the police investigation is based on "actual behaviour or *on information about suspected activity by someone who meets the description of a specific individual.*"[49] Similarly, in a recently proposed private member's bill — *An Act to Eliminate Racial Profiling* (Canada) — there is a specific exemption for circumstances where race is part of the suspect's description:

> 3.(2) Reliance on criteria such as race, colour, ethnicity, ancestry, religion or place of origin is not considered to be racial profiling if it is used by an enforcement officer in

combination with other identifying factors to search for and apprehend a specific suspect whose race, colour, ethnicity, ancestry, religion or place of origin *is part of the description of the suspect.*[50]

Our courts have also treated race and suspect descriptions as an exception to the general constitutional rule prohibiting the use of race in policing. For example, in *R. v. Smith*, the trial judge observed:

The use of race as a descriptor of an individual or group of individuals, where there are other reasons to differentiate or select on the basis of race, may or may not contravene the principles of fundamental justice. This will depend on whether there are legitimate reasons which arise from the combination of race and other factors which make it legitimate to use race as a descriptor in the course of selecting a person, or groups of persons, for scrutiny. *An obvious example would be where the victim of a crime describes the perpetrator in part by reference to the perpetrator's race.*[51]

The Supreme Court of Canada decision in *R. v. Mann*[52] tacitly approves the use of race when tracking a known suspect. In *Mann*, the police received a call shortly before midnight that a break and enter was in progress in a neighbouring district of downtown Winnipeg. Apparently, the district was known as a "high-crime" area. The suspect was described as twenty-one years old, Aboriginal, male, 5 feet 8 inches, 165 pounds, and wearing a black jacket with white sleeves. He was thought to be someone named "Zachary Parisienne."[53] A few blocks from the crime scene, the police saw Philip Mann, who is Aboriginal, walking down the street. The police decided to detain Mann because, in their words, he matched the description of the suspect to a "tee." Following a search, they found a small quantity of marijuana and charged him with a drug offence.

In concluding that the police had reasonable grounds to detain Mann, Justice Iacobucci, on behalf of a majority of the Supreme Court, held that "[h]e closely matched the description of the suspect given by radio dispatch, and was only two or three blocks from the scene of the reported crime."[54] Although it did not specifically address the issue, the Court was presumably content with the fact that the officer took into account the fact that Mann was Aboriginal. However, the physical description of the suspect was not that detailed—young, male, Aboriginal, approximately 5 feet 8 inches tall, and weighing 165 pounds. When you factor in the proximity of Mann to the crime scene, this generalization becomes less of a concern. But, more significant, there was a discrepancy in the description of the clothing. The police were looking for a suspect wearing "a black jacket with white sleeves." Mann, however, was wearing "a pullover sweater with a kangaroo pouch pocket in the front."[55] This difference raises the very real concern that Mann was stopped simply because he was a young Aboriginal male walking in a high-crime area.[56]

It is unclear why we have been so quick to accept that suspect descriptions should be exempt from the general prohibition against using race in policing. It is ironic that "the controversy about racial profiling has generated the staunchest defenses of law enforcement use of race-based suspect descriptions. The effort to delegitimize one form of race-based suspect selection has fortified another."[57] There are a number of possible explanations. First, the use of race in suspect descriptions is related, in theory, to physical appearance rather than the social construction of race or racialization. As such, it is used as an individual identifier rather than as a stereotypical marker. Consequently, it is seen as more reliable and less likely to result in abuse. Second, in theory, suspect descriptions apply equally to everyone. In other words, since all suspects are identified, in part, based on race, all groups share the burden of having race relied upon in the police investigation.[58] Third, suspect descriptions usually come from victims or witnesses rather than the police and may, therefore, be seen as neutral and free from possible state or police bias.[59] And, finally, the use of suspect descriptions almost always arises in cases of completed crimes usually involving violence, such as murder, robbery, or sexual assault.[60]

THE DANGERS OF RACE-BASED SUSPECT DESCRIPTIONS

PERMITTING THE POLICE TO use race to track identified racialized suspects is not, however, without its problems. In the narratives presented, death, false arrest, and harassment are but some of the damage caused by its use. Race is an inherently unreliable physical identifier. Cross-racial identifications are now recognized as a leading cause of wrongful convictions.[61] Moreover, as the Manitoba Aboriginal Justice Inquiry noted:

> Mentioning a suspect's race does little to assist the officers on the street, in our opinion. If they are to look for people with a certain skin colouring, then we believe that the description of the suspect's complexion should suffice. Aboriginal people come in all shapes and sizes, and have skin colouring that can range from dark to fair. It seems illogical, therefore, to assume that by stating that a person is "native," one can conclude how that person looks. If a police officer is directed to look for a "native" male, the question arises: What type of person is he or she looking for? The facial characteristics of Aboriginal people are not sufficiently distinctive from those of other racial groups to justify the use of the category in police broadcasts. The retention of such a practice will continue to lead to situations, we believe, where Aboriginal people are confronted by police officers solely or primarily because of their race.
>
> To advise police officers that a suspect in an offence is a native is a licence to commit racism. That should not be condoned.[62]

Consequently, neither law enforcement nor equality interests are necessarily advanced by using race to track known suspects.

The police will sometimes waste valuable resources in uncovering a large number of false positives and will miss the real perpetrator because the person does not accord with the police officer's conception of a Black or an Arab or Aboriginal person. And because of the dangers of overbroad application, the equality interests of the racialized community are jeopardized. In this sense, the use of race in suspect descriptions suffers from being "overbroad" and "overly restrictive."[63] Given our history of overt and systemic racism, there is the additional danger that anytime race is permitted to influence the exercise of discretion, the decision maker will consciously or unconsciously rely on stereotypes. "Out of place" thinking, clothing, or vehicle preferences become justifications for investigating suspects who only vaguely can be said to resemble the known suspect. The following narratives reveal these dangers.

Being "Out of Place" in Toronto

Peter Owusu-Ansah

SHORTLY AFTER MIDNIGHT ON September 14, 2002, the police reportedly received word of a robbery involving upwards of twenty Black men in a neighbourhood in mid-town Toronto. No other physical characteristics were identified. Approximately fifteen to twenty minutes later, Peter Owusu-Ansah and seven or eight of his friends were waiting at a bus stop at Bayview and Eglinton Avenues, many blocks away from the scene of the robbery. They had been playing basketball and had just finished a late snack at McDonald's. Even though they had nothing to do with the incident, they were Black and attracted the attention of the police, who likely saw them as "out of place." Owusu-Ansah and his friends were also hearing impaired, and this disability created significant confusion as the police attempted to question the group.

Owusu-Ansah was eventually arrested for failing to cooperate and driven to a deserted school yard, where, on his evidence, he was assaulted by a police officer while his partner watched. When Owusu-Ansah reported what had happened, the two officers were charged with assault. At trial, the officers denied that Owusu-Ansah was assaulted. The officers were ultimately acquitted, even though the trial judge rejected most, if not all, of the evidence of the officer who had allegedly assaulted Owusu-Ansah—including the reason he gave for taking the complainant to a deserted location in the middle of the night.[64] The trial judge acquitted because he rejected much of Owusu-Ansah's evidence. The manner in which he did is troubling. For example, the trial judge treated Owusu-Ansah's understandable anger at having been stopped seventeen previous times in two years by the police as evidence of animus.[65]

Being "Out of Place" in Vancouver

Cornelius Muojekwe

IN OCTOBER 1991 CORNELIUS Muojekwe, a doctoral student at the University of British Columbia, was practising for his driver's licence with his friend in a car marked "student driver." They were in the vicinity of a pizza restaurant that had just been robbed. Before they knew it, they were suddenly surrounded by police with their guns drawn. The men were arrested in a "high-risk" takedown. However, other than the fact that they were Black men, they did not match the description of the suspects. Muojekwe filed a complaint with the police. A disciplinary panel exonerated the officers, concluding that they had the requisite reasonable and probable grounds to arrest the men because they were young Black men "who happened to be in the approximate area and time of an armed robbery"[66] In her dissenting opinion, board member Yasmin Jiwani wrote: "[The arrest] was predicated on the assumption based on the racial identity of the suspects, rather than on any other detail of their appearance. Were the same situation to have involved two white men, the focus would have been on the other details of their appearance."[67]

In a subsequent media interview, Chuck Lew, a lawyer and chair of the panel, provided the real motivating reason behind the majority's decision. As he put it, "You don't see that many blacks in the city"[68] and "I really feel that if something happens on the street tonight and a black man is involved, the police are going to stop the next black guy that they see downtown. I think it's more than reasonable."[69] He later added: "I want this city to be a safe place. I want to be able to walk down a street safely."[70] Val Romilly, a former member of the city's race-relations committee, noted: "There are lots of blacks in the Lower Mainland. If Mr. Lew can't see us, he has blinkers on."[71]

Jon Alan Yamanaka

On October 13, 1995, the police were investigating reports of loud noises described as gunfire in the early morning hours in an affluent neighbourhood in West Vancouver. The first officer at the scene saw Jon Alan Yamanaka, a young Japanese Canadian, and a friend standing by an "old model vehicle." When asked if they had heard any gunfire, they advised the officer that they had not but that their car had broken down and had backfired several times. A second officer arrived at the scene. He became suspicious because he did not think that Yamanaka "and his companion *belonged* in the neighbourhood."[72] After being told that there were "electrical tools" in the athletic bag that Yamanaka was holding, the officer asked to look inside to ensure that it did not contain any firearms. No firearms were found.

The police did apparently find other items, and Yamanaka was charged with being in possession of instruments suitable for the purpose of breaking into a coin-operated device. On the appeal from his conviction, Chief Justice McEachern, for the British Columbia Court of Appeal, held that the detention and search complied with the *Canadian Charter of Rights and Freedoms* because, in part, "the appellant and his co-accused seemed to be *out of place* in the neighbourhood at 5:30 A.M."[73] Although *Yamanaka* is more of a traditional racial-profiling case, the appellate court's endorsement of the "out of place" doctrine was soon applied in a suspect description case.

Eton Greaves

ON JUNE 26, 2000, the police were investigating an assault involving a Black victim at a liquor store in an area of Southeast Vancouver. The incident occurred sometime after 7:30 p.m. One of the assailants was described as Black, the other five as White. The police dispatcher further advised that the suspects had fled eastbound. A police officer responded to the call and was at the scene within five minutes. He started to drive around the neighbourhood. He saw Eton Greaves, a Black male, accompanied by two White males walking out of Central Park, a very large public park that houses a professional soccer stadium and a swimming pool.[74] The group was heading in the direction of the liquor store.

Greaves did not resemble the suspect. The suspect was described as eighteen years old and skinny; Greaves was in his mid-thirties, with a stocky build. He also had a distinctive appearance: a very prominent gap between his two front teeth. Moreover, none of the other circumstances were consistent with the information that the officer had been given.[75] Nevertheless, the officer decided to investigate the group. In his mind, their mixed racial composition was "unique"[76] for the area. This grouping, along with the fact that they appeared to be carrying beer bottles and tried to avoid him as he approached, led him to believe they were involved in the assault. As it turned out, Greaves was not the suspect, and he was never charged with assault. However, he was detained for over forty minutes, interrogated, handcuffed, and repeatedly searched. Eventually, the police discovered a cell phone that linked him with an unsolved robbery, and he was arrested for that offence.

Greaves challenged the constitutionality of his detention and search. The primary issue was whether there were reasonable grounds to suspect he was involved in the assault. The trial judge accepted, as objectively reasonable, the police officer's "out of place" justification and relied, in support, on *Yamanaka*.[77] On appeal, the British Columbia Court of Appeal affirmed the trial judge's reasoning and conclusion. Justice Lowry, for the court, held:

> It is clear that [the officer] was acting on more than an intuitive hunch. His suspicion that the persons detained may have been involved in the assault was supported by objective facts and was reasonable in the circumstances. Although there may not be objective data to support his belief that the combination of one black and two white males was "unique" in this area, the testimony of both he and Cst. Law was consistent with the fact that this was the *only* group of males—whether black, white or some combination of the two—observed in the area at the time. After hearing the testimony of [the officer], the trial judge was satisfied that his conduct was not racially motivated.[78]

Why did the officer think it was "unique" for Greaves to have been in the company of Whites? As a matter of logic, since Greaves did not match the description of the suspect, how does the mixed racial composition of the group add to the reasonable suspicion calculus? Why did the trial judge and the Court of Appeal say that the detention was not racially motivated, when the officer explicitly articulated that he used race and "out of place" reasoning as one of the factors in deciding to detain Greaves? While the Court of Appeal did begin to address the use of race by the police officer, it nevertheless seemed satisfied to leave the issue once it determined that he was not acting as an overt racist.[79] This, however, ignores the larger problem of systemic racism and the unconscious differential treatment of racialized individuals. As a matter of policy, to suggest that shared use of public spaces in Canada by members of racialized communities, or that a racially diverse group is inherently suspicious, is very troubling and violates all the fundamental principles underlying the *Charter* and our system of justice. Like all forms of racism, this particular manifestation harms the dignity of members of racialized communities.

It promotes exclusionary thinking and limits the ability of individuals to move freely within our cities. It perpetuates the belief that racialized individuals are under constant surveillance.[80] The Supreme Court of Canada refused to hear a further appeal.[81]

A MODEST PROPOSAL

ALL THESE DANGERS ARE substantial and are, in part, the reasons that some have argued against using race in suspects descriptions.[82] The Aboriginal Justice Inquiry of Manitoba, for example, recommended in its report on the J.J. Harper shooting that "[t]he Winnipeg Police Department cease the practice of using race as a description in police broadcasts."[83] Is the banning of race in suspect descriptions, however, a workable recommendation? A complete ban on the use of race is unlikely to find political, public, police, or judicial support. Moreover, there is no denying that race can be a relevant physical identifier in guiding police investigations, if nothing else than as a means of excluding suspects. That is precisely why even the Manitoba Aboriginal Justice Inquiry recognized that the police should still be able to use complexion as part of the description.[84] This recommendation may not, however, prevent misuse. There is always the danger that even more racialized individuals may get entangled in the web of suspicion if the suspect is described, for example, as having a dark complexion. Moreover, given the relevance of race in our society, it will inevitably be constructed through complexion, name, or eye colour.[85]

Instead of a ban, the answer may lie in identifying a zone of misuse and recognizing that this zone should fall within the racial-profiling prohibition. The narratives presented in this chapter suggest that abuse is likely (or perhaps more accurately will occur) where race is used as the dominant feature of the suspect description. When this occurs, it is often difficult to determine whether the victim was stopped because of stereotypical thinking or because the suspect description was negligently used. It seems to be logical to refer to this zone of abuse as racial profiling. Indeed, as we have seen, there are many similarities between the use of racial profiles and racialized suspect descriptions:

> [T]hese two forms of race-based suspect selection are functionally similar; both are ... especially burdensome to innocent members of certain minority groups. Profiles and suspect descriptions both couple race and suspicion, burdening individuals on account of race in a manner that violates the usual nondiscrimination norm. Second, both types of suspect selection are subject to misuse and error. Third, the placement of actual practices into one category or the other is often riddled with uncertainty. The categories do not neatly and unambiguously map onto discrete sets of actual practices.[86]

Finally, given the disapprobation now linked to the term "racial profiling," it is appropriate to use the phrase as a normative concept to capture all misuse and abuse of race in policing.

Having identified a risk zone, the next step is to flush out how we can identify when race has become the dominant characteristic, both to prevent discriminatory treatment before it occurs and to provide a remedy when it does, in fact, occur. The key is to examine the degree of detail, specificity, and significance of the non-racial attributes of the suspect description given to the police. The less detailed, specific, and significant the non-racial identifiers, the more likely it is that race will be used as the dominant feature. A detailed description should include:

- gender;
- approximate age, height, build, and weight;
- complexion;
- hair length, style, and colour;
- presence or absence of facial hair;
- presence or absence of eyeglasses;
- any distinguishing features such as a scar or tattoo, large nose or ears;

- colour, type and nature of clothing; and
- location and time of offence.

In addition, we need to develop standards and protocols on just how specific and detailed the description needs to be in order to prevent race from becoming the dominant feature.

In civil, criminal, or disciplinary cases where there is an allegation of a discriminatory stop, there are three additional factors that can help identify whether race was used as the dominant feature. These include whether there is a significant discrepancy between the description of the suspect and the victim; the extent to which the police attempted to obtain a detailed description from the victim or witness; and whether there were any additional circumstances that may have invited the police to engage in stereotyping (e.g., the individual's presence in an expensive car or "high-crime" neighbourhood; the wearing of baggy or other so-called distinctive clothing). Thinking about race in the context of suspect descriptions reveals that, whenever we talk about the use of race in policing, we need to question continually whether the rules we create and apply will perpetuate systemic racism. Are they open to abuse? Will they serve to stigmatize? Are they an open invitation for the use of racialized stereotypes? Will they result in a large number of false positives? One of the legacies of our history of slavery and segregation is that "[t]here is no policy choice that would avoid the imposition of racial inequality. Any choice is a choice among inequalities. That is the tragedy of race."[87]

Legislative Reform

IT IS TIME FOR our governments to act. There is now compelling evidence that racial profiling is a serious problem in Canada, one that is jeopardizing the physical and psychological integrity and dignity of racialized communities across this country. It is also clear that police and security forces have no intention of taking the necessary steps to determine whether, and to what extent, racial profiling is a problem within a particular police service. No police chief, for example, has agreed to follow the lead of Chief Closs of the Kingston Police. Consequently, the burden falls on the shoulders of our elected officials to take action. Our governments have a moral and constitutional obligation to act, and, in addition, international law commitments demand it. Canada is a signatory to the *International Convention on the Elimination of All Forms of Racial Discrimination*.[1] Article 2 of the *International Convention* mandates that all State Parties "undertake to pursue by all appropriate means and without delay a policy of eliminating racial discrimination in all its forms ..." Canada is also a signatory to the *International Covenant on Civil and Political Rights*.[2] Article 4 of the *Covenant* is particularly significant in that it permits State Parties to derogate from their obligations during times of emergencies except where that derogation would result in discrimination.

There appears to be some political momentum for legislative reform. At the federal level, for example, Prime Minister Paul Martin has spoken out against racial profiling in the domestic and terrorism contexts.[3] On March 29, 2005, Multiculturalism Minister Raymond Chan announced a multi-million–dollar initiative to address racially biased policing through a federal program called Law Enforcement Aboriginal and Diversity Network (LEAD).[4] More than half of the money will come from the Department of Canadian Heritage's new action strategy to address racism, including racial profiling.[5] On November 18, 2004, Libby Davies introduced a private member's bill — *An Act to Eliminate Racial Profiling*.[6] In addition to defining racial profiling, the bill prohibits federal agencies such as the RCMP and Customs officers from using racial profiling. It also requires the collection of data on "routine investigatory activities to determine if any enforcement officer has engaged in racial profiling." While the Act would not apply to provincial or municipal police forces, it provides a blueprint for provincial legislation. Davis has also been instrumental in the creation of a website — www.stopracialprofiling. ca — where individuals can get more information about profiling and also report incidents.[7] Other politicians, including Senators Mobina Jaffer and Donald Oliver, have individually called for anti-racial-profiling legislation.[8] And, on March 21, 2005, Members of Parliament from all three opposition parties gathered and demanded legislation to ban racial profiling.[9]

ANTI-RACIAL-PROFILING LEGISLATION

ANTI-RACIAL-PROFILING LEGISLATION would send an important message to racialized communities, the police, and the public that this practice will not be tolerated. It would also reflect a recognition by Parliament that profiling *is* a problem. What would federal and provincial anti-racial-profiling legislation look like? As part of a preamble, the legislation should recognize that racial profiling is a serious problem in Canada and that it is a violation of human rights and the equality guarantee in our Constitution. It should also emphatically state that it is ineffective as a law-enforcement strategy. The first section of the Act should clearly define racial profiling, following the guidelines from chapter 1. The second section should contain a comprehensive ban on the use of racial profiling by all law-enforcement and state actors and agencies.[10] Part of the ban should also include a prohibition on the use of pretext traffic stops, given the experience in the United States and Canada that these stops have become the means by which profiling is carried out. In the United States, Montana and West Virginia have included bans on pretext stops in their legislation.[11] Anti-racial-profiling legislation should also have the following components.

Mandatory Data Collection

THE LEGISLATION MUST CONTAIN a mandatory data-collection requirement for all law-enforcement encounters, whether they be, for example, on the street, at the border or airport, or at work.[12] In its racial-profiling inquiry report, the Ontario Human Rights Commission urged that, "where anecdotal evidence of racial profiling exists, the organization involved should collect data for the purpose of monitoring its occurrence and to identify measures to combat it."[13] The commission reiterated this position two years later in its *Policy and Guidelines on Racism and Racial Discrimination*.[14] It went farther and held that, "where a *prima facie* complaint of discrimination is made out, the Commission will consider the failure to collect and analyze data as part of its analysis of whether the respondent has met its duty to ensure it is not in violation of the *Code*." It also noted that, "in cases where the collection of data was clearly warranted, the failure to collect accurate and reliable data may foreclose a respondent from making a credible defence that it did not discriminate."[15]

With the exception of the Kingston project (and the Canada Customs project described below), Canada currently stands alone in its failure to address claims of racial profiling through data collection. In the United States, data collection is the norm. Only four of its fifty states (North Dakota, Missouri, Hawaii, and Vermont) do not (or have not previously) collect(ed) data either voluntarily or pursuant to legislation.[16] In England, a number of jurisdictions, including the Metropolitan Police Federation (London), are currently collecting stop data, and that number is expected to grow.[17]

As noted above, Canada Customs is also about to implement a data-collection project. On May 24, 1999, Selwyn Pieters, a thirty-one-year-old law student and employee of the Immigration and Refugee Board of Canada, was on his way back home to Toronto from New York City. He had decided to take the train that weekend. At the Fort Erie border, a student Canada Customs inspector boarded his train car. There were approximately seventy people on board, and he was the only Black person. The Customs official decided to search his luggage, and Pieters did not see him search any other luggage. When he complained about what he felt was racial profiling, a supervisor called him "Billy Jack," a bigot-fighting character from the B movies of the 1970s.[18] Pieters was humiliated; as he said, "[i]t went to the very heart of my dignity, to who I was." He filed a complaint with the Canadian Human Rights Commission.[19]

The Customs official would later offer four reasons why he had decided to search Pieters's luggage: "He was travelling alone; he had been out of the country a short time; he had visited New York, which Canada Customs sees as a drug-source city; and he seemed anxious to avoid having his bags searched."[20] This explanation had all the hallmarks of racial profiling as generic reasons, and misinterpreted behaviour formed the basis of the suspicion. Canada Customs eventually settled the complaint, but not before Pieters had succeeded in bringing about important systemic changes. In addition to a ban on racial profiling at the border, a requirement that passengers be told why they are being selected for secondary inspection, Customs agreed to hire an expert to conduct anti-racism training.[21] But perhaps, most significant, Customs agreed to collect race-based data on who is selected for inspection.[22] Meanwhile, Pieters is now a successful human rights and civil litigation lawyer in Toronto, having graduated from Osgoode Hall Law School in 2003.

What is data collection? It is a requirement that the police and security officials record, either electronically or in writing, those whom they stop and investigate. What would the process look like? The information collected would include perceived age, gender, racial and ethnic background, where the stop takes place, the reasons for the stop, what investigative measures were taken (e.g., a search), and the results. To promote accountability and transparency, the police should be required to give the person stopped a ticket confirming that they were stopped, the reasons, and the name of the officer(s). Funding should be tied to compliance. The legislation should require the ministry responsible for policing in the province to publish an annual report on the results of the data collection. Alternatively, a provincial Racial Diversity Secretariat as proposed by the Ontario Human Rights Commission could be established not only to report annually on racial profiling but on all issues of racism. For example, this secretariat could also be empowered to review and report on the implementation of the recommendations of the numerous systemic racism commissions that have been made over the last fifteen years.[23]

Unfortunately, there are a number of misconceptions about what kind of data should be collected to address the issue of racial profiling. We must always be cognizant of the optics and ethics of compiling race-based statistics. Statistics can be misleading, and they may serve to further stereotype a particular community. For example, the historical problem with race statistics is that they have focused on arrests, and therefore have given us only part of the picture — namely, who is caught and prosecuted. This data is misleading because, to the extent that it shows that certain groups are overrepresented for certain offences, it cannot tell us whether that overrepresentation is due to greater group criminality, over-policing, or other systemic factors. Race-based stop data, which is what is being proposed, is different from arrest data because it looks at who the police stop, as opposed to who is arrested. Its primary purpose is to identify whether particular groups attract more police attention than other groups.

A second concern about race-based statistics is that they can be easily manipulated and used for an improper purpose. That is why data collection was originally banned in Toronto by the Toronto Police Services Board in 1989, following a speech by then Staff-Inspector Julian Fantino to a race-relations committee in North York, Ontario.[24] In his speech, Fantino proclaimed that, based on statistics he had himself compiled, Blacks accounted for most of the crime in the Jane-Finch corridor, and that it was this criminal element that was responsible for the "bad blood between police and blacks."[25] Sufficient safeguards, however, can be taken to protect the reliability, integrity, and use of the collection of stop data.[26] For example, the design should be left to the experts, in-cluding anti-racism experts, and there should be consultation with the relevant communities and the relevant Human Rights Commission.[27] Safeguards to ensure compliance and honest re-porting could include the installation of video-cameras in all po-lice cars;[28] a requirement that all stops be called into the dispatch; or a requirement, as in England, that the police issue a written confirmation that the individual was stopped, the reasons for the stop, and the name of the officer.[29]

Why is stop data so important in the fight against racial pro-filing? As we noted earlier in the book, the breeding ground for racial profiling is the day-to-day proactive and crime-detection po-licing that occurs on our streets. These "opportunity," or "fishing expedition," encounters are used by the police to find contraband such as drugs or weapons, to monitor the activities of "suspicious" individuals, and, generally, to engender respect from those groups perceived to be in need of order maintenance.[30] Data collection will identify to what degree the police are focusing their attention on certain groups. It also reflects a commitment to transparency and will, therefore, go some way in restoring faith in the police and justice system. Tracking stops will permit senior officials to monitor the performance of their officers, information that, in addition to identifying which officers are in need of further anti-racism training, may serve to deter them from conducting unjustified stops.

Some preliminary results from England suggest that a recording obligation has made officers more likely to "think twice" before acting inappropriately.[31] That is important, because one of the best protections against racial profiling is for officers to realize that their view of events is often distorted by stereotypes and for them to think about why they are making the stop before they do so.[32] Some police officials have argued that this consideration is precisely why data should not be collected.[33] Indeed, one of the emerging criticisms of racial-profiling research and discourse is that it will have a negative impact on police effectiveness. For example, it has been suggested that police will be hesitant to do "their job" out of fear of being called racist, if the data should later reveal a higher percentage of stops of Blacks or other racialized groups.[34] The idea, however, that the police are going to stop investigating objectively suspicious behaviour because of such a requirement is not persuasive, particularly since this hypothetical outcome has not been a problem in the United States or Britain.[35]

Finally, data collection will allow officials to keep track of "hit" rates. A hit rate is the likelihood that contraband will be found within a particular group following a police stop. As noted earlier in the book, hit-rate data in the United States has severely undermined the myth that has fuelled profiling (that the usual drug offender is Black or Hispanic). In the event that legislation is not passed and police forces do not voluntarily collect this data, the burden will fall on courts or human rights commissions to order such collection. In its anti-racism policy, the Ontario Human Rights Commission stated that it would seek "data collection and analysis as a public interest remedy in litigation and settlements."[36]

Other Proactive Measures

ANTI-RACIAL-PROFILING LEGISLATION should impose an obligation on the police and all levels of government to take other proactive measures to address racially-biased policing. At a minimum they should include issuing a written protocol defining and banning the use of racial profiling. Kingston and Montreal have done so.[37] Additional proactive measures include anti-racism training and, in particular, anti-racial-profiling training that is both comprehensive and effective.[38] In Quebec, for example, courses on racial profiling are now part of the training at all police academies.[39] This new policy is one of a number of recommendations from a racial-profiling task force set up by the Quebec government. All police forces should be required to hire an anti-racism expert to conduct an external audit of the current training measures in place. The hiring and promoting of visible minority officers must also be made a priority.[40] Legislation should emphasize the need for an accountable and transparent police complaints process and stress that it is a shared responsibility of the police, civilian oversight bodies, and government to ensure that there is a fair complaints process.

A Racial-Profiling Tort

AN ANTI-PROFILING LAW SHOULD create a racial-profiling tort (i.e., a civil wrong) to reflect the pernicious nature of this conduct. It should, regardless of whether a specific tort is created, also provide a jurisdictional basis for aggrieved individuals to seek a civil remedy in court.[41] Possible remedies could include damages, mandatory data collection, anti-racial-profiling training, and community service.[42] Given the problems of proof identified in chapter 8, the legislation should reverse the onus of proof where there is evidence that a disproportionate number of racialized individuals are being stopped by the officer or members of his or her division or police service. This reverse onus would place the burden on the police to prove that the plaintiff was not the victim of racial profiling. Section 4(2) of the *Elimination of Racial Profiling Act*, for example, states: "Proof that the routine investigatory activities of an enforcement officer have had a disparate impact on racial, religious or ethnic minorities is, in the absence of evidence to the contrary, proof that the officer has engaged in racial profiling."[43]

A Racial-Profiling Crime

SOME CONSIDERATION SHOULD BE given to amending the *Criminal Code* to include a crime of racial profiling, as has been suggested by the Canadian Race Relations Foundation.[44] Because racial profiling is often unconscious, we might want to limit the application of the criminal law to cases where the officer is a repeat offender.[45] In New Jersey, racial profiling is now a criminal offence. Under the prohibition, a person must commit two acts of profiling before he or she can be found guilty. Up to five years imprisonment and/or a $15,000 fine can be imposed. The penalty increases to a maximum of ten years' imprisonment if someone is injured.[46] Racial profiling is also a crime in Oklahoma.[47]

BEYOND LEGISLATION

EFFECTIVE CIVILIAN OVERSIGHT AND an objective and transparent police complaints process are two important mechanisms that must be in place to ensure that complaints against the police and security officials are treated fairly and to restore and maintain confidence in the system. Victims of racial profiling must feel confident that they have a place to complain about police misconduct and that their complaints will be treated fairly. No one should be surprised that Aboriginal people and members of the Black, Arab, or Muslim communities would not want to file a racial-profiling complaint in circumstances where state officials continue to deny the existence of profiling. For example, as of June 17, 2005, only two complaints by Muslims have apparently been filed with the Commission for Public Complaints against the RCMP. As Shirley Heafey, the commission's chair, recently pointed out in a speech in Alberta:

I've been told of Muslims being visited at work by the RCMP. They were being asked questions like: Do you pray 5 times a day and what do you think about "Al Quaeda." And then being told they don't need a lawyer. Told to co-operate and be good citizens. These are stories that people have told me. I haven't investigated these stories because, with two exceptions, no one is telling me this stuff has lodged a complaint with my Commission.

... many people are just too afraid of retaliation to complain. That's not hard to understand. To lodge a complaint is to invite more attention, from police and government officials.[48]

This fear is very unfortunate. In the criminal justice system, Parliament and our courts have spent the last decade trying to make the system more sensitive and accessible for victims. To that end, a number of measures have been taken to reduce revictimization and to promote the reporting of incidents, particularly in the sexual-assault context. This same philosophy needs to be incorporated to address racial profiling in this country. There are some signs of encouragement. Police complaints in Saskatchewan are now vetted and administered by a five-person Public Complaints Commission.[49] The commission, which must include both First Nations and Métis representation at the commission levels, has expansive jurisdiction, including the ability to conduct its own investigations into a particular complaint. It is, in part, a result of the Neil Stonechild Inquiry and its recommendation for improved procedures to deal with police complaints.[50]

In Ontario, former Chief Justice Patrick Lesage was appointed to review the police complaints process in Ontario.[51] In a report released on April 25, 2005, Justice Lesage concluded that the current system is "flawed."[52] To ensure greater transparency and accountability, Justice Lesage made a number of recommendations, including the creation of a new independent civilian oversight body. This new body would be, among other things, responsible for education, promoting access, taking and screening complaints, and deciding whether it or the police should investigate the complaint.[53]

At the decision-making stage, Justice Lesage recommended that the government develop a body of independent adjudicators to preside over *Police Services Act* disciplinary hearings.[54]

Similarly, part of the mandate of the Arar Inquiry is to make recommendations on a mechanism for reviewing the national security activities of the RCMP.[55] In its submissions to the inquiry, the Commission for Public Complaints (CPC) against the RCMP recommended that it be given greater access to information and an audit power, which the Security Intelligence Review Committee (SIRC), the oversight body of the Canadian Security Intelligence Service (CSIS), currently has.[56] An audit power would enable the CPC to investigate RCMP conduct without the need of an individual complaint.[57] The CPC also made an alternative recommendation: the creation of a National Security Review Commission that would have the jurisdiction to review all federal agencies involved in national security operations.[58]

Some consideration should be given to establishing a national commission on racial profiling that could act as an oversight body for federal agencies and as an advisory body for provincial law enforcement. As a civilian oversight body for the RCMP, for example, the commission would be able, with proper audit powers, to fully investigate the training materials used by Operation Pipeline/ Convoy/Jetway as well as the intelligence reports prepared by related organizations such as the Criminal Intelligence Service Canada.[59] This national commission could provide expert assistance to courts, police complaints mechanisms, or human rights commissions. It could also be responsible for promulgating the data-collection standards that could be used by police forces as well as providing a mechanism to interpret and even publish the data.

The commission could also have a significant public educative function. It is critical that the public be educated about the harm caused by racial profiling and why it is an ineffective and troubling law-enforcement technique that has served only to continue our legacy of discrimination. The more we become aware of the destructive nature of racial profiling, the greater the likelihood that we will see meaningful reform. Part of that educative process is for us to try to put ourselves in the shoes, as best we can, of those who experience it. In identifying the damage caused by racial profiling, the Ontario Human Rights Commission and others listened carefully to those who came forward with their stories.[60]

Sam, a young Black youth, is a composite of these lived experiences. I want to end the book by considering what life with racial profiling is like for Sam, who lives in a largely racialized community in the north part of Toronto. As he wakes up each morning, Sam faces the prospect of a regular interaction, or "routine check," as it is sometimes called, with the police. This encounter could take place on the way to school, at school, in the parking lot of the McDonald's where he eats lunch, in the shopping mall, or on his way home.[61] The check usually involves questions such "Where are you going?" or "Do you have any drugs on you?" then a request for identification and a computer check to verify his name, the filling out of a "208" card, and a "pat down."[62] When Sam leaves his house, he always has to remember to bring some identification, for fear of being further detained if he does not have it when the police ask for it. As *Globe and Mail* columnist John Barber discovered in his interviews of Black youth in Toronto, "[t]hese kids are ecstatic about going a whole month without having been stopped, questioned and checked out on the criminal database.... "I'm *lovin'* it, Jay exclaimed.... "I can walk to the store with no I.D.!"[63] As Sam leaves his house, he is acutely aware of the police presence. Even when they don't stop him, he sees them looking at him. He knows they are waiting for some kind of a cue and, no matter whether he looks at them or away from them, it will generate suspicion. His friends call this "tagging and clocking."[64]

Sam tries his best to minimize his exposure and the consequences of being stopped. On the weekend, when he takes his girlfriend to a movie, they have to allot an extra 30 minutes to compensate for a likely police stop. Sam has an 11:00 P.M. curfew. He also has to plan in advance what route he is going to take, to avoid certain areas that will make a stop for being "out of place" more likely.[65] When Sam does get stopped, the police lights are flashing. Fear and humiliation consume him.[66] Will he become the next young Black male shot?[67] Why does this checking keep happening to me? he asks himself. How do I get them to stop? As the officer leaves his cruiser, Sam remains as still as he can, as he knows that any sudden movement could cost him his life. He has been taught this reaction by his parents, as Royson James so poignantly pointed out in his column "Why I Fear for My Sons":

> Whenever [I] was stopped by the police, and as the officer approached the car, sometimes checking the holster, the kids were told to watch how Dad responded to the interrogation and model that behaviour. Even when their father suspected racial profiling, it was never brought up as a cause for the police contact. Don't be lippy. Keep your hands on the steering wheel. Ask before you go to your pocket for your licence or to the glove compartment for the insurance and ownership. Keep your passengers calm and quiet.[68]

On those occasions when Sam is courageous enough to ask why he is being stopped, he is usually told that "he fit the description" of someone they were looking for.[69] Other times he is told "because we are the law." If, at any time, Sam makes a mistake that all kids his age are prone to do, such as giving an acquaintance who has drugs a lift, he faces a much greater chance of being caught than if he were White. If he is caught, he will be burdened with a criminal record. And, even if he does not get into trouble, Sam will likely develop a chip on his shoulder, an attitude, or a distrust of authority—all of which will be interpreted negatively by those who have no appreciation for his lived experience. Paranoia and post-traumatic stress disorder may also set in.[70] This scenario is the lived experience of most racialized youth in this country. It is time for action.

Notes

INTRODUCTION

1 *Report of the Commission on Systemic Racism in the Ontario Criminal Justice System* (Toronto: Queen's Printer for Ontario, 1995), ix [*Ontario Systemic Racism Report*].

2 See Scot Wortley and Julian Tanner, "Inflammatory Rhetoric? Baseless Accusations? A Response to Gabor's Critique of Racial Profiling Research in Canada," *Canadian Journal of Criminology and Criminal Justice* 47 (2005): 590–95 ["Inflammatory Rhetoric"].

3 See Philip Mascoll and Jim Rankin, "Racial Profiling Exists," *Toronto Star*, 31 March 2005, A1.

4 See, for example, Betsy Powell, "Video Convicts Officer," *Toronto Star*, 29 July 2005, A1; Dale Anne Freed, "Constable Convicted of Assault," *Toronto Star*, 19 October 2004, A4; "Winnipeg Police Accused of Brutality Against Aboriginals," *Guardian*, 9 November 2002, A5; Scot Wortley, "Hidden Intersections: Research on Race, Crime and Criminal Justice in Canada," *Canadian Ethnic Studies* 35 (2003): 105; and Gabriella Pedicelli, *When Police Kill: Police Use of Force in Montreal and Toronto* (Montreal: Véhicule Press, 1998), 75–77.

5 See *R. v. Munson* (2003), 172 CCC (3d) 515 (Sask. CA); *Report of the Commission of Inquiry into Matters Relating to the Death of Neil Stonechild* (October 2004), online: Neil Stonechild Inquiry http://www.stonechild-

inquiry.ca/finalreport/default.shtml (date accessed 4 August 2005), 1; and *Legacy of Hope: An Agenda for Change*, vol. 1 (June 21, 2004), online: Commission on First Nations and Metis Peoples and Justice Reform http://www.justicereformcomm.sk.ca/volume1.gov (date accessed 4 August 2005), 5-1-5-2.

6 See Michelle Shephard, "Are We Ready for Torture by Proxy," *Toronto Star*, 17 July 2005, A6.

7 See "Inflammatory Rhetoric," 600.

8 See Gail Kellough and Scot Wortley, "Remand for Plea: Bail Decisions and Plea Bargaining as Commensurate Decisions," *British Journal of Criminology* 42 (2002): 194–97, 201; *Report of the Aboriginal Justice Inquiry of Manitoba*, vol. 1 (Winnipeg: Queen's Printer, 1991), 102–3, 221–24, 595; *Ontario Systemic Racism Report*, 123–24, 142–44, 251, 277; *R. v. Gladue* (1999), 133 CCC (3d) 385 at 412 (para. 65) (SCC); Kent Roach, *Due Process and Victims' Rights: The New Law and Politics of Criminal Justice* (Toronto: University of Toronto Press, 1999), 225; Scot Wortley and Gail Kellough, "Racializing Risk: Police and Crown Discretion and the Over-Representation of Black People in the Ontario Criminal Justice System," in Anthony Harriott et al., eds., *Crime and Criminal Justice in the Caribbean and Among Caribbean Peoples* (Kingston, Jamaica: Arawak Publications, 2004), 173–205; Cynthia Peterson, "Institutionalized Racism: The Need for Reform of the Criminal Jury Selection Process," *McGill Law Journal* 38 (1993): 147; Toni Williams, "Sentencing Black Offenders in the Ontario Criminal Justice System," in Julian V. Roberts and David P. Cole, eds., *Making Sense of Sentencing* (Toronto: University of Toronto Press, 1999), 211–12; and Sanjeev S. Anand, "Expressions of Racial Hatred and Racism in Canada: An Historical Perspective," *Canadian Bar Review* 77 (1998): 190. See also Nova Scotia, Royal Commission on the Donald Marshall, Jr., Prosecution, *Findings and Recommendations*, vol. 1 (Halifax: The Commission, 1989).

9 This figure is approximately 17 percent of the Canadian population. See "Aboriginal Identity Population 2001," online: Statistics Canada http://www12.statcan.ca/english/census01/products/highlight/Aboriginal/Page.cfm?Lang=E&Geo=PR&View=1a&Table=1&StartRec=1&Sort=2&B1=Counts01&B2=Total (date accessed 4 July 2005); and Statistics Canada, "Visible Minority Populations, Provinces and Territories" (2001 Census), online: Statistics Canada http://www40.statcan.ca/l01/cst01/demo52a.htm (date accessed 18 June 2005).

10 *Policy and Guidelines on Racism and Racial Discrimination*, 9, online: Ontario Human Rights Commission http://www.ohrc.on.ca/english/pub-

lications/racism-and-racial-discrimination-policy.pdf (date accessed 5 July 2005).

11 See *Ontario Systemic Racism Report*, 40–41.

CHAPTER 1: WHAT IS IT?

1 See *Board of Inquiry Decision*, 26 September 1995 (Ontario) [on file with the author], 1–6 [*Board of Inquiry Decision*]. See also *Ontario (Police Complaints Commissioner) v. Hannah*, [1997] OJ No. 1411 at para. 2 (Gen. Div., Div. Ct.) [*Hannah*]. See also Philip Mascoll, "Police Cleared in 'Take Down,'" *Toronto Star*, 27 September 1995 ["Police Cleared"].

2 See *Board of Inquiry Decision*, 6.

3 This history of police shootings is chronicled in chapter 9.

4 See "Young Black Men," *Toronto Star*, 2 October 1995, A16 ["Young Black Men"].

5 Cecil Foster, *A Place Called Heaven: The Meaning of Being Black in Canada* (Toronto: HarperCollins, 1996), 7. See also Cecil Foster, "Blacks Learn Futility of Complaint," *Toronto Star*, 3 October 1995, A19.

6 See Clayton Ruby, "Police Complaints a Monster We Can't Control," *Toronto Star*, 4 October 1995, A21.

7 RSO 1990, c. P.15.

8 See Rosie DiManno, "Attacks on Kerr a Punishment for Breaking Ranks," *Toronto Star*, 30 January 1995, A6, discussing the police union's motion of non-confidence.

9 See Rosie DiManno, "Scary Rogue Police Law unto Themselves," *Toronto Star*, 27 January 1995, A6; Philip Mascoll, "Police Only Had 'Hunch'," *Toronto Star*, 28 January 2005, A4 ["Police Only Had 'Hunch'"]; and John Duncanson and Michelle Shephard, "Police Union Chief Calling It Quits," *Toronto Star*, 11 September 2002, A2.

10 See *Board of Inquiry Decision*, 3–4.

11 Philip Mascoll, "Skin Color Reason for 'Take-Down'," *Toronto Star*, 31 March 1995, A22 ["Reason for 'Take-Down'"].

12 As quoted in Rosie DiManno, "TV Editor Fears 'Open Season' on Black Men," *Toronto Star*, 27 September 1995, A7 ["Open Season"]. See also *Hannah*, para. 10.

13 See "Police Only Had 'Hunch'"; and *Board of Inquiry Decision*, 7–8.

14 "Police Only Had 'Hunch'"; and *Board of Inquiry Decision*, 4.

15 See *Board of Inquiry Decision*, 5–7.

16 *Ibid*. See also Bruce DeMara, "Officer Never Sought Witness," *Toronto Star*, 30 March 1995, A7; "Open Season"; and "Young Black Men."

17 As reported in the *Toronto Star*. See "Reason for 'Take Down.'"

18 The board consisted of Fernando Costa (a lawyer), Edward Clarke (founding director of the National Black Coalition), and Keith Aiken (retired police officer). See "Police Cleared."

19 *Board of Inquiry Decision*, 11.

20 *Ibid.*, 10. See also *Hannah*, para. 15.

21 *Board of Inquiry Decision*, 11 (emphasis added).

22 *Ibid.*, 10–11.

23 *Ibid.*, 10.

24 For example, in its reasons, the board noted that it "shares a special sensitivity to subtle and covert racism." See *Board of Inquiry Decision*, 11.

25 As quoted in "Police Cleared," and "Open Season."

26 See Carl James, "'Up to No Good': Black on the Streets and Encountering Police," in Vic Satzewich, ed., *Racism and Social Inequality in Canada: Concepts, Controversies and Strategies of Resistence* (Toronto: Thompson Education, 1998), 157.

27 Jennifer Lewington, "Councillor's Racial Remark Sparks Furor," *Globe and Mail*, 17 August 2005, A15.

28 See *Hannah*.

29 See, generally, the discussion in Sujit Choudhry, "Protecting Equality in the Face of Terror: Ethnic and Racial Profiling and s. 15 of the *Charter*," in Ronald J. Daniels et al., eds., *The Security of Freedom: Essays on Canada's Anti-Terrorism Bill* (Toronto: University of Toronto Press, 2001), 368–70 ["Protecting Equality"].

30 Kent Roach, "Making Progress on Understanding and Remedying Racial Profiling," *Alberta Law Review* 41 (2003): 896.

31 See also *Paying the Price: The Human Cost of Racial Profiling*, 21 October 2003, online: Ontario Human Rights Commission http://www.ohrc. on.ca/english/consultations/racial-profiling-report.pdf (date accessed 21 June 2005), 6 [*Paying the Price*]; and Canadian Bar Association, "Resolution 04-07-A, Racial Profiling and Law Enforcement," online: Canadian Bar Association http://www.cba.org/CBA/resolutions/pdf/04-07-A.pdf (date accessed 10 June 2005).

32 Beverly Cross, "A Time for Action," in Tammy Johnson, Jennifer E. Boyden, and William J. Pittz, eds., *Racial Profiling and Punishment in U.S. Public Schools: How Zero Tolerance Policies and High Stakes Testing Subvert Academic Excellence and Racial Equity* (Applied Research Centre, 2001), 5, online: Applied Research Centre http://www.arc.org/erase/downloads/ profiling.pdf (date accessed 26 September 2005).

33 See Chief Justice Beverley McLachlin, "Racism and the Law: The Canadian Experience," *Journal of Law & Equality* 1 (2002): 10–14; "Policy and
Guidelines on Racism and Racial Discrimination," 9 June 2005, 5–8,
online: Ontario Human Rights Commission http://www.ohrc.on.ca/
english/publications/racism-and-racial-discrimination-policy.pdf (date
accessed 11 August 2005) ["Policy and Guidelines on Racism"]; Sanjeev
S. Anand, "Expressions of Racial Hatred and Racism in Canada: An His-
torical Perspective," *The Canadian Bar Review* 77 (1998): 187–92; Carol
A. Aylward, *Canadian Critical Race Theory: Racism and the Law* (Halifax:
Fernwood, 1999), 39–49; Barry Cahill, "Slavery and the Judges of Loyal-
ist Nova Scotia," *University of New Brunswick Law Journal* 43 (1994): 73;
H.T. Holman, ed., "Slaves and Servants on Prince Edward Island: The
Case of Jupiter Wise," *Acadiensis* 12 (1982): 100; James Walker, *"Race,"
Rights and the Law in the Supreme Court of Canada* (Waterloo: Wilfrid
Laurier University Press, 1997); Constance Backhouse, *Colour-Coded:
A Legal History of Racism in Canada, 1900–1950* (Toronto: University of
Toronto Press, 1999); Robin Winks, *The Blacks in Canada* (New Haven,
Conn.: Yale University Press, 1971); Constance Backhouse, "Racial Seg-
regation in Canadian Legal History: Viola Desmond's Challenge, Nova
Scotia, 1946," *Dalhousie Law Journal* 17 (1994): 299; "Looking Forward,
Looking Back," in *People to People, Nation to Nation: Highlights from the
Report of the Royal Commission on Aboriginal Peoples* (1996) online: Indian
and Northern Affairs Canada http://www.ainc-inac.gc.ca/ch/rcap/rpt/
lk_e.html (date accessed 20 November 2004); John S. Milloy, *A National
Crime: The Canadian Government and the Residential School System, 1879
to 1986* (Winnipeg: University of Manitoba Press, 1999); and "The Residential School System Historical Overview," online: Indian Residential
Schools Resolution Canada http://www.irsr-rqpi.gc.ca/english/history.
html (date accessed 21 November 2004).

34 William M. Carter Jr., "A Thirteenth Amendment Framework for Com-
bating Racial Profiling," *Harvard Civil Rights — Civil Liberties Law Review*
39 (2004): 20. See also N. Jeremi Duru, "The Central Park Five, the
Scottsboro Boys, and the Myth of the Bestial Black Man," *Cardozo Law
Review* 25 (2004): 1322–43.

35 It is now generally accepted that targeting an individual for investigation
based on race is contrary to section 9 of the *Charter*. See, for example,
Brown v. Durham Regional Police Force (1998), 131 CCC (3d) 1 at 17 (Ont.
CA) ("[o]fficers who stop persons intending to conduct unauthorized
searches, or who select persons to be stopped based on their ... colour ... all
act for an improper purpose"); and *R. v. Richards* (1999), 26 CR (5th) 286

at 293–95 (Ont. CA) ("… if the demand for the appellant's driver's licence and identification was racially motivated the demand was unlawful …"). In *R .v. Smith* (2004), 26 CR (6th) 375 at 384–85 (Ont. SCJ), the Court held that racial profiling also violates section 7 of the *Charter,* which guarantees that the state will not deprive someone of life, liberty, or security of the person except in accordance with principles of fundamental justice.

36 *Law v. Canada (Minister of Employment and Immigration),* [1999] 1 SCR 497 at para. 51, Iacobucci J. See "Protecting Equality," for a discussion of the section 15(1) analysis.

37 See, for example, the *International Convention on the Elimination of All Forms of Racial Discrimination,* 21 December 1965, 660 United Nations Treaty Series (UNTS) 195 (entered into force 4 January 1969, accession by Canada 14 October 1970); and the *International Covenant on Civil and Political Rights,* 16 December 1966, 999 UNTS 171 (entered into force 23 March 1976, accession by Canada 19 May 1976).

38 See, for example, the cases of Neil Stonechild and Darryl Night. These cases and the "starlight tours" phenomenon are discussed in more detail in chapter 2.

39 Systemic racism is present in every social institution in Canadian society. See the discussion in *Anti-Black Racism in Canada: A Report on the Canadian Government's Compliance with the International Convention on the Elimination of All Forms of Racial Discrimination* (Toronto: African Canadian Legal Clinic, 2002) [on file with the author]; *Report of the Commission on Systemic Racism in the Ontario Criminal Justice System* (Toronto: Queen's Printer for Ontario, 1995), chapter 3 [*Ontario Systemic Racism Report*]; Multiculturalism and Citizenship Canada, *Eliminating Racial Discrimination in Canada* (Ottawa: Minister of Supply & Services Canada, 1989), 3–7; W. Head and D.H. Clairmont, *Discrimination Against Blacks in Nova Scotia* (Halifax: Royal Commission on the Donald Marshall, Jr. Prosecution, 1989); Canada, *Findings and Recommendations, The Royal Commission on the Donald Marshall, Jr. Prosecution,* vol. 1 (Halifax: Royal Commission on the Donald Marshall, Jr. Prosecution, 1989) (Chair: T.A. Hickman); Law Reform Commission of Canada, *Report on Aboriginal Peoples and Criminal Justice: Equality, Respect and the Search for Justice* (Ottawa: Law Reform Commission of Canada, 1991); and Royal Commission on Aboriginal Peoples, *Bridging the Cultural Divide: A Report on Aboriginal People and Criminal Justice in Canada* (Ottawa: Minister of Supply & Services Canada, 1996). See also the discussion in *R. v. Williams,* [1998] 1 SCR 1128 at paras. 20–31; *R. v. Gladue,* [1999] 1 SCR 688 at paras. 58–74; and *R. v. Parks* (1993), 84 CCC (3d) 353 (Ont. CA).

40 *Ontario Systemic Racism Report*, 39.

41 *Ibid.*, 40. See also Anthony C. Thompson, "Stopping the Usual Suspects: Race and the Fourth Amendment," *New York University Law Review* 74 (1999): 983–86 ["Stopping the Usual Suspects"]. See further Alan W. Mewett, "Secondary Facts, Prejudice and Stereotyping," *Criminal Law Quarterly* 42 (1999): 319; and Marilyn MacCrimmon, "Developments in the Law of Evidence: The 1995–96 Term: Regulating Fact Determination and Commonsense Reasoning," *Supreme Court Law Review* 8 (2d) (1997): 368–74.

42 *Paying the Price*, 6.

43 Miro Cernetig, "Looking Over Their Shoulders," *Toronto Star*, 13 February 2005, A8; and Roberto Rocha, "Police Admit to Racial Profiling," Montreal *Gazette*, 29 January 2005, A1.

44 Chris Sorensen, "Ottawa Police, Deputy Chief at Odds Over Racial Profiling," *Toronto Star*, 2 March 2003, A1.

45 *R. v. Singh* (2003), 15 CR (6th) 288 at 295–96 (Ont. SCJ) [*Singh*].

46 Alan Young, *Justice Defiled: Perverts, Potheads, Serial Killers & Lawyers* (Toronto: Key Porter Books, 2003).

47 Alan Young, "'Racial Profiling' a Misnomer for Racism," *Toronto Star*, 26 September 2004, F7 ["Misnomer for Racism"].

48 *Ibid.*

49 The Criminal Intelligence Service Alberta (CISA) is described on its website as follows:

> CISA exists to facilitate the exchange of criminal intelligence between intelligence units, enforcement units and CISC Provincial Bureau where collection, evaluation, collation, analysis, re-evaluation, and dissemination can be made to effectively combat the spread of organized crime in Canada. CISA and its Alberta *regular member police agencies* are also responsible for implementing the Provincial Organized and Serious Crime strategy to combat the spread of organized and serious crime in Alberta.
>
> In carrying out its mandate, CISA is involved in intelligence sharing, strategic analysis, operational support, and training. CISA's Executive Committee is made up of the chiefs of police from cities across the province. "About CISA," online: Criminal Intelligence Service Canada http://www.cisalberta.ca/faq.asp; and http://www.cisalberta.ca/mandate.htm (date accessed 18 October 2005).

50 The Annual Report of Criminal Intelligence Service Alberta, 2004/2005, 9–10, online: Criminal Intelligence Service Alberta http://www.

cisalberta.ca/Annual%20&%20Semi%20Annual%20Reports/
2004-2005%20annual%20report.pdf (date accessed 20 September 2005).

51 The Criminal Intelligence Service Canada (CISC) is an organization that "provides facilities to unite the criminal intelligence units of Canadian law enforcement agencies in the fight against organized crime and other serious crime in Canada." CISC consists of a Central Bureau, in Ottawa, and ten provincial bureaux located in each province. CISC is funded by the RCMP through its National Police Services. The Executive Committee of CISC is headed by the commissioner of the RCMP and is composed of twenty-two leaders from Canadian law enforcement. See "About CISC," online: Criminal Intelligence Service Canada http://www.cisc.gc.ca/about/about_CISC_e.htm (date accessed 21 September 2005).

52 Annual Report of Criminal Intelligence Service Canada, 2003, 5, 8, 15, online: Criminal Intelligence Service Canada http://www.cisc.gc.ca/annual_reports/AnnualReport2003/Document/CISC_annual_report_2003.pdf (date accessed 20 September 2005).

53 *Ibid.*, 2.

54 *Singh*, 295–96. The trial judge ultimately concluded that no racial profiling had occurred.

55 David A. Harris, *Profiles in Injustice: Why Racial Profiling Cannot Work* (New York: The New Press, 2002), 101.

56 *Ibid.*

57 RCMP Criminal Intelligence Brief (volume 8, no. 25), 18 September 2001, 2 [on file with the author]. This document was filed at the Arar Inquiry as part of Exhibit P-85. See Transcript of Proceedings, 30 June 2005, 8184–86, online: Commission of Inquiry into the Actions of Canadian Officials in Relation to Maher Arar http://www.stenotran.com/commission/maherarar/2005-06-30%20volume%2033.pdf (date accessed 23 August 2005) [Transcript of Arar Proceedings].

58 I say perception because, in chapter 7, I address why racial profiling is of no practical utility in the fight against terrorism.

59 See James Gordon, "A-O Canada: The RCMP'S Hunt for al-Qaida," Regina *Leader-Post*, 2 August 2005, A5; Jim Bronskill, "RCMP Targeted Another Engineer," *Toronto Star*, 10 August 2005, A8 ["RCMP Targeted Another Engineer"]; and Michelle Shephard, "Arar Deportation Surprised RCMP," *Toronto Star*, 27 November 2004, A4.

60 See Transcript of Arar Proceedings, 8187, 1.3-8.

61 "Misnomer for Racism."

62 This resistence is chronicled in chapter 2.

63 Policy and Guidelines on Racism, 13–14.

64 See "A Racist Is a Racist," editorial, *Ottawa Citizen*, 30 June 2005, C4; Nicholas Keung, "New Rights Guide Targets Racism Not Racists," *Toronto Star*, 29 June 2005, A11; and Avvy Go and Michael Kerr, "New Racism Policy Falls Short," *Toronto Star*, 7 July 2005, A20.

65 Tamsin McMahon and Frank Armstrong, "Police Chief 'Sorry' for Racial Profiling," *Kingston Whig-Standard*, 27 May 2005, 1. But see Frank Armstrong, "Officers Suffering in Wake of Racial-Profiling Study," *Kingston Whig-Standard*, 17 June 2005, 3; and Tamsin McMahon, "Officers 'Wounded' by Publicity Given to Racial-Profiling Study," *Kingston Whig-Standard*, 31 May 2005, 1.

66 "Stopping the Usual Suspects," 987, 991. See also David M. Tanovich, "The Colourless World of Mann," *Criminal Reports* (CR) 21 (6th) (2004): 52–54.

67 See Scott Plous, *The Psychology of Judgment and Decision Making* (New York: McGraw-Hill, 1993).

68 See *R. v. S.(C.)* (1997), 13 CR (5th) 375 (Ont. CJ); *R. v. Safadi*, [2005] AJ No. 559 (QB); *R. v. Heslop*, [2005] OJ No. 2072; *R. v. Snape*, [2002] OJ No. 714 (SCJ); *R. v. Burgher*, [2002] OJ No. 5316 (SCJ); *R. v. Peck*, [2001] OJ No. 4581 (SCJ); *R. v. Ramdeen*, [2000] OJ No. 5350 (CJ); *R. v. Griffiths* (2003), 11 CR (6th) 136 (Ont. CJ); *R. v. Carty*, [1995] OJ No. 2322 (PD); *R. v. Genus*, [1993] OJ No. 2821 (Prov. Div.); and *R. v. Hoang*, [2000] AJ No. 1630 at para. 6 (SC).

69 See *R. v. Ferdinand* (2004), 21 CR (6th) 65 at 72 (Ont. SCJ).

70 Jeffrey Rosen, "The Need to Test Evidence," *New York Times*, 13 October 2002.

71 *Ibid.*

72 See "Ottawa Muddled as Syria Squeezed," editorial, *Toronto Star*, 25 April 2005, A20.

73 See Michelle Shephard, "Canada Failed to Aid Arar Documents," *Toronto Star*, 22 April 2005, A1; Graham Fraser, "Arar's Syrian Hell," *Toronto Star*, 5 November 2003, A1 ["Arar's Syrian Hell"]; and Kate Jaimet, "Arar Applauds Public Inquiry," Saskatoon *StarPhoenix*, 13 February 2004, C5.

74 See Maher Arar, "I Want My Life Back," *Globe and Mail*, 30 April 2005, F3.

75 See Michelle Shephard, "Untangling Tale of Tortured Canadian," *Toronto Star*, 1 May 2004, A1.

76 As the Canadian Bar Association has pointed out in its brief to the Special Senate Committee on the *Anti-Terrorism Act*:

> Mr. Arar and at least four other Canadians have stated that they were detained and in three cases tortured when the information that led to their arrest is believed to have been received from

Canadian security agencies: Ahmad El-Maati; Abdullah Almalki; Muayyed Nureddin; and Kassim Mohammed.

See "Submission on the Three Year Review of the *Anti-Terrorism Act*," May 2005, 17, note 39, online: Canadian Bar Association http://www.cba. org/CBA/submissions/pdf/05-28-eng.pdf (date accessed 19 August 2005). See also the discussion in Michelle Shephard, "Are We Ready for Torture by Proxy," *Toronto Star*, 17 July 2005, A6; Colin Freeze, "Fears of Terror Cell Fade as Two Are Freed," *Globe and Mail*, 20 March 2004, A16; and Thomas Walkom, "New Torture Claim Shows Arar's Case Isn't Unique," *Toronto Star*, 26 February 2004, A1.

77 See Jeff Salot, "Once a Mujahed Who Took Flying Lessons, Ahmad El-Maati Seemed to Fit the Profile of a Terrorist," *Globe and Mail*, 29 August 2005, A1; Jeff Sallot, "For the First Time, Abdullah Almalki Tells His Story," *Globe and Mail*, 29 August 2005, A1; and "RCMP Targeted Another Engineer."

78 See "Maher's Story," Maher Arar Website online: http://www.maherarar. ca/mahers%20story.php (date accessed 24 August 2005).

79 *Ibid.* See also Colin Freeze, "Fears of Terror Cell Fade as Two Are Freed," *Globe and Mail*, 20 March 2004, A16; Shelley Page, "Collateral Damage," *Ottawa Citizen*, 15 December 2004, A1; and "Arar's Syrian Hell," A1.

80 Shirley Heafey, "The Need for Civilian Review of the RCMP on National Security Issues," speech delivered to the Access & Privacy Conference, 17 June 2005, online: Commission for Public Complaints Against the RCMP http://www.cpc-cpp.gc.ca/DefaultSite/Whatsnew/index_ e.aspx?ArticleID=776 (date accessed 17 August 2005).

81 See "Arar Commission: About the Inquiry," online: Commission of Inquiry into the Actions of Canadian Officials in Relation to Maher Arar http://www.ararcommission.ca/eng/ (date accessed 19 August 2005).

82 Richard Mackie, "Head of Arar Inquiry Hailed as 'A Judge Beyond Reproach,'" *Globe and Mail*, 29 January 2004, A13.

83 *Report of Professor Stephen J. Toope, Fact Finder*, 14 October 2005, 13, 17, 19, 23, online: Commission of Inquiry into the Actions of Canadian Officials in Relation to Maher Arar http://www.ararcommission.ca/eng/17. htm (date accessed 29 October 2005).

84 See Doug Saunders, "Shoot-to-Kill Error Causes U.K. Uproar," *Globe and Mail*, 18 August 2005, A2; Rosie Cowan, Duncan Campbell, and Vikram Dodd, "London Police Subdued Man, Then Shot Him Point-Blank," *Globe and Mail*, 17 August 2005, A1.

85 See Michelle Shephard and Betsy Powell, "How Terror Probe Slowly Unfolded," *Toronto Star*, 6 September 2003, A1 ["How Terror Probe Slowly

Unfolded"]; and Stewart Bell, "We Are Still Trying to Hide," *National Post*, 7 February 2004, A1.

86 See Michelle Shephard and Sonia Verma, "They Only Arrested the Muhammads," *Toronto Star*, 30 November 2003, A6 ["They Only Arrested the Muhammads"]; and Michelle Shephard, "19 Jailed Men Suspected of Links to Al-Qaeda," *Toronto Star*, 27 August 2003, A1 ["19 Jailed Men"].

87 See Michael Higgins, "RCMP Checked Out Suspect After 9/11," *National Post*, 27 August 2003, A7; and David Rider, "Ontario Cites Terror Threat to Nuclear Plants," *Ottawa Citizen*, 23 August 2003, A4 ["Ontario Cites Terror Threat"].

88 See Michelle Shephard and Betsy Powell, "Police Arrest 19 in Terror Probe," *Toronto Star*, 22 August 2003, A1 ["Police Arrest 19"].

89 See Stewart Bell, "'Network' Eyed Tower," *National Post*, 27 August 2003, A1; "Ontario Cites Terror Threat"; "Police Arrest 19."

90 See "Police Arrest 19." Two men were already in custody, having been arrested in May. A third man who fled his apartment during the police raids that led to the arrest of the nineteen eventually turned himself into police in September. Some have suggested that a twenty-fourth man was detained in October in relation to the investigation. See Michelle Shephard, "RCMP Clears Itself in 'Terror Cell' Sweep," *Toronto Star*, 6 October 2004, A1 ["RCMP Clears Itself"].

91 See "19 Jailed Men"; and "They Only Arrested the Muhammads."

92 SC 2001, c. 27. Section 58(1)(c) permits an individual's detention to enable the minister to take necessary steps to inquire whether there is reasonable suspicion that he or she is inadmissible on grounds of security.

93 See Michelle Shephard, "Detained Students Seek Refugee Status," *Toronto Star*, 11 October 2003, A8; and Thomas Walkom, "Ottawa Must Make Amends," *Toronto Star*, 28 October 2003, A21.

94 Thomas Walkom, "Slender Threads Tie 19 to Terror," *Toronto Star*, 26 August 2003, A21.

95 See "RCMP Clears Itself."

96 Joseph Hall, "Project Thread 'Coming Undone,'" *Toronto Star*, 26 September 2003, A1.

97 See Stewart Bell, "Canadian Sites Have Likely Been Scouted," *National Post*, 8 July 2005, A4. See also Michelle Shephard, "Agents Feared Attack on Toronto Subway," *Toronto Star*, 13 November 2004, A23.

98 See Anne Sutherland, "'National Security Threat' Just Taking Photos of Metro," *The Gazette*, 19 May 2004, A7; and Anne Sutherland, "Transit, City Officials Deny Racial Profiling," *The Gazette*, 20 May 2004, A9.

99 See the discussion of incidents in Calgary and Montreal in Mario
    Toneguzzi and Sherri Zickefoose, "Racial Profiling Charges Aimed at
    Clubs: Bars Deny Picking Patrons by Race," *Calgary Herald*, 2 September
    2004, A1; and Ann Carroll, "Few Local Bars Charge Blacks Extra," *The
    Gazette*, 1 September 2004, A6.

100 See *The Public Health Amendment Act*, SM 2002, c. 38. This legislation
    was never enacted. See also "Sniff Law Dangerous," editorial, *Winnipeg
    Free Press*, 27 June 2002, A14; and Scott Edmonds, "Sniff Laws Raise
    Rights Concerns," Victoria *Times-Colonist*, 27 December 2002, A6.

101 See David Kuxhaus and Mary Agnes Welch, "Solvent Rules Racism
    Complaint," *Winnipeg Free Press*, 2 December 2002, A3; and Mary Agnes
    Welch, "Native Woman Gets Apology from Food Store," *Winnipeg Free
    Press*, 3 December 2002, A9.

102 See Phinjo Gombu, "Muslim Files Suit Over Loss of Atomic Energy Job,"
    Toronto Star, 10 November 2001, A16.

103 See Michelle Shephard, "CSIS Angered by Imam's Campaign," *Toronto
    Star*, 27 July 2005, A1.

104 See Phinjo Gombu, "Fired Nuclear Worker Heading Back to Job," *Toronto
    Star*, 27 November 2001, A8; and "Overzealous Policing," editorial, *To-
    ronto Star*, 25 November 2001, A12.

105 SO 2000, c. 12 [Bill 81, 2000]. Enacted in full on 1 September 2001.

106 See Theresa Boyle, "Trustees Defer Vote on Race Statistics," *Toronto Star*,
    20 May 2004, B7; Jonathan Fowlie, "Safe Schools Act Deemed Unfair to
    Racial Minorities," *Globe and Mail*, 11 May 2004, A5; Louise Brown and
    Kristin Rushowy, "Safe Schools Report Calls for Racial Data," *Toronto
    Star*, 11 May 2004, A4; and Richard Brennan and Theresa Boyle, "Race-
    Based School Stats Won't Help: Kennedy," *Toronto Star*, 12 May 2004, B5.

107 In a letter to the board's director of education, the Ontario Principals'
    Council stated:

>   While there will always be some people who hold biases, and
>   we must assume that some school administrators do as well,
>   the clear majority of school administrators have dedicated their
>   careers to educating students, regardless of ability, race, first lan-
>   guage, culture, religion or ethnicity. ...
>   The labelling of a group of dedicated employees as racists and/
>   or discriminators is unproductive, offensive and untrue.

    See Caroline Alphonso, "Principals React Angrily to Claims of Racism,"
    Globe and Mail, 22 May 2004, A12; and "Student Sanctions Applied Im-
    partially," *Toronto Star*, 15 May 2004, H7.

108 *Paying the Price*, 18. On November 14, 2005, the Ontario Human Rights Commission announced a settlement with respect to a complaint it launched against the Toronto District School Board on July 7, 2005. The complaint concerned the impact of the *Safe Schools Act* on racialized and disabled students. As part of the settlement, the board agreed to end "zero tolerance" and to collect data on who is suspended or expelled. See Louise Brown, "Toronto School Board to End 'Zero Tolerance'," *Toronto Star*, 14 November 2005, A1.

109 See, for example, Jeff Brazil and Steve Berry, "Color of Driver Is Key to Stops in I-95 Videos," *Orlando Sentinel*, 23 August 1992, A1; Sam Vincent Meddis, "Suit Says Suspect 'Profiles' Are Racist," *USA Today*, 1 September 1994, 3A; Andrew Fegelman, "Suit Charges State Police Improperly Stop Minorities," *Chicago Tribune*, 31 August 1994, 4;·Mark Pazniokas, "Discrimination by Police Often Hard to Prove," *Hartford Courant*, 2 May 1994, A11; Robert Jackson, "Minorities Win Suit Over Unfair I-70 Stops," *Rocky Mountain News*, 10 November 1995, 4A; Robert D. McFadden, "Police Singled Out Black Drivers in Drug Crackdown, Judge Says," *New York Times*, 10 March 1996 33; and Michael Schneider, "State Police I-95 Drug Unit Found to Search Black Motorists 4 Times More Often than White," *Baltimore Sun*, 23 May 1996, B2. Particular attention was given to the issue early on in New Jersey and Maryland. As David Harris has observed, "In the late 1980s and early 1990s, African-Americans often complained that police stopped them on the New Jersey Turnpike more frequently than their numbers on that road would have predicted. ... In 1994, the problem was brought to the state court's attention in *State v. Pedro Soto*." See David A. Harris, "The Stories, the Statistics, and the Law: Why 'Driving While Black' Matters," *Minnesota Law Review* 84 (1999): 277. In Maryland, Harvard Law School graduate David Wilkins filed a lawsuit against the Maryland Police. See the discussion of the *Wilkins* case in David A. Harris, "'Driving While Black' and All Other Traffic Offenses: The Supreme Court and Pretextual Traffic Stops," *Journal of Criminal Law and Criminology* 87 (1997): 563–66. See also Jerome H. Skolnick and Abigail Caplovitz, "Guns, Drugs, and Profiling: Ways to Target Guns and Minimize Racial Profiling," *Arizona Law Review* 43 (2001): 419, note 36.

CHAPTER 2: EXPOSED

1 See the discussion of how the media perpetuates the racialization of crime in Frances Henry and Carol Tator, *Discourses of Domination: Racial*

Bias in the Canadian English-Language Press (Toronto: University of Toronto Press, 2002), chapter 9 [*Discourses of Domination*].

2 See Timothy Appleby, "Police Unit Seeks Out the Worst of the Worst," *Globe and Mail*, 20 July 2005, A9; and "The Truth About Racial Profiling," *National Post*, 30 May 2005, A18.

3 See Ron Laffin, "Don't Blame the Police," *National Post*, 30 May 2005, A18. This most-wanted list was also discussed in Margaret Wente, "Is the Real Problem Here Crime or Systemic Racism?" *Globe and Mail*, 31 May 2005, A17.

4 See Laurence L. Motiuk and Ben Vuong, "Homicide, Sex, Robbery and Drug Offenders in Federal Corrections: An End-of-2003 Review," Research Brief, January 2004, online: Correctional Service of Canada, http://www.csc-scc.gc.ca/text/research_e.shtml (date accessed 21 July 2005).

5 See Jim Rankin et al., "Singled Out," *Toronto Star*, 19 October 2002, A1 ["Singled Out"].

6 See, for example, "Police Target Black Drivers," *Toronto Star*, 20 October 2002, A1 ["Police Target Black Drivers"]; "Black Arrest Rates Highest," *Toronto Star*, 26 October 2002, A2; and "Life and Death on Mean Streets," *Toronto Star*, 27 October 2002, A2.

7 Mary Deanne Shears, "Our Duty: Examine All Issues," *Toronto Star*, 19 October 2002, A2.

8 See "Police Target Black Drivers."

9 See "Singled Out."

10 For example, the *Report of the Commission on Systemic Racism in the Ontario Criminal Justice System* (Toronto: Queen's Printer for Ontario, 1995), 143, 277 [*Ontario Systemic Racism Report*] documented that

- in 1989/90, Blacks charged with drug offences were less likely than Whites to be released by police and more likely to be detained after a bail hearing;
- for Blacks convicted of drug offences, race had a small but statistically significant influence on sentencing decisions.

The creation of the Commission and its findings on the issue of racial profiling in police stops are discussed in chapter 4.

11 See "Voices: Racial Profiling and the Police," *Toronto Star*, 23 October 2002, A6 ["Voices"]. Similar narratives were documented by the Ontario Human Rights Commission in *Paying the Price: The Human Cost of Racial Profiling*, 21 October 2003, on-line: Ontario Human Rights Commission www.ohrc.on.ca/english/consultations/racial-profiling-report.pdf

(date accessed 17 August 2005) [*Paying the Price*]. In the United States, some of the narrative evidence has been reported in the media and in law journal articles. See David A. Harris, "The Stories, the Statistics, and the Law: Why Driving While Black Matters," *Minnesota Law Review* 84 (1999): 269–75.

12 See Royson James, "Why I Fear for My Sons," *Toronto Star*, 21 October 2002, A1. See also Royson James, "Statistics Only Lend Weight to Experience," *Toronto Star*, 23 October 2002, B1.

13 "Voices."

14 *Ibid.*

15 "Racism Was a Gun at His Head," *Toronto Star*, 22 October 2002, A6. This account was given to the reporter by a police officer who did not want to be identified.

16 *Ibid.*

17 See Jennifer Morrison, "Star Report on Racial Profiling Wins Award," *Ottawa Citizen*, 11 April 2003, A11; and "*Toronto Star* Wins NNA for Its Series on Racial Profiling by Police," *Guardian*, 5 May 2003, A5.

18 See Frances Henry and Carol Tator, "A Discourse of Denial," *Toronto Star*, 24 October 2002, A31.

19 See "There Is No Racism. We Do Not Do Racial Profiling," *Toronto Star*, 19 October 2002, A14; John Deverell, "Chief Defends His Force; Police Act Powers Enough to Curb Any 'Bad Apples'; 'We're Not a Bunch of Corrupt, Racist No-Goods': Fantino," *Toronto Star*, 4 June 2003, B5; Colin Perkel, "Ontario Chiefs Back Fantino's Profiling Denial," *Toronto Star*, 29 October 2002; Philip Mascoll, "No Racial Profiling by Police: Gardner," *Toronto Star*, 18 November 2002, B4; and Catherine Porter, "Police Union Urges Star Boycott," *Toronto Star*, 22 October 2002, A6.

20 Edward B. Harvey, "An Independent Review of the *Toronto Star* Analysis of Criminal Information Processing System (CIPS) Data Provided by the Toronto Police Service (TPS)," online: Toronto Police Service www.torontopolice.on.ca/publications/files/reports/harveyreport.pdf (date accessed 19 July 2005). The integrity of Harvey's review is challenged by Scot Wortley and Julian Tanner in "Data, Denials and Confusion: The Racial Profiling Debate in Toronto," *Canadian Journal of Criminology and Criminal Justice* 45 (2003): 367. See also Harold Levy, "Police Rebuttal Called Flawed," *Toronto Star*, 10 June 2003, A1.

21 Paul Moloney, "Police Attack Star's Race Articles," *Toronto Star*, 21 February 2003, A1; "Text from Toronto Police Service Website," *Toronto Star*, 21 February 2003, A19; and Catherine Porter, "Act, Don't Fight, Police Told," *Toronto Star*, 21 February 2003, B1. See also Jonathan Kay, "When 'Junk

Science' Hurts Minorities," *National Post*, 26 February 2003, A18; Alan D. Gold, "Media Hype, Racial Profiling and Good Science," *Canadian Journal of Criminology and Criminal Justice* 45 (2003): 391; Ron Melchers, "Do Toronto Police Engage in Racial Profiling," *Canadian Journal of Criminology and Criminal Justice* 45 (2003): 457; and Thomas Gabor, "Inflammatory Rhetoric on Racial Profiling Can Undermine Police Services," *Canadian Journal of Criminology and Criminal Justice* 46 (2004): 457.

22 See Peter Small, "Police Union Sues Star Over Race-Crime Series," *Toronto Star*, 18 January 2003, A6.

23 See *Gauthier v. Toronto Star Daily Newspapers Ltd.*, [2003] OJ No. 2622 (SCJ), Cullity J, upheld [2004] OJ No. 2686 (CA). Leave to appeal to the Supreme Court of Canada dismissed January 27, 2005. See [2004] SCCA No. 411.

24 See Philip Mascoll and Jim Rankin, "Racial Profiling Exists," *Toronto Star*, 31 March 2005, A1 ["Racial Profiling Exists"].

25 See "Racial Profiling Exists"; and "Big Breakthrough on Racial Profiling," editorial, *Toronto Star*, 2 April 2005, F6.

26 See "Racial Profiling Exists."

27 See Ron Fanfair, "Inspector 'Profiled,' Investigated," online: Share, www.sharenews.com/2005_Archives/3-31-05-news6.htm (date accessed 10 September 2005).

28 See "Racial Profiling Exists."

29 See Jim Rankin and Philip Mascoll, "Officers' Feud Ends on Handshake," *Toronto Star*, 2 April 2005, A16.

30 *Ibid.*

31 Royson James, "New Chief, New Hope, Blair Offers an Honest Take," *Toronto Star*, 8 April 2005, B1.

32 See *Paying the Price*, 1.

33 News Release, "Paying the Prices: The Human Cost of Racial Profiling," Ontario Human Rights Commission Releases Report, 9 December 2003, online: Ontario Human Rights Commission http://www.ohrc.on.ca/english/news/e_pr-racial_profiling-report.shtml (date accessed 9 October 2005).

34 *Ibid.*, 9–10.

35 *Ibid.*, 17–66.

36 Tracey Tyler, "Holding Court on Life in Law," *Toronto Star*, 12 April 2004, A6.

37 *Ibid.*

38 *R. v. Brown* (2003), 9 CR (6th) 240 at 246 (Ont. CA) [*Brown*].

39 *Ibid.*, 246.

40 *Ibid.*, 267.

41 E-mail correspondence of March 13, 2004 [on file with the author].

42 *Brown*, 254. This evidence included (i) the fact that Brown was a young Black male wearing a baseball hat and jogging clothes and driving an expensive new car; (ii) Brown's evidence that the officer looked into the car before he followed and stopped him; (iii) evidence of a second set of notes prepared by the officer once he became aware that the person he had arrested was a celebrity; (iv) a licence check that the officer made before the stop; and (v) discrepancies between the time recorded in his notebook and those he gave to the breathalyzer technician." *Ibid.*

43 See Tracey Tyler, "Ex-Raptor Pleads Guilty," *Toronto Star*, 26 June 2003, B4.

44 *R. v. Watson* (2004), 191 CCC (3d) 144 (Ont. CA).

45 *Ibid.*, 148.

46 *Johnson v. Halifax (Regional Municipality) Police Service*, [2003] NSHRBID No. 2 at paras. 5–6 (P. Girard, Chair) (QL) [*Johnson*].

47 *Ibid.*, paras. 1, 18, 32, 40.

48 See Monty Mosher, "Johnson Floored," *Halifax Herald*, 7 December 2003. See also John Gregg, "Klitschko Crushes Out of Shape Johnson in Two," *The Boxing Times*, December 6, 2003, online: The Boxing Times http://www.boxingtimes.com/analyses/2003/031206klitschko_johnson.html (date accessed 21 August 2005).

49 *Johnson*, para. 97.

50 He did not accept Fraser's evidence that the window was open, but he was nevertheless satisfied that there was still sufficient light outside to enable the officer to see the occupants as they passed him. *Ibid.*, paras. 30–32.

51 *Ibid.*, para. 41.

52 *Ibid.*, paras. 41, 111, 112. These reports are available online: Halifax Regional Police http://www.police.halifax.ns.ca/menu.asp (date accessed 21 August 2005).

53 See "Johnson Receives Police Apology," *Toronto Star*, 20 January 2004, E1.

54 See Sidhartha Banerjee, "Community Leaders Urge Cops to Tackle Racial Profiling," *The Gazette*, 3 February 2005, A1. See also Patrick Dare, "Black Teen Lodges Race Profiling Complaint," *Ottawa Citizen*, 6 July 2005, B1.

55 See Matthew Wuest, "Johnson: 'It's Not Over,'" Halifax *Daily News*, 6 June 2005, 15.

56 See Janet Bagnall, "Justice Denied," Montreal *Gazette*, 26 November 2004, A23 ["Justice Denied"].

57 See *Report of the Commission of Inquiry into Matters Relating to the Death of Neil Stonechild* (October 2004), 191–94, 212, online: Stonechild Inquiry http://www.stonechildinquiry.ca/finalreport/default.shtml (date accessed 19 August 2005).

58 See "Justice Denied"; and Katherine Harding, "Two Police Officers Fired in Stonechild Case," *Globe and Mail*, 13 November 2004, A6.

59 *R. v. Munson* (2003), 172 CCC (3d) 515 at 519 (Sask. CA).

60 *R. v. Munson*, [2001] SJ No. 714 (QB).

61 *R. v. Munson*, [2001] SJ No. 735 (QB).

62 "Neil Stonechild: Timeline," *CBC News*, 12 November 2004, online: CBC News Online http://www.cbc.ca/news/background/stonechild/timeline.html (date accessed 8 October 2005).

63 Another Aboriginal man, Lloyd Joseph Dustyhorn, was found deceased in Saskatoon on January 19, 2000. He had been in police custody the night before. A coroner's inquest concluded that his death was accidental. *Ibid.*

64 See "Justice Denied"; and "The Story of Four Aboriginal Men Found Abandoned on the Outskirts of Saskatoon," *Canadian Press Newswire*, 7 September 2003.

65 See "Backgrounder," online: Commission of Inquiry into the Death of Neil Stonechild http://www.stonechildinquiry.ca/backgrounder.shtml (date accessed 3 March 2004); Lori Coolican, "Jury Calls for Better Police Relations with Native Citizens," *Edmonton Journal*, 4 November 2001, A5; and Craig Wong, "Jury Shrugs over Cause of Death," *Windsor Star*, 15 February 2002, B1.

66 See "Wegner Inquiry Can't Find Answers," *CBC News*, February 2002, online: CBC Online News http://sask.cbc.ca/newsinreview/sask_content_february.html (date accessed 4 March 2004).

67 See also, for example, the Manitoba case of Garrett Barthelette. He alleges that, on April 15, 2003, he and two other Aboriginal men were driven to the outskirts of town by the Winnipeg police. See "Native Man Accuses Winnipeg Police of Abandoning Him Outside City," Saskatoon *StarPhoenix*, 4 June 2003, A11.

68 See Susanne Reber and Robert Renaud, *Starlight Tour: The Last, Lonely Night of Neil Stonechild* (Toronto: Random House, 2005); "Starlight Tours," *CBC News*, online: CBC News Online http://www.cbc.ca/news/indepth/firstnations/starlighttours.html (date accessed 5 March 2004); and *Legacy of Hope: An Agenda for Change*, vol. 1, 5-1–5-2 (June 2004), online: Commission on First Nations and Metis Peoples and Justice Reform http://www.justicereformcomm.sk.ca/volume1.gov (date accessed 19 Au-

gust 2005) [*Legacy of Hope*]. See also Graeme Smith, "Fear and Suspicion Linger in Saskatoon," *Globe and Mail*, 28 October 2004, A1.

69 See Amy Carmichael, "Dumping Drunks on Town Outskirts Called 'Good Tool' by Police Chief," *Kingston Whig-Standard*, 22 January 2004, 13. See also the recent case of Glen Shuter, who alleges that he was assaulted by two RCMP officers in British Columbia and dropped off in the bush to walk back home. See Rod Mickleburgh, "RCMP Probe Alleged Assault by Officer," *Globe and Mail*, 3 September 2005, A9; and Jeff Lee and Darah Hansen, "2 Mounties Suspended Over Beating," *Vancouver Sun*, 3 September 2005, B1.

70 *Amnesty International Report 2001*, online: Amnesty International http://web.amnesty.org/web/ar2001.nsf/webamrcountries/ CANADA?OpenDocument (date accessed 22 August 2005). See also Stephen Thorne, "Amnesty Targets Police Treatment of Canada's Natives," *Toronto Star*, 31 May 2001, A8.

71 See Betty Ann Adam, "Police Sometimes 'Unarrest' People," *StarPhoenix*, 25 September 2003, A1; Shannon Boklaschuk, "Saskatoon Police Admit Abandoning Native Woman in '76," *Edmonton Journal*, 10 June 2003, A3; and Betty Ann Adam, "Police Linked to Teen," *StarPhoenix*, 10 March 2004.

72 See Tim Cook, "Police-Dropping Issue in Spotlight," *Kingston Whig-Standard*, 9 December 2004, 29.

73 See, for example, *Justice on Trial: Report of the Task Force on the Criminal Justice System and Its Impact on the Indian and Metis People of Alberta* (Edmonton: The Task Force, 1991), 2-48–2-49 [*Justice on Trial*]; *Report of the Aboriginal Justice Inquiry of Manitoba*, vol. 1 (Winnipeg: Queen's Printer, 1991), 595 [*Manitoba Justice Inquiry*]; and Law Reform Commission of Canada, *Report on Aboriginal Peoples and Criminal Justice: Equality, Respect and the Search for Justice* (Report 34) (Ottawa: LRCC, 1991), 45, 47. See also the discussion in Benjamin L. Berger, "Race and Erasure in *R. v. Mann*" (2004), 21 CR (6th) 58 at 59; Kent Roach, *Due Process and Victims' Rights: The New Law and Politics of Criminal Justice* (Toronto: University of Toronto Press, 1999), 256–58 [*Due Process*]; Tim Quigley, "Some Issues in Sentencing of Aboriginal Offenders," in Richard Grosse et al., eds., *Continuing Poundmaker and Riel's Quest* (Saskatoon: Purich, 1994), 273; *Legacy of Hope*, 5-1– 5-7; Dion Spotted Eagle, "First Nations Want Fair Treatment," Regina *Leader-Post*, 2 May 2005, B8; and "Police Racism in the Spotlight," *Leader-Post*, 26 February 2000, A4.

74 See *Justice on Trial*, 2-49.

75 See *Manitoba Justice Inquiry*, 595. The establishment of the inquiry is discussed in chapter 9.

76 See Tracey Tyler, "Why Being a Cop Prosecutor Means You Just Can't Win," *Toronto Star*, 11 June 1993, A25.

77 See Wendy Darroch, "Police Shooting Victim Stole Purse, Court Told," *Toronto Star*, 8 May 1993, A19.

78 See section 634(1) of the *Criminal Code*, RSC 1985, c. C-46. The number of challenges given to the parties depends on the seriousness of the offence. In this case, the Crown and the defence would have been entitled to twelve challenges (see section 634(2)(b)).

79 See *R. v. Lines*, [1993] OJ No. 3284 (GD) at para. 26. The prosecution team did, however, convince the trial judge to strike down as unconstitutional a provision of the *Criminal Code* that permits police officers to use as much force as necessary to apprehend a fleeing felon even in circumstances where the suspect is not a danger. *Ibid.* One year later, Parliament introduced a more limited deadly force justification. The police can now use force only where necessary to prevent imminent or future death or grievous bodily harm: see section 25 of the *Criminal Code*, RSC 1985, c. C-46. See *Due Process*, 230–33.

80 See Tracey Tyler, "Should Juries Reflect Society's Racial Mix?" *Toronto Star*, 22 May 1993, D4.

81 See Wendy Darroch, "Officer Cleared in Shooting of Teen Suspect," *Toronto Star*, 18 May 1993, A2; and Tracey Tyler, "Crown Appeal Dropped in Officer's Acquittal," *Toronto Star*, 15 November 1994, A19. On the issue of the dispositions of police shootings, see Ian D. Scott, "Addressing Police Excessive Use of Force: A Proposal to Amend the Mandate of the Special Investigations Unit," *Criminal Law Quarterly* 49 (2005): 357–60. Two exceptions to the general acquittal rule include *R. v. Deane* (2000), 143 CCC (3d) 84 (Ont. CA) affd. [2001] 1 SCR 279; and *R. v. Levert*, [1994] OJ No. 2627 (CA).

82 For a discussion of the racialized aspects of the case, see *Discourses of Domination*, 168–95.

83 See *R. v. Brown*, [1999] OJ No. 4867 at para. 6 (GD).

84 See *R. v. Brown* (2002), 162 CCC (3d) 27 (Ont. SCJ).

85 *R. v. Peck*, [2001] OJ No. 4581 (SCJ) at para. 18 [*Peck*]. Justice Trafford further held that he was satisfied that "the race of the defendant and his appearance was a factor that consciously led to the belief of Constable Murphy [that he had illegal drugs on him]." *Ibid.*, paras. 18, 21.

86 *Ibid.*, paras. 13–15. This evidence included purportedly seeing Peck holding a plastic bag in his hand, closing his hand, and then putting the bag in his pocket. Peck also supposedly walked away quickly as he passed the officer.

87 *Ibid.*, para. 21.

88 See Graeme Hamilton, "Judge Acquits Man Despite Drug Find," *National Post*, 3 February 2005, A9. The case was *R. v. Campbell*, [2005] QJ No. 394 (CQ (Crim. and Pen. Div.)) [*Campbell*], which is discussed later in this chapter.

89 See *R. v. Chung* (1994), 23 WCB (2d) 579 (Ont. PC), Greco J [*Chung*].

90 As of September 30, 2005. In addition to *Peck* and *Chung*, there are *Johnson*; *R. v. Khan* (2004), 24 CR (6th) 48 (Ont. SCJ) [*Khan*]; *Campbell*; and *R. v. Safadi*, [2005] AJ No. 559 (QB).

91 *Khan*, 69–70.

92 *Ibid.*, 72.

93 See Shannon Kari, "Man Sues Toronto Police Over Racial Profiling," *The Gazette*, 14 May 2005, A18.

94 See Nick Pron, "2nd Case Scrapped for Racial Profiling," *Toronto Star*, 20 October 2004, A19. In *Khan* the defence called Sheldon Jackson as a similar act witness, but Justice Molloy did not rely on this evidence in her decision. See *Khan*, 63–66.

95 See Andy Riga, "A Passion for Justice," *The Gazette*, 3 February 2005, A4; Don MacPherson, "Judge in Racial Profiling Case Has Made Her Mark," *The Gazette*, 3 February 2005, A21; and Cecil Foster, *A Place Called Heaven: The Meaning of Being Black in Canada* (Toronto: HarperCollins, 1996), 92–99.

96 See "Dean of Law, Juanita Westmorelant-Traoré, Appointed Judge of the Court of Quebec in Montreal," 12 April 1999, online: *University of Windsor's Daily News* http://web4.uwindsor.ca/units/pac/a_dailynews. nsf/o/231a737e4f8cbc38852567510005f007?OpenDocument (date accessed 21 August 2005).

97 "Judge Juanita Westmoreland-Traoré Honoured with 2005 Touchstone Award," 12 August 2005, online: Canadian Bar Association http://www. cba.org/CBA/News/2005_Releases/2005-08-12_touchstone.aspx (date accessed 21 August 2005).

98 *Campbell*, para. 59. See also the discussion at paras. 37–40.

99 See Monique Beaudin, "Man Ruled Target of Racial Profiling," *The Gazette*, 2 February 2005, A1. See also Brenda Branswell, "How Blacks See Encounters with the Police," *The Gazette*, 13 February 2005, D1; and Sidhartha Banerjee, "Community Leaders Urge Cops to Tackle Racial Profiling," *The Gazette*, 3 February 2005, A1.

100 I say "generally speaking" because, as we will see later in the book, there are still calls for its use in the fight against terrorism.

101 See Gabe Gonda and Isabel Teotonio, "Police, Politicians Reject Idea to Fight Gun 'Crisis,'" *Toronto Star*, 17 August 2005, C1.

102 See the discussion in Frances Henry, Carol Tator, Winston Mattis, and Tim Rees, *The Colour of Democracy: Racism in Canadian Society*, 2nd ed. (Toronto: Nelson, 1998), 1–3 [*The Colour of Democracy*]; Clayton James Mosher, *Discrimination and Denial: Systemic Racism in Ontario's Legal and Criminal Justice Systems, 1892–1961* (Toronto: University of Toronto Press, 1998); Jeffrey Reitz and Raymond Breton, *The Illusion of Difference: Realities of Ethnicity in Canada and the United States* (Toronto: C.D. Howe Institute, 1994); and Bohdan G. Szuchewycz, "Re-pressing Racism: The Denial of Racism in the Canadian Press," *Canadian Journal of Communications* 25 (2000): 497.

103 See Susan Delacourt, "Canadians Must Fight Racism," *Toronto Star*, 6 April 2004, A1.

104 See *The Colour of Democracy*, 1.

CHAPTER 3: ADJUSTING OUR LENS

1 See J.C. Smith, "*Regina v. Drybones* and Equality Before the Law," The *Canadian Bar Review* 49 (1971): 167; and "Section of *Indian Act* Is Ruled Discriminatory by Appeal Court," *Globe and Mail*, 29 August 1967, 4.

2 RSC 1952, c. 149. Section 94 of the *Indian Act* read:

94. An Indian who

(a) has intoxicants in his possession,
(b) is intoxicated, or
(c) makes or manufactures intoxicants

off a reserve, is guilty of an offence and is liable on summary conviction to a fine of not less than ten dollars and not more than fifty dollars or to imprisonment for a term not exceeding three months or to both fine and imprisonment.

3 See, for example, section 31(4) of the *Liquor Licence Act*, RSO 1990, c. L.19.

4 See RONWT 1956, c. 60, s. 19(1)(a).

5 See the discussion in J.W. Morrow, ed., *Northern Justice: The Memoirs of Mr. Justice William G. Morrow* (Toronto: University of Toronto Press, 1995), 145–46 [*Northern Justice*].

6 See Jan Alexander Smith and Sherrlyn J. Kelly, "William G. Morrow: A Bench with a View," *Alberta Law Review* 28 (1990): 809–13 [*A Bench with a View*].

7 *Ibid.*, 813. The title of the lecture was "The Criminal Justice System and Its Application to the Problems of Native Peoples in the Territories."

8 See section 718.2(e), RSC 1985, c. C-46; and *R. v. Gladue* (1998), 133 CCC (3d) 385 (SCC).

9 As described in *R. v. Drybones* (1969), 9 DLR (3d) 473 (SCC) at 478 [*Drybones*] and in *Northern Justice*, 146.

10 SC 1960, c. 44. Section 1(b) states:

It is hereby recognized and declared that in Canada there have existed and shall continue to exist without discrimination by reason of race, national origin, colour, religion or sex, the following human rights and fundamental freedoms, namely,

(b) the right of the individual to equality before the law and the protection of the law.

11 *Northern Justice*, 146.

12 See *R. v. Drybones* (1967), 60 WWR 321 (NWT Terr. Ct.).

13 See *R. v. Gonzales* (1962), 132 CCC 237 (BCCA).

14 *Drybones*, 484.

15 *Ibid.*

16 *Brown v. Board of Education*, 347 U.S. 483 (1954). *Brown* overruled *Plessy v. Ferguson*, 163 U.S. 537 (1896), which had established the "separate but equal" doctrine.

17 *Drybones*, 486–87.

18 See, for example, David A. Harris, who observes in his book *Profiles in Injustice: Why Racial Profiling Cannot Work* (New York: The New Press, 2002), 10 [*Profiles in Injustice*] that "[r]acial profiling grew out of a law enforcement tactic called *criminal* profiling."

19 See Clayton James Mosher, *Discrimination and Denial: Systemic Racism in Ontario's Legal and Criminal Justice Systems, 1892–1961* (Toronto: University of Toronto Press, 1998), 126–37 [*Discrimination and Denial*]; Yasmin Jiwani, "The Criminalization of 'Race,' the Racialization of Crime," in Wendy Chan and Kiran Mirchandani, eds., *Crimes of Colour: Racialization and the Criminal Justice System in Canada* (Peterborough: Broadview Press, 2002), 67 [*Crimes of Colour*]; Kiran Mirchandani and Wendy Chan, "From Race and Crime to Racialization and Criminalization," in *Crimes of Colour*, 9–22; Carl E. James, "'Up to No Good': Black on the Streets and Encountering Police," in Victor Satzewich, ed., *Racism and Social Inequality in Canada* (Toronto: Thompson Educational Publishing, 1998); and Carl E. James, "The Distorted Images of African Canadians: Impact, Implications, and Responses," in Charles Green, ed., *Globalization and*

Survival in the Black Diaspora: The New Urban Challenge (Albany: State
University of New York Press, 1997), 307.

20 Gabriella Pedicelli, *When Police Kill: Police Use of Force in Montreal and
Toronto* (Montreal: Vehicule Press, 1998), 16 [*When Police Kill*]. See also
Caroline Brown and Lorne Brown, *An Unauthorized History of the* RCMP
(Toronto: James Lorimer, 1978), 11–12, 22.

21 *Discrimination and Denial*, 128–29.

22 *Ibid.*, 129. This racialization of crime ultimately led to over-policing, as
reflected in the arrest rates. From 1892 to 1961, Blacks and Aboriginals
made up 23 percent of all arrests in Ontario for public order offences.
And, as noted below, Chinese were overrepresented in arrests for drug
offences. *Ibid.*, 161–62 and 166–74.

23 *Ibid.*, 129.

24 See *An Act to Prohibit the Importation, Manufacture and Sale of Opium for
Other than Medical Purposes*, SC 1908, c. 50.

25 See *Opium and Drug Act*, SC 1911, c. 17.

26 See *Opium and Narcotic Drug Act*, SC 1923, c. 22.

27 See the discussion in *Discrimination and Denial*, 139–51; Melvyn Green,
"A History of Canadian Narcotics Control: The Formative Years," *University of Toronto Faculty of Law Review* 37 (1979): 52–58 ["Canadian Narcotics
Control"]; and P.J. Giffen, Shirley Endicott, and Sylvia Lambert, *Panic and
Indifference: The Politics of Canada's Drug Laws* (Ottawa: Canadian Centre
on Substance Abuse, 1991), 11–17, 53–61. See also *R. v. Clay* (2000), 146
CCC (3d) 276 at 291 (Ont. CA), where Justice Rosenberg held that "it has
to be conceded that origins of the marihuana prohibition in Canada are
not based in good public policy. While the objective was to protect Canadians from harm caused by marihuana use, the supposed evidence of
that harm was based on racism and irrational, unproven and unfounded
fears." A similar motivation lay behind America's drug prohibition. See
Discrimination and Denial, 139; David F. Musto, *The American Disease*
(New Haven: Yale University Press, 1987); and John Helmer, *Drugs and
Minority Oppression* (New York: The Seabury Press, 1975).

28 *Discrimination and Denial*, 147.

29 See Roy Miki and Cassandra Kobayashi, *Justice in Our Time: The Japanese
Canadian Redress Settlement* (Vancouver: Talonbooks, 1991) [*Justice in
Our Time*]; Ken Adachi, *The Enemy That Never Was: A History of Japanese
Canadians* (Toronto: McClelland & Stewart, 1976) [*The Enemy That Never
Was*]; K. Victor Ujimoto, "Japanese," in B. Singh Bolaria and Peter S. Li,
Racial Oppression in Canada (Toronto: Garamond Press, 1985) [*Racial
Oppression*]; and Franco Iacovetta, Roberto Perin, and Angelo Principe,

eds., *Enemies Within: Italian and Other Internees in Canada and Abroad* (Toronto: University of Toronto Press, 2000) [*Enemies Within*]. Not all historians agree with this official interpretation. See Patricia E. Roy, J.L. Granatstein, Masako Iino, and Hiroko Takamura, *Mutual Hostages: Canadians and Japanese During the Second World War* (Toronto: University of Toronto Press, 1990), 214–18 [*Mutual Hostages*]; and J.L. Granatstein, *Who Killed Canadian History?* (Toronto: HarperCollins, 1998), 96–100, for an argument that the relocation and internment was motivated, in large part, by perceived military necessity. For a critical review of *Mutual Hostages*, see Reg Whitaker, book review in *Canadian Historical Review* 72 (1991): 224 [Book review].

30 *Justice in Our Time*, 16, 37. Approximately 75 percent of the 22,000 were naturalized or Canadian citizens. *Ibid.*, 16.

31 See *The Enemy That Never Was*, 251–52; and *Racial Oppression*, 127–28. But see *Mutual Hostages*, chapter 5 and page 193, where this characterization is questioned. The authors write that "[i]nternment was different from evacuation, a fact that has become confused or forgotten in recent histories and in the Canadian press. The Japanese Canadians who were moved to the BC interior were not held behind barbed wire by armed guards and, though subject to strict controls and less than favourable conditions, they could move with relative freedom."

32 *Justice in Our Time*, 37–41, 55.

33 *Ibid.*, 55. See also *Reference Re: Persons of Japanese Race*, [1946] SCR 248. In 1988 the Canadian government acknowledged and apologized for the wrongs committed and provided reparations. See *Justice in Our Time*, 143–54.

34 See "Other Canadian Internees: Drawing Distinctions," in *Enemies Within*, 122, 124.

35 Book review, 226.

36 See Alan Jeffers, "RCMP Spied on Blacks in '60s," Montreal *Gazette*, 11 April 1994, A1. See also Charles Saunders, "RCMP Snooping No Surprise," Halifax *Daily News*, 17 April 1994, 22; Dean Beeby, "Mounties 'Sorry' for Spying on Blacks," *Vancouver Sun*, 21 July 1994, A9.

37 We are now learning more about the scope of spying by the RCMP in the name of national security. For a discussion of other vulnerable and marginalized groups that were targeted, including gays, lesbians, and Aboriginals, see Gary Kinsman et al., eds., *Whose National Security? Canadian State Surveillance and the Creation of Enemies* (Toronto: Between the Lines, 2000); Gary Kinsman, "'Character Weaknesses' and 'Fruit Machines': Towards an Analysis of the Anti-Homosexual Security Campaign

in the Canadian Civil Service," *Labour/Le Travail* 35 (1995): 133; John Sa-
watsky, *Men in the Shadows: The* RCMP *Security Service* (Toronto: Double-
day, 1980), chapters 10–11; and Steve Hewitt, *Spying 101: The* RCMP's
Secret Activities at Canadian Universities, 1917–1997 (Toronto: University
of Toronto Press, 2002).

38 See Kathy English, "Metro Police Probed Black 'Activists,'" *Toronto Star*,
11 February 1994, A1 ["Metro Police"]. See also "Why Is Metro Police
Probing Its Critics," editorial, *Toronto Star*, 14 February 1994, A16; Lisa
Wright, "Police Report on Blacks Under Attack," *Toronto Star*, 18 Febru-
ary 1994, A6; Gail Swainson, "Report Slams Metro Police for Dossiers on
Black Activists," *Toronto Star*, 24 June 1994, A7.

39 See *When Police Kill*, 71.

40 See "Metro Police."

41 See Charles C. Smith, *Crisis, Conflict and Accountability* (Toronto: African
Canadian Community Coalition on Racial Profiling, 2004), 4–25 [*Conflict
and Accountability*], for a concise history of the relationship between the
Black community and the police in Toronto. Smith correctly points out
that, over the last thirty years, this issue has been "studied to death," with
little meaningful change (7–10). Some of these reports are highlighted
in Nicholas Keung, "Studies and More Studies on Racial Profiling Issue,"
Toronto Star, 26 October 2002, B5.

42 *Conflict and Accountability*, 29.

43 The profiles generated by these intelligence-gathering bodies are discussed in more detail in chapters 5 and 6.

44 On the issue of necessity, see David Gelerntier, "Profiling Only Makes
Sense," *The Gazette*, 4 August 2005, A19; Bruce Garvey, "Finally, Canad-
ians Begin to Wake Up," *National Post*, 27 July 2005, A16; "Racial Profil-
ing a Proper Weapon Against Terrorism," editorial, *The Vancouver Sun*, 7
June 2002, A14; Ed Morgan, "Terrorism Challenges the Profiling Taboo,"
National Post, 2 January 2002, A14; "Profiling Is No Crime: Properly
Used, This Investigative Tool Can Help Stop Law-Breakers," editorial,
Ottawa Citizen, 6 November 2002, A18; and "Profiling Makes Sense,"
editorial, *National Post*, 6 October 2001, A16.

45 See Philip Mascoll, "No Racial Profiling by Police: Gardner," *Toronto Star*,
18 November 2002, B4 (emphasis added). See also the comments of Craig
Bromell, who, while president of the Toronto Police Association, stated
that "[police] look at the crime, [we] don't look at the race, [we] look at the
crime. ... [We can't be] politically correct." See Nick McCabe-Lokos, "Police
Can't Be 'Politically Correct,'" *Toronto Star*, 11 November 2002, A1.

46 Thomas Gabor, "Inflammatory Rhetoric on Racial Profiling Can Undermine Police Services," *Canadian Journal of Criminology and Criminal Justice* 46 (2004): 462 ["Inflammatory Rhetoric Undermine Police Services"]. Gabor's conception of an "informed criminal profile" also appears to be a manifestation of the informed statistical generalization argument.

47 See Lea Winerman, "Criminal Profiling: The Reality Behind the Myth," *Monitor on Psychology* 35 (July/August 2004), online: American Psychological Association http://www.apa.org/monitor/julaug04/criminal.html (date accessed 12 August 2005).

48 See *R. v. Ranger* (2003), 178 CCC (3d) 375 at 388 (Ont. CA) [*Ranger*]. See also the discussion in *The Commission on Proceedings Involving Guy Paul Morin*, The Honourable Fred Kaufman, commissioner (Toronto: Queen's Printer for Ontario, 1998), 834–47, 1225–26 [*Morin Inquiry*].

49 See Daniel Girard, "Hunt on for a Serial Killer," *Toronto Star*, 18 June 2005, A1; Jim MacDonald, "Police Release Serial-Killer Profile," *Vancouver Sun*, 18 June 2005, A4; and Katherine Harding, "Mounties Finally Admit Serial Killer Is Prowling Edmonton," *Globe and Mail*, 18 June 2005, A1.

50 Royal Canadian Mounted Police News Release — Alberta, "Project KARE Offers Reward for Information on Sex Trade Worker Homicides," 17 June 2005, online: Royal Canadian Mounted Police http://www.RCMP-grc. gc.ca/ab/news/2005/KARE_Reward_Jun16-05.htm (date accessed 9 August 2005).

51 See *R. v. Eng*, [1995] BCJ No. 2509 (SC).

52 See *R. v. Cox* (1999), 132 CCC (3d) 256 at 261 (NBCA).

53 See *R. v. Calderon* (2004), 23 CR (6th) 1 at 23–24 (Ont. CA), Laskin JA [*Calderon*]; *R. v. Lam*, [2002] AJ No. 1623 (QB); *R. v. Truong* (2002), 168 CCC (3d) 132 (BCCA); and David M. Tanovich, "Operation Pipeline and Racial Profiling" (2002), 1 CR (6th) 52 ["Operation Pipeline"]. For a discussion of the use of the drug courier profile in the United States, see Michael R. Cogan, "The Drug Enforcement Agency's Use of Drug Courier Profiles: One Size Fits All," *Catholic University Law Review* 41 (1992): 943; Charles L. Becton, "The Drug Courier Profile: 'All Seems Infected That th' Infected Spy, As All Looks Yellow to the Jaundic'd Eye," *North Carolina Law Review* 65 (1987): 417; and Joseph P. D'Ambrosio, "The Drug Courier Profile and Airport Stops: Reasonable Intrusions or Suspicionless Seizures," *Nova Law Review* 12 (1987): 273.

54 See *R. v. Monney* (1999), 133 CCC (3d) 129 at 153–55 (SCC) [*Monney*].

55 See *R. v. Mohan* (1994), 89 CCC (3d) 402 (SCC) [*Mohan*]; and *R. v. J. (J.L.)* (2000), 148 CCC (3d) 487 (SCC).

56 *R. v. Marin*, [1994] OJ No. 1280 (GD) [*Marin*].
57 *Ibid.*, para. 12. *Marin* was subsequently quoted with approval by the Supreme Court of Canada in *R. v. Jacques* (1996), 110 CCC (3d) 1 at 11–12 (SCC) [*Jacques*] for its reliance on a generalized profile in assessing suspicion. In *Jacques*, the police were responding to a call that there had been a border crossing at an uncontrolled point of entry in New Brunswick. As the officer got close to the entry to the Trans-Canada Highway, he saw two vehicles. One was being driven by a woman approximately sixty years old. The other was a Dodge pick-up truck with a Quebec licence plate. When asked why he targeted the Quebec vehicle, the officer responded that the other vehicle "didn't look like … your suspicious vehicle … she didn't look like somebody that would be smuggling or jumping the border" (16). He also stated that the Quebec vehicle looked out of place and was consistent with vehicles used by smugglers. A search of the car revealed boxes of liquor. The Court held by a slim 3 to 2 majority that the officer had reasonable suspicion to target the Quebec vehicle.
58 For this reason, many courts have held that criminal profiles are not admissible in criminal trials as circumstantial evidence in support of the Crown or the defence case. See *Ranger* and *Mohan*.
59 See *Morin Inquiry*, 846.
60 *Ibid.*, 1225.
61 Both incidents are discussed in *Threat and Humiliation: Racial Profiling, Domestic Security, and Human Rights in the United States* (New York: Amnesty International USA, 2004), 22, online: Amnesty International http://www.amnestyusa.org/racial_profiling/report/rp_report.pdf at 28 (date accessed 11 August 2005) [*Threat and Humiliation*].
62 The officers attended an OPP drug interdiction course in 1997 at the Provincial Police Academy in Brampton, Ontario.
63 See Tracey Tyler, "Ruling Curbs Police Profiling," *Toronto Star*, 26 August 2004, A2. But see *R. v. Hoang*, [2000] AJ No. 1630 (PC), where the officer in charge of the Calgary branch of Operation Jetway, an RCMP drug interdiction program, testified that, "in a week his Unit may stop eight people and engage them in conversation. Of that eight, three to four may be asked for permission to search their baggage and two to three of them give consent. … [approximately] 70% of those two or three prove positive for illicit drugs," para. 21.
64 See *Calderon*, 505.
65 See Steve Coughlan, "Annotation to *R. v. Calderon*" (2004), 23 CR (6th) 3 at 4.
66 *Calderon*, 23–24.

67 *R. v. Calderon*, [2002] OJ No. 2583 (SCJ), paras. 68–69.

68 *Calderon*, 24.

69 See Tracey Tyler, "'Loo Searches' Facing Setback," *Toronto Star*, 6 April 2004, A13.

70 See *Report of the Commission on Systemic Racism in the Ontario Criminal Justice System* (Toronto: Queen's Printer for Ontario, 1995), 83–90 [*Ontario Systemic Racism Report*]; and *R. v. Hamilton* (2003), 8 CR (6th) 215 at 224–25, 245–52, 272–73 (Ont. SCJ), Hill J.

71 See online: Criminal Intelligence Service Canada http://www.cisc.gc.ca/ annual_reports/AnnualReport1998/Cisc1998en/cocaine98.htm (date accessed 18 September 2005).

72 *Ontario Systemic Racism Report*, 83. See also the discussion of Operation Pipeline/Convoy/Jetway in chapter 5.

73 This data and the link between the importer profile and race provide compelling evidence for the Supreme Court of Canada to overrule its decision in *Monney*. In that case, the Court not only approved of the use of an importer profile but set the standard of belief to submit a traveller for a drug "loo" search far too low (at reasonable suspicion rather than probable cause).

74 Margaret Wente, "Is the Real Problem Here Crime or Systemic Racism?" *Globe and Mail*, 31 May 2005, A17. See also Ron Laffin, "Don't Blame the Police," *National Post*, 30 May 2005, A18; Martin Loney, "Show Us the Numbers," *National Post*, 30 May 2005, A18; "Smearing Toronto's Cops," editorial, *National Post*, 11 November 2002, A19.

75 See Julian V. Roberts and Ronald Melchers, "The Incarceration of Aboriginal Offenders: Trends from 1978–2001," (*Canadian Journal of Criminology and Criminal Justice* 45 (2003): 212 [*Trends*].

76 *Ibid.*, 227.

77 See Julian V. Roberts, "Racism and Collection of Statistics Relating to Race and Ethnicity," in *Crimes of Colour*, 102.

78 *Ontario Systemic Racism Report*, 90.

79 See, for example, the summary of these economic arguments and studies in Bernard E. Harcourt, "Rethinking Racial Profiling: A Critique of the Economics, Civil Liberties, and Constitutional Literature, and of Criminal Profiling More Generally," *University of Chicago Law Review* 71 (2004): 1276–77, 1284–1314. See also the discussion in *Inflammatory Rhetoric Undermines Police Services*, 462–63; Robin Shepard Engel, Jennifer M. Calnon, and Thomas J. Bernard, "Theory and Racial Profiling: Shortcomings and Future Directions in Research," *Justice Quarterly* 19 (2002): 250; and *Profiles in Injustice*, 73–78. For a more general discussion

and defence of using informed generalizations, see Frederick Schauer, *Profiles, Probabilities and Stereotypes* (Cambridge, Mass.: Harvard University Press, 2003), chapter 7. Schauer appears to stop short of advocating the use of statistically valid racial profiles in the terrorism and domestic policing contexts because of his concern that the racial component will be overused and may further perpetuate ethnic and racial stigmatization.

80 See Dinesh D'Souza, "Sometimes Discrimination Can Make Sense," *USA Today*, 2 June 1999, 15A. See the discussion of discrimination and differential insurance rates in *Zurich Insurance Co. v. Ontario (Human Rights Commission)*, [1992] 2 SCR 321.

81 *Little Sisters Book and Art Emporium v. Canada* (2002), 150 CCC (3d) 1 (SCC) [*Little Sisters*].

82 *Ibid.*, 49, paras. 120–21.

83 *Ibid.*

84 The reasonable limit section is section 1, which states: "The *Canadian Charter of Rights and Freedoms* guarantees the rights and freedoms set out in it subject only to such reasonable limits prescribed by law as can be demonstrably justified in a free and democratic society." See *R. v. Oakes* (1986), 24 CCC (3d) 1 (SCC). The implications of *Little Sisters* for assessing the constitutionality of statistically informed racialized profiles in the context of section 15(1) and section 1 is considered by Sujit Choudhry in "Protecting Equality in the Face of Terror: Ethnic and Racial Profiling and s. 15 of the *Charter*," in Ronald J. Daniels et al., eds., *The Security of Freedom: Essays on Canada's Anti-Terrorism Bill* (Toronto: University of Toronto Press, 2001), 375–77.

85 *R. v. Smith* (2004), 26 CR (6th) 375 at 385 (Ont. SCJ).

86 See *Profiles in Injustice*, chapter 9, for a discussion of the self-fulfilling prophecy in this context. See also Scot Wortley and Julian Tanner, "Inflammatory Rhetoric? Baseless Accusations? A Response to Gabor's Critique of Racial Profiling Research in Canada," *Canadian Journal of Criminology and Criminal Justice* 47 (2005): 600.

87 See the discussion in *Threat and Humiliation*, 22–23. See also Tim Quigley, *Procedure in Canadian Criminal Law* (Toronto: Carswell, 1997), 116–17, note 19, who observes: "The fact that the police use personal attributes, such as ethnicity, as indicators for where to patrol or whom to stop partially accounts for the apparently high criminality among marginalized minority groups."

88 *Ontario Systemic Racism Report*, 99. See also Thomas Gabor, *Everybody Does It: Crime by the Public* (Toronto: University of Toronto Press, 1994).

89 Olivia Ward, "'Epidemic' Makes Control Difficult," *Toronto Star*, 31 December 2005, A20.

90 See Andrew Chung, "A Call for 'Separateness,'" *Toronto Star*, 8 October 2005, A1.

91 This figure is based on 2001 statistics. It is likely much higher today. See 2001 Community Profile Toronto, online: Statistics Canada http://www12.statcan.ca/english/profil01/Details/details1pop2.cfm?SEARCH= BEGINS&PSGC=35&SGC=35535&A=&LANG=E&Province=35&PlaceNa me=toronto&CSDNAME=Toronto&CMA=&SEARCH=BEGINS&DataTy pe=1&TypeNameE=Census%20Metropolitan%20Area&ID=853 (date accessed 28 September 2005).

92 See *Law v. Canada (Minister of Employment and Immigration)*, [1999] 1 SCR 497 at 530–31 (paras. 53–54).

93 See *Ontario Systemic Racism Report*, 98–99 and notes 24–27, for a discussion of the social and economic inequality arguments. See also Kent Roach, *Due Process and Victims' Rights: The New Law and Politics of Criminal Justice* (Toronto: University of Toronto Press, 1999), 229–30; and *R. v. Gladue* (1999), 133 CCC (3d) 385 at 412–13, paras. 65, 67–68 (SCC).

CHAPTER 4: SOCIAL SCIENCE AND BEYOND

1 *Report of the Commission on Systemic Racism in the Ontario Criminal Justice System* (Toronto: Queen's Printer for Ontario, 1995), 1 [*Ontario Systemic Racism Report*].

2 *Ibid.*, 1–2.

3 See "May 4, 1992 Yonge St. Riot," *Toronto Star*, 27 August 2005, B4; Andrew Duffy, Joseph Hall, and Bruce DeMara, "Hundreds Riot Downtown after Anti-Racism Protest," *Toronto Star*, 5 May 1992, A1; and Gerald Utting, "Protest Sparks Yonge Rampage," *Toronto Star*, 10 May 1992, B4.

4 The verdicts were delivered on April 8, 1992. See Farrell Crook, "Officers Cleared in Fatal Shooting of Teenager in Car," *Toronto Star*, 9 April 1992, A1.

5 The verdict was delivered on April 29, 1992. See "Police Officers Acquitted," Halifax *Daily News*, 30 April 2002, 10.

6 The shooting occurred on May 2, 1992. See Gabriella Pedicelli, *When Police Kill: Police Use of Force in Montreal and Toronto* (Montreal: Véhicule Press, 1998), 73.

7 Ontario, *Report of the Advisor on Race Relations to the Premier of Ontario* (Toronto: Advisor on Race Relations, 1992) (Advisor: Hon. S. Lewis).

8 The other commissioners included Toni Williams, a law professor at Osgoode Hall Law School and author of the report, Sri-Guggan Sri-Skanda-Rajah, Moy Tam, and Ed Ratushny.

9 See Philip C. Stenning, "Policing the Cultural Kaleidoscope: Recent Canadian Experience," *Police and Society* 7 (2003): 27.

10 See Clyde H. Farnsworth, "Canada's Justice System Faces Charges of Racism," *New York Times*, 28 January 1996, section 1, 3.

11 *Ontario Systemic Racism Report*, ix, 13–14, 352–55.

12 *R. v. Brown* (2003), 9 CR (6th) 240 at 246 (Ont. CA).

13 See "The Usual Suspects: Race, Police Contact and Perceptions of Criminal Injustice," *Criminology* ["Usual Suspects"], forthcoming.

14 *Ibid.*

15 Tamsin McMahon, "Battling Racial Bias," *Kingston Whig-Standard*, 17 September 2005, 1.

16 See Scot Wortley and Julian Tanner, "Inflammatory Rhetoric? Baseless Accusations? A Response to Gabor's Critique of Racial Profiling Research in Canada," *Canadian Journal of Criminology and Criminal Justice* 47 (2005): 586–87 ["Inflammatory Rhetoric"]. For more detail about the survey, see Scot Wortley and Julian Tanner, *The Toronto Youth Crime and Victimization Survey: Overview Report* (Toronto: Centre of Criminology, 2002).

17 "Inflammatory Rhetoric," 589.

18 *Ibid.*, 593–95.

19 Scot Wortley and Julian Tanner, "Data, Denials, and Confusion: The Racial Profiling Debate in Toronto," *Canadian Journal of Criminology and Criminal Justice* 45 (2003): 372–73.

20 In their interpretation of the results, Wortley and Tanner observe that "critics might question the use of survey methods to measure racial profiling. For example, they might claim that problems with respondent recall (i.e., telescoping) may lead to exaggerated estimates of police contact or less than accurate reporting of personal involvement in criminal activity." However, as the authors rhetorically ask, "[C]an such methodological concerns, however reasonable, completely invalidate the considerable racial differences in police stops ...?" See "Inflammatory Rhetoric," 597.

21 See Sonia Verma, "Kingston Police to Gather Race Data," *Toronto Star*, 19 July 2004, A1 ["Kingston Police"].

22 See *ibid.*

23 The officer involved was exonerated at a disciplinary proceeding. See Tamsin McMahon and Genevieve Perreault, "Acted in 'Good Faith,' Officers Cleared," *Kingston Whig-Standard*, 9 December 2004, 1; and Paul

Schliesmann, "Police Inquiry Was Flawed," *Kingston Whig-Standard*, 11 December 2004, 6.

24 See Greg McArthur, "How Kingston Police Will Keep Stats on Race," *Kingston Whig-Standard*, 18 July 2003, 1 ["Stats on Race"].

25 See Sidhartha Banerjee, "Community Leaders Urge Cops to Tackle Racial Profiling," Montreal *Gazette*, 3 February 2005, A1.

26 See Tamsin McMahon, "High-Risk Takedown of Black Youths Was First Step in Road to Racial Profiling Study," *Kingston Whig-Standard*, 31 May 2005, 6.

27 "Stats on Race."

28 See Ann Lukits, "Police Officers Oppose Chief on Collection of Race Stats," *Kingston Whig-Standard*, 21 November 2003, 1; and Paul Schliesmann, "Police Union Must Explain," *Kingston Whig-Standard*, 22 November 2003, 6.

29 See "Kingston Police."

30 See Tamsin McMahon, "Police Decide Against Job Action in Protest Over Race Data," *Kingston Whig-Standard*, 10 April 2004, 1.

31 See "Stats on Race."

32 See Ann Lukits, "Closs Lauded for Race Project," *Kingston Whig-Standard*, 27 May 2004, 1. See also Ann Lukits, "Closs Called a 'Visionary' for Stance on Collection of Race Statistics," *Kingston Whig-Standard*, 25 November 2003, 1.

33 See Tasmin McMahon and Frank Armstrong, "Police Chief Sorry," *Kingston Whig-Standard*, 27 May 2005, 1.

34 See Tamsin McMahon, "Wallen Family Accuses Police of Setup," *Kingston Whig-Standard*, 4 July 2005, 1.

35 See Scot Wortley and Lysandra Marshall, *Bias-Free Policing: The Kingston Data Collection Project (Final Results)* (15 September 2005), online: Kingston Police http://www.police.kingston.on.ca/Data%20Collection%20Final%20Report%202005-09-15.pdf (date accessed 20 September 2005) [*Bias-Free Policing*].

36 See John Lamberth, "Benchmarking and Analysis for Ethnic Profiling Studies," in *Ethnic Profiling by Police in Europe*, Justice Initiatives (June 2005), 59, online: Open Society Initiative http://www.soros.org/resources/articles_publications/publications/juticeinit_20050610/justiceinit_200506.pdf (date accessed 17 August 2005) [Ethnic Profiling by Police in Europe].

37 *Bias-Free Policing*, 11.

38 *Ibid.*, 12.

39 *Ibid.*, 61.

40 See the discussion in Robin Shepard Engel and Jennifer M. Calnon, "Comparing Benchmark Methodologies for Police-Citizen Contacts: Traffic Stop Data Collection for the Pennsylvania State Police," *Police Quarterly* 7 (2004): 97 ["Comparing Benchmark Methodologies"]; Candice Batton and Colleen Kadleck, "Theoretical and Methodological Issues in Racial Profiling Research," *Police Quarterly* 7 (2004): 30; Robin Shepard Engel, Jennifer M. Calnon, and Thomas J. Bernard, "Theory and Racial Profiling: Shortcomings and Future Directions in Research," *Justice Quarterly* 19 (2002): 256–59; Lorie Fridell, Robery Lunney, Drew Diamond, and Bruce Kubu, *Racially Biassed Policing: A Principled Response* (Washington, DC: Police Executive Research Forum, 2001); David A. Harris, *Profiles in Injustice: Why Racial Profiling Cannot Work* (New York: New Press, 2002), 186–87; and Deborah Ramirez, Jack McDevitt, and Amy Farrell, *Resource Guide on Racial Profiling Data Collection Systems: Promising Practices and Lessons Learned* (Washington, DC: U.S. Department of Justice, 2000).

41 See "Comparing Benchmark Methodologies," 101; and *Bias-Free Policing*, 79–80. Other benchmarks include using traffic violators or observations of the racial make-up of a particular location.

42 See Frank Armstrong, "Academic Assails Racial-Profiling Results," *Kingston Whig-Standard*, 20 September 2005, 1.

43 See *Bias-Free Policing*, 27, 33, 39, 50. Wortley also attempted to use an observation benchmark — watching locations and assessing racial diversity. Here the odds ratio varied from 1 to 1.56, depending on the location, but, given the limited duration of the observations, Wortley cautions against drawing conclusions from the results. *Ibid.*, 61–62.

44 See Lorie A. Fridell, *By the Numbers: A Guide for Analyzing Race Data from Vehicle Stops* (Washington, DC: Police Executive Research Forum, 2004), chapter 5. See also *Bias-Free Policing*, 80–82.

45 The report stated that 27.1 percent of Whites were ticketed, compared to 17.8 percent of Blacks, and 6.9 percent of Blacks were charged or arrested, compared to 3.8 percent of Whites. *Bias-Free Policing*, 71.

46 This was discovered to be the case with the Aboriginal data. As the study notes, "native overrepresentation in police stops is eliminated once we control for individuals who have been stopped on numerous occasions." *Ibid.*, 74.

47 *Ibid.*, 39.

48 See Curt T. Griffiths, Richard B. Parent, and Brian Whitelaw, *Community Policing in Canada* (Scarborough: Nelson Thomson Learning, 2001), 19, 178–200; James Stribopoulos, "A Failed Experiment? Investigative

NOTES

Detention: Ten Years Later," *Alberta Law Review* 41 (2003): 341; and Richard V. Ericson, *Reproducing Order: A Study of Police Patrol Work* (Toronto: University of Toronto Press, 1982), 16–17, 200–1. See also Peter Crosby, "Community Policing, in Its Many Forms, Is Here to Stay," *Ottawa Citizen*, 20 May 2002, D4.

49 Jeff Goldberg, "The Color of Suspicion," *New York Times Magazine*, 20 June 1999, quoting Sgt. Mike Lewis of the Maryland State Police.

50 Discretion is an important part of policing because limited resources make full enforcement impossible. As Justice LaForest recognized in *R. v. Beare* (1988), 45 CCC (3d) 57 at 76 (SCC), "Discretion is an essential feature of the criminal justice system. A system that attempted to eliminate discretion would be unworkably complex and rigid. Police necessarily exercise discretion in deciding when to lay charges, to arrest and to conduct incidental searches."

51 See, for example, "Police Launch Crackdown on West-End Crime," *Edmonton Journal*, 23 February 2001, B2; Steve Berry, "Crackdown on Crime on Drive Returns Commercial to People," *Vancouver Province*, 2 May 2004, A10.

52 See David M. Tanovich, "Racial Profiling and Operation Pipeline," (2002), 1 CR (6th) 52.

53 See, for example, Sonia Verma, "400 Face Arrest in New War on Crime; Police Chief Plans to Sweep Streets of Worst Offenders," *Toronto Star*, 6 August 2003, A1; and Emma Poole, "Police Swoop in on Gangs," *Calgary Herald*, 27 June 2003, B1.

54 See *R. v. Sterling*, [2004] OJ No. 3355 (SCJ).

55 See Heba Aly, "Groups Demand Public Hearings into Police Bias," *The Gazette*, 17 June 2005, A6 ["Police Bias"]. This is one manifestation of a relatively new style of policing known as "broken windows." The thrust of broken windows, or "quality of life," policing involves the cracking down on vandalism, public intoxication, graffiti, panhandling, loitering, squeegeeing, and subway infractions (e.g., turnstile jumping) in an effort to stop disorder before it engenders more serious criminality. See Bernard Harcourt, "The Broken-Windows Myth," *New York Times*, 11 September 2001. See also George L. Kelling and Catherine M. Coles, *Fixing Broken Windows: Restoring Order and Reducing Crime in Our Communities* (New York: Martin Kessler Books, 1996); and Bernard E. Harcourt, *Illusion of Order: The False Promise of Broken Windows Policing* (Cambridge, Mass.: Harvard University Press, 2001).

56 See "Police Bias." See also Anne Sutherland, "Black Youth Group Proposes Ideas to Counter Racial Profiling," *The Gazette*, 8 March 2004, A7;

and Brenda Branswell, "Minority Youths Feel Targeted," *The Gazette*, 23 March 2004, A4.

57 See Adebbie Parkes, "Teenager Accuses Police of Racial Profiling," *The Gazette*, 13 August 2005, A11; Phillip Todd, "Group Demands That City End Alleged Racial Profiling by Transit Security Guards," *The Gazette*, 30 May 2003, A8; "Mothers Raise Racism Concerns," *The Gazette*, 6 February 2003, A7; Lynn Moore, "Protesters Charge Police Racism," *The Gazette*, 8 October 2003, A7; CRARR Press Release, "Racial Harassment and Profiling: CRARR Helps Minority Public Housing Tenants Sue Police and Housing Authorities for $750,000," 14 September 2003 [on file with the author].

58 See Threat and Humiliation: Racial Profiling, Domestic Security, and Human Rights in the United States (New York: Amnesty International USA, 2004), 1–2, 28, online: Amnesty International http://www.amnestyusa.org/racial_profiling/report/rp_report.pdf (date accessed 11 August 2005). See also Eric Lichtblau, "Profiling Report Leads to a Demotion," *New York Times*, 24 August 2005, online: New York Times Website http://www.nytimes.com/2005/08/24/politics/24profiling.html (date accessed 24 August 2005); and Bureau of Justice Statistics, *Contacts Between the Police and the Public: Findings from the 2002 National Survey*, online: U.S. Department of Justice http://www.ojp.usdoj.gov/bjs/pub/pdf/cpp02.pdf (date accessed 24 August 2005). According to this 2002 data, while there were not significant differences in the likelihood of Blacks, Hispanics, and Whites being stopped by the police, Black and Hispanic drivers were far more likely to be searched and have force used against them, compared to White drivers. See also *Ethnic Profiling by Police in Europe*.

59 See "Police Still Search More Black People," 7 November 2002, online: BBC News, http://news.bbc.co.uk/1/hi/uk/2413979.stm (date accessed 8 October 2005).

60 "Ethnic Groups 'Accept Searches,'" 1 August 2005, online: BBC News, http://news.bbc.co.uk/1/hi/england/london/4734725.stm (date accessed 11 August 2005).

61 "Muslim Police Stops 'More Likely,'" March 2, 2005, online: BBC News http://news.bbc.co.uk/1/hi/uk_politics/4309961.stm (date accessed 11 August 2005); and "Searches to Target Ethnic Groups," 31 July 2005, online: BBC News http://news.bbc.co.uk/1/hi/england/london/4732465.stm (date accessed 11 August 2005). See also "Random Searches Divide New York," 9 August 2005, online: BBC News http://news.bbc.co.uk/1/hi/world/americas/4747463.stm (date accessed 11 August 2005).

62 "Spotty Progress on Racial Profiling," *Toronto Star,* 9 December 2004, A33. See also Royson James, "Statistics Only Lend Weight to Experience," *Toronto Star,* 23 October 2003, B1, in relation to the *Toronto Star* data.

63 See Kiran Mirchandani and Wendy Chan, "From Race and Crime to Racialization and Criminalization," in Wendy Chan and Kiran Mirchandani, eds., *Crimes of Colour: Racialization and the Criminal Justice System in Canada* (Peterborough: Broadview Press, 2002), 15 [*Crimes of Colour*]. See also Nob Doran, "Making Sense of Moral Panics: Excavating the Cultural Foundations of the 'Young, Black Mugger,'" in *Crimes of Colour,* 157–75.

64 One example outside the context of race was the order-in-council passed during the Second World War that made it "illegal for Jehovah's Witnesses to worship God as they wished — and the law was vigorously enforced." See William Kaplan, *State and Salvation: The Jehovah's Witnesses and Their Fight for Civil Liberties* (Toronto: University of Toronto Press, 1989), xi–xii.

65 See the discussion in Reg Whitaker, "Before September 11 — Some History Lessons," and in Desmond P. Morton, "Canada's Responses to Past Serious Threats," in David Daubney et al., eds., *Terrorism, Law & Democracy: How Is Canada Changing Following September 11?* (Montreal: Canadian Institute for the Administration of Justice, 2002).

66 See Campbell Clark, "Canadians Want Strict Security, Poll Finds," *Globe and Mail,* 11 August 2005, A1.

67 See Andrew Duffy, "Ontarians Approve Racial Profiling, Poll Suggests," *National Post,* 24 May 2003, A8.

CHAPTER 5: THE WAR ON DRUGS

1 See *Report of the Commission on Systemic Racism in the Ontario Criminal Justice System* (Toronto: Queen's Printer for Ontario, 1995), 83–90 [*Ontario Systemic Racism Report*]; and David A. Harris, *Profiles in Injustice: Why Racial Profiling Cannot Work* (New York: The New Press, 2002), 48–52 [*Profiles in Injustice*].

2 See *Ontario Systemic Racism Report,* 82–83. For example, in setting a sentencing tariff of 3 to 5 years for first-time offenders who import quantities of cocaine under 1 kilogram, and 6 to 8 years for larger amounts, the Ontario Court of Appeal observed in 1996 that "in many instances, couriers tend to be weak and vulnerable, thereby becoming easy prey to those who engage in drug trafficking on a commercial basis. Sympathetic though we are to the plight of many couriers, such concerns must give way to the

need to protect society from the untold grief and misery occasioned by the illicit use of hard drugs." See *R. v. Cunningham* (1996), 104 CCC (3d) 542 at 546–47 (Ont. CA), Finlayson JA. See also *R. v. Madden* (1996), 104 CCC (3d) 548 (Ont. CA); *R. v. H. (C.N.)* (2002), 170 CCC (3d) 253 (Ont. CA); *R. v. Hamilton* (2004), 186 CCC (3d) 129 (Ont. CA); and *R. v. Spencer* (2004), 186 CCC (3d) 181 (Ont. CA).

3 See, generally, Bruce Alexander, *Peaceful Measures: Canada's Way Out of the War on Drugs* (Toronto: University of Toronto Press, 1990).

4 *Ontario Systemic Racism Report,* 83.

5 In 1999, approximately 50,000 individuals were charged with drug offences under the *Controlled Drug and Substances Act,* SC 1996, c. 19. According to the 2001 report of the Auditor General of Canada, "90 percent of the charges related to cannabis and cocaine. Cannabis accounted for two-thirds of the charges and about half of all charges were for possession." See "Illicit Drugs — The Federal Government's Role," 2001 Report of the Auditor General of Canada, 11.13, online: Office of the Auditor General of Canada http://www.oag-bvg.ca/domino/reports.nsf/html/0111ce.html (date accessed 18 June 2005).

6 See "Canada Can and Should Find Alternatives to Prohibition of Pot," editorial, *Vancouver Sun,* 25 June 2005, E6, which refers to a 2004 Canadian Addiction Survey. The editorial also refers to a Canadian Centre on Substance Abuse survey, which revealed that 51 percent of British Columbians reported having tried marijuana. For additional data, see Janice Tibbetts, "Marijuana Use Doubles, 57% Back Legalization," *Ottawa Citizen,* 25 November 2004, A1; and Michael Tjepkema, "Use of Cannabis and Other Illicit Drugs," *Health Reports* 15 (2004): 44.

7 *Ontario Systemic Racism Report,* 83. This finding was judicially noted in *R. v. Borde* (2003), 172 CCC (3d) 225 at 231–32 (Ont. CA). See also David M. Tanovich, "Race, Sentencing and the 'War on Drugs,'" (2004), 22 CR (6th) 45 at 53–55; and Clayton James Mosher, *Discrimination and Denial: Systemic Racism in Ontario's Legal and Criminal Justice Systems, 1892–1961* (Toronto: University of Toronto Press, 1998), 199. For a discussion of the American experience, see Kenneth B. Nunn, "Race, Crime and the Pool of Surplus Criminality: Or Why the 'War on Drugs' Was a 'War on Blacks,'" *Iowa Journal of Gender, Race and Justice* 6 (2002): 381; Kathleen R. Sandy, "The Discrimination Inherent in America's Drug War: Hidden Racism Revealed by Examining the Hysteria over Crack," *Alabama Law Review* 54 (2003): 665; Joseph E. Kennedy, "Drug Wars in Black and White," *Law & Contemporary Problems* 66 (2003): 153; and D.J. Silton,

"U.S. Prisons and Racial Profiling: A Covertly Racist Nation Rides a Vicious Cycle," *Law & Inequality* 20 (2002): 53.

8 *Ontario Systemic Racism Report*, 82–83. See Kent Roach, "Systemic Racism and Criminal Justice Policy," *The Windsor Yearbook of Access to Justice* 15 (1996): 236.

9 This figure is the combined average for the Toronto Jail, the Metro West Detention Centre, and the Metro East Detention Centre. Trafficking includes importing charges. These data come from Scot Wortley, "The Usual Suspects: Race, Police Contact and Perceptions of Criminal Injustice," *Criminology*, forthcoming ["Usual Suspects"], and *Ontario Systemic Racism Report*, 79–81. This information is the only provincial data available for public consumption.

10 See "Usual Suspects."

11 I have used the same categories of estimating the Black population in Toronto as were used by the Ontario Racism Commission. See Statistics Canada, *Census Canada, 1986 — Population and Dwelling Counts — Provinces and Territories*, table 9, Catalogue 92-114 (Ottawa: Statistics Canada, 1987) (identifying the Toronto population in 1986 as 3,345,121), and Statistics Canada, *Census Canada, 1986 — Profile of Ethnic Groups: Dimensions — Census of Canada 1986*, table 1, Catalogue 93-154 (Ottawa: Statistics Canada, 1989) (identifying Black population in Toronto in 1986 as 123,705 [*Profile of Ethnic Groups*].

12 See "Usual Suspects."

13 I have used the same categories of estimating the Black population in Toronto as were used by the Ontario Racism Commission. See Statistics Canada, *Census Canada, 1991– Nation — Ethnic Origin*, Catalogue 93-315 (Ottawa: Statistics Canada, 1993) (identifying Black population in Toronto in 1991 as 161,875) [*Ethnic Origin*]; and Statistics Canada, *Census Canada, 1991 — Profile of Census Tracts in Toronto, Part A*, Catalogue 93-353 (Ottawa: Statistics Canada, 1993) (identifying Toronto population in 1991 as 3,806,234).

14 See "Usual Suspects."

15 The population growth figures come from *Ethnic Origin* and *Profile of Ethnic Groups*.

16 *Ontario Systemic Racism Report*, 84.

17 See Scot Wortley and Julian Tanner, "Inflammatory Rhetoric? Baseless Accusations? A Response to Gabor's Critique of Racial Profiling Research in Canada," *Canadian Journal of Criminology and Criminal Justice* 47 (2005): 591 ["Inflammatory Rhetoric"].

18 See *Ontario Systemic Racism Report*, 83.

19 Arrest rates are completely reversed. Whites make up only 5.7 percent (for crack) and 18.2 percent (for powder) of all cocaine arrests. African-Americans account for 84.2 percent of cocaine and 30.3 percent of crack cocaine arrests. See National Household Survey on Drug Abuse (Substance Abuse and Mental Health Services Administration, 2000) and Sourcebook of Federal Sentencing Statistics (U.S. Sentencing Commission, 2000), as documented in *Threat and Humiliation: Racial Profiling, Domestic Security and Human Rights in the United States,* September 2004 (New York: Amnesty International USA, 2004), online: Amnesty International http://www.amnestyusa.org/racial_profiling/report/rp_report.pdf at 22 (date accessed 5 June 2005).

20 See K. Jack Riley, "Crack, Powder Cocaine, and Heroin: Drug Purchase and Use Patterns in Six U.S. Cities" (National Institute of Justice & Office of National Drug Control Police, 1997), Research Report, 1, online: National Criminal Justice Reference Service http://www.ncjrs.org/pdffiles/167265.pdf (date accessed 4 August 2005).

21 See Laurence L. Motiuk and Ben Vuong, "Homicide, Sex, Robbery and Drug Offenders in Federal Corrections: An End-of-2003 Review Research Brief (January 2004), online: Correctional Service of Canada http://www.csc-scc.gc.ca/text/rsrch/briefs/b35/b35_e.pdf (date accessed 9 August 2005), 14.

22 For more detailed discussion of the hit-rate results, see David M. Tanovich, "E-Racing Racial Profiling," *Alberta Law Review* 41 (2004): 917. See also "2004 Annual Report — Missouri Vehicle Stops," online: Missouri Attorney General's Office http://www.ago.mo.gov/racialprofiling/racialprofiling.htm (date accessed 2 June 2005).

23 See David Cole and John Lamberth, "The Fallacy of Racial Profiling," *New York Times,* 13 May 2001, A13.

24 See *R .v. Dinh,* [2001] AJ No. 302 at para. 38 (PC).

25 See *R. v. Lam* (2003), 178 CCC (3d) 59 at 77 (Alta. CA).

26 Operation Pipeline/Convoy was formally launched in September 1995. In early 1998, Jetway was added. See "RCMP Best Practices — Pipeline/Convoy/Jetway," online: Royal Canadian Mounted Police http://www.RCMP-learning.org/bestdoc/english/fsd/drugs/pipeline.htm (date accessed 11 May 2004) ["RCMP Best Practices"].

27 Joanna Kerr, "Securing the Right of Passage: Pipeline, Convoy, Jetway Program Gaining Ground Across the Force," online: Royal Canadian Mounted Police www.RCMP-grc.gc.ca/online0106c.htm (date accessed 23 May 2002) ["Securing the Right of Passage"]. See also Shannon Boklaschuk, "RCMP Make Big Pot Bust," Saskatoon *StarPhoenix,* 30

January 2004, A8; Doug Nairne, "Winnipeg Battles Flow of Illegal Goods," *Vancouver Sun*, 4 July 1996, A4. In addition to the cases cited earlier, see the discussion of the use of opcj in *R. v. France* (2002), 1 CR (6th) 27 at 32 (NWTSC); *R. v. Arabi* (2002), 1 CR (6th 75 at 78–80 (Alta. PC) [*Arabi*]; *R. v. Kane*, [1998] NSJ No. 553 (SC); *R. v. Ferrari*, [2001] SJ No. 431 (QB) appeal dismissed [2002] SJ No. 32 (CA) [*Ferrari*]; and *R. v. Miller*, [2000] AJ No. 962 (PC).

28 There are conflicting reports as to how many police officers in Canada have been trained on opcj methodology. One report suggested that, as of 1999, Pipeline/Convoy had trained 1,900 RCMP officers and 350 officers from provincial and municipal enforcement agencies. Operation Jetway was said to have trained 193 RCMP officers and 65 enforcement officers from other agencies. See "RCMP Best Practices." A 2002 RCMP report suggested that Corporal Rob Ruiters had trained over 10,000 officers in this program. See "Securing the Right of Passage."

29 "RCMP Best Practices."

30 See, in particular, *R. v. Truong* (2002), 168 CCC (3d) 132 (BCCA); *R. v. Lam*, [2002] AJ No. 1623 (QB); and *R. v. Hoang*, [2000] AJ No. 1630 (PC). For other cases invloving OPCJ and racialized individuals, see *R. v. Rajaratnam*, [2005] AJ no. 1346 (QB) and *R. v. Kang-Brown* (2005), 31 CR (6th) 231 (Alta. QB).

31 See David A. Harris, "Driving While Black: Racial Profiling on Our Nation's Highways," 7 June 1999 (ACLU Special Report) online: American Civil Liberties Union http://www.aclu.org/RacialEquality/RacialEquality. cfm?ID=18163&c=133 (date accessed 11 October 2005). See also *Profiles in Injustice*, 48–52.

32 See Jeffrey Goldberg, "The Color of Suspicion," *New York Times Magazine*, 20 June 1999.

33 See Gary Webb, "DWB," *Esquire*, April 1999, 118.

34 See "Operation Pipeline," Report of the Legislative Task Force on Government Oversight, California (29 September 1999), online: ACLU http://www.aclunc.org/discrimination/webb-report.html (date accessed 29 July 2005); "History of Racial Profiling Controversy," online: Racial Profiling Data Collection Resource Center at Northeastern University http://racial-profilinganalysis.neu.edu/article.php?article_type=history (date accessed 11 May 2004); David Kocieniewski, "New Jersey Argues That the U.S. Wrote the Book on Race Profiling," *New York Times*, 29 November 2000; and Dunstan McNichol and Ron Marsico, "An Idea About Race and a War on Drugs Went Hand in Hand," New Jersey *Star Ledger*, 28 November 2000, 26.

35 *Profiles in Injustice*, 48–49.

36 *Ibid.*

37 See "Canadian 'Mounties' Join Georgia Troopers for Contraband Crackdown Training March 11, 2002," online: Georgia Office of Homeland Security http://www.gahomelandsecurity.com/news/news_releases/Canadian%20Mounties%203-11-02a.htm (date accessed 11 September 2005).

38 See Jana G. Pruden, "Drug Busts Just Tip of Iceberg," Regina *Leader-Post*, 15 November 2004, A5.

39 See, for example, where a claim of privilege was successful in *Ferrari*. See also *R. v. Kim*, [2003] AJ No. 1215 (QB). In *Kim*, the trial judge ordered production of the training instructions received by the officer involved in the case, but he refused to order production of opcj's general training materials.

40 Online: Criminal Intelligence Service Canada http://www.cisc.gc.ca/annual_reports/documents/1998_annual_report.pdf (date accessed 11 October 2005). See chapter 1 for a discussion of the disclaimer included in CISC reports and how it further encourages the use of racial profiling.

41 See 2004 Annual Report on Organized Crime in Canada, 5–6, online: Criminal Intelligence Service Canada http://www.cisc.gc.ca/annual_reports/AnnualReport2004/Document/CISC_2004_Annual_Report.pdf (date accessed 11 October 2005) [2004 CISC Annual Report]. See also the 2005 Annual Report on Organized Crime in Canada, 36, online: Criminal Intelligence Service http://www.cisc.gc.ca/annual_reports/annualreport2005/document/annual_report_2005_e.pdf (date accessed 18 September 2005) [2005 CISC Annual Report].

42 See 1997 Annual Report on Organized Crime in Canada, online: Criminal Intelligence Service Canada http://www.cisc.gc.ca/annual_reports/AnnualReport1997/Cisc1997en/cocaine.htm (date accessed 18 September 2005).

43 See, for example, 2005 CISC Annual Report, 37.

44 *Ibid.*

45 See, for example, 2004 CISC Annual Report, 20–21, 30.

46 *Ibid.*, 5; and 2005 CISC Annual Report, 39.

47 *R. v. Safadi*, [2005] AJ No. No. 559 (QB) [*Safadi*]. See also Vernon Clement Jones, "Police Violated Man's Charter Rights," *Edmonton Journal*, 2 April 2005, B1.

48 As the trial judge held "upon observing the Lebanese male with cell phones in the car, [the officer] developed a hunch far short of reasonable grounds to detain, that drugs might be involved." See *Safadi*, paras. 29, 30, 34. See also *Arabi*.

49 2002–2003 CISA Annual Report, 8, online: Criminal Intelligence Service Alberta http://www.cisalberta.ca/Annual%20&%20Semi%20Annua l%20Reports/Annual%20Report%20April%202002%20to%20March%2 02003.PDF (date accessed 11 October 2005).

50 *Ibid.*, 6–9.

CHAPTER 6: THE WAR ON GANGS

1 See Nicholas Kohler, "Gun Crime Biggest Fear," *National Post*, 25 October 2005, A1; Julius Strauss, "Street Gangs and Random Violence," *Globe and Mail*, 17 October 2005, A1; "Gunfire in Toronto," editorial, *Globe and Mail*, 29 July 2005, A16; "Gunsmoke Masks an Ever Safer City," editorial, *Toronto Star*, 28 July 2005, A20; Linda Slobodian, "New Kind of Gang Brings Terror to Streets," *Calgary Herald*, 6 March 2005, B1 ["New Kind of Gang"]; Jason van Rassel, "Police Declare War on Gang Violence," *Calgary Herald*, 28 February 2005, A1; Cal Miller, "Gang Battle Erupts Over Pot," *Toronto Star*, 23 October 2003, B5; and Mark Reid and Linda Slobodian, "Innocents Caught in Gang Turf Wars," *Calgary Herald*, 8 June 2003, A1 ["Innocents Caught in Gang Turf Wars"].

2 See Sikander Hashmi, "Guns, Gangs and Getting Tough," *Toronto Star*, 7 August 2005, A4; Linda Slobodian, "City's Gang Warfare Tip of Iceberg," *Calgary Herald*, 17 July 2005, A1; Betsy Powell, Scott Roberts, and Curtis Rush, "Police Plan Anti-Gang Blitz, Chief Says," *Toronto Star*, 2 June 2005; "New Kind of Gang"; Betsy Powell, "Police Vow War After Subway Shots," *Toronto Star*, 3 June 2005, B5; "More Charges Laid in Toronto Gang War," Victoria *Times-Colonist*, 30 April 2005, A7; Renata D'Aliesio, "Gang Violence Eludes Solutions," *Edmonton Journal*, 23 December 2004, B1; Miro Cernetig, "Montreal's Streets Turn Mean," *Toronto Star*, 14 August 2004, H2; Nick Pron and Moira Walsh, "Sweep Takes Aim at Malvern Crew," *Toronto Star*, 13 May 2004, A1; "Strike Against Gangs," editorial, *Toronto Star*, 14 May 2004, A20; Anne Kyle, "Gangs Moving to Small Cities," Regina *Leader-Post*, 30 March 2004, A1; Tom Blackwell, "Toronto Police Raid Tamil Gangs," *National Post*, 19 October 2001, A5; Bill Dunphy, "Police Call for Tough Anti-Gang Laws," *Toronto Star*, 31 March 2001, K7; and Michelle Shephard, "Gang Wars Leave Six Dead," *Toronto Star*, 24 October 2000, A1.

3 See "Organized Crime — National Priorities and Areas of Concern — Street Gangs," online: Public Safety and Emergency Preparedness Canada http://www.psepc.gc.ca/policing/organized_crime/Priorities/ StreetGangs_e.asp (date accessed 21 November 2004) (emphasis added).

4 Noel Fraser, "Latin Youth Offended by Police Union Ad," *Toronto Star*, 22 June 1999, 1; Paul Moloney, "Police Union Ad Incites Hatred, Ethnic Groups Say," *Toronto Star*, 2 June 1999, 1; "Offensive Campaign Ad," *Toronto Star*, 1 June 1999, 1; and Peter Small, "Police Stand Firm on Poster," *Toronto Star*, 31 May 1999, 1.

5 The 2002 Canadian Police Survey on Youth Gangs was obtained by the *National Post* and is discussed in Allan Woods, "Toronto and Its Gangs," *National Post*, 3 June 2004, A4 ["Toronto and Its Gangs"]. For a further discussion of how the police racialize gangs, see Gladys L. Symons, "Police Constructions of Race and Gender in Street Gangs," in Wendy Chan and Kiran Mirchandani, eds., *Crimes of Colour: Racialization and the Criminal Justice System in Canada* (Peterborough: Broadview Press, 2002), 115.

6 See chapter 1 for a discussion of the disclaimer included in CISC reports and how it further encourages the use of racial profiling.

7 CISC Annual Report, 2004, 20–21, 30–31. Online: Criminal Intelligence Service Canada http://www.cisc.gc.ca/annual_reports/AnnualReport2004/Document/CISC_2004_Annual_Report.pdf (date accessed 21 November 2004).

8 "Toronto and Its Gangs."

9 See "New Kind of Gang." See also "Innocents Caught in Gang Turf Wars."

10 See Ai Lin Choo, "Police Target Indo-Canadian Gang Violence," *Vancouver Sun*, 6 May 2004, B1.

11 See Allan Chambers, "Local Task Force Links 2,300 Natives to Gangs in Edmonton," *Edmonton Journal*, 11 April 2003, B5.

12 See René Bruemmer, "Montrealer Loses Hand in Machete Attack," *National Post*, 6 July 2005, A7.

13 See Lee Greenberg, "Chinese Gang Member Was Ring's CEO, Police Allege," *Ottawa Citizen*, 1 April 2004, A4.

14 See "Vietnamese Gang Wars Escalate: Calgary, Edmonton, B.C. Police Join Forces," *Calgary Herald*, 28 February 2000, A9.

15 See "Asian Gangs Deemed Biggest Threat," *Calgary Herald*, 5 January 2004, A4.

16 See Christie Blatchford, "Police Identify Gangs as 'Latino,'" *National Post*, 8 July 1999, B2.

17 See Darryl Philip, "Why Not Report on 'White-on-White' Crime?" *Toronto Star*, 3 August 2001, A23.

18 *R. v. B.(K.)*, [2003] MJ No. 248 (PC) at para. 1 (emphasis added) [*B.(K.)*]. See also *R. v. Flett*, [2002] MJ No. 439 (PC).

19 B.(K.), paras. 43–44.

20 See R. v. B.(K.) (2004), 186 CCC (3d) 491 at 507–8 (Man. CA).

21 See Tracy Huffman, "Shooting of 4-Year-Old Kick-Starts Police Action," *Toronto Star*, 4 August 2005; Sikander Z. Hashmi and Bob Mitchell, "Shootings 'Spike' as 3 Slain," *Toronto Star*, 1 August 2005, B5; Joe Friesen, "Seven Shootings in 13 Hours Shake GTA," *Globe and Mail*, 27 July 2005, A10; Timothy Appleby, "Gang-Related Killings Show Dramatic Increase," *Globe and Mail*, 30 September 2004, A12.

22 See Gabe Gonda and Isabel Teotonio, "Police, Politicians Reject Idea to Fight Gun Crisis," *Toronto Star*, 17 August 2005, C1; Royson James, "A Repugnant, Divisive Suggestion," *Toronto Star*, 17 August 2005, C1; "'Target' Black Youth, Councillor Urges," *Toronto Star*, 16 August 2005; and "Thompson's Comments Divide Readers," *Toronto Star*, 16 August 2005. See also James Q. Wilson, "Just Take Their Guns Away," *New York Times*, 20 March 1994.

23 "Hot spot" policing involves the identification of areas or pockets of high crime and the mobilization of resources to these locations. See *R. v. Griffiths* (2003), 11 CR (6th) 136 (Ont. CJ); and Jennifer Lewington, "A Crime Wave in Reverse," *Globe and Mail*, 19 March 2005, M1.

24 Community policing involves initiatives where the police and the community work together to identify priorities and strategies in an effort to solve and deter particularly visible crimes such as gang violence and drug trafficking. As the Ontario Systemic Racism Commission observed: "A community policing approach emphasizes peacekeeping, problemsolving, crime prevention, reducing barriers between the police and the community, constructive alternatives to law enforcement for dealing with some offences or offenders, and inclusion of citizens in these and other policing activities." It is designed to empower disadvantaged communities and to give them a voice in how their communities should be policed. See *Report of the Commission on Systemic Racism in the Ontario Criminal Justice* System (Toronto: Queen's Printer for Ontario, 1995), 336.

25 See Unnati Gandhi, "'Anybody Can Have a Gun' in Northwest Toronto," *Globe and Mail*, 10 August 2005, A1, quoting a community activist: "It's like we're under occupation."

26 R. v. Ferdinand (2004), 21 CR (6th) 65 (Ont. SCJ) [*Ferdinand*].

27 See online: City of Toronto http://www.city.toronto.on.ca/demographics/pdf2/cpa22.pdf (date accessed 15 February 2005).

28 Ferdinand, 70.

29 *Ibid.*, 71–72.

30 See Scot Wortley and Julian Tanner, "Social Groups or Criminal Organ-
    izations: The Extent and Nature of Youth Gangs in Toronto," in Bruce
    Kidd and Jim Phillips, eds., *From Enforcement and Prevention to Civic En-
    gagement: Research on Community Safety* (Toronto: Centre of Criminology,
    2004), 76 [*Civic Engagement*].

31 See Debra Black, "London Police Hero to Speak on Terror," *Toronto Star*,
    15 August 2005, B4.

32 See *Paying the Price: The Human Cost of Racial Profiling*, 21 October 2003,
    22–29, online: Ontario Human Rights Commission http://www.ohrc.
    on.ca/english/consultations/racial-profiling-report.pdf (date accessed 14
    June 2005) [*Paying the Price*]; Scot Wortley, "The Usual Suspects: Race,
    Police Contact and Perceptions of Criminal Injustice," *Criminology*, forth-
    coming ["Usual Suspects"]; and Scot Wortley and Julian Tanner, "Inflam-
    matory Rhetoric? Baseless Accusations? A Response to Gabor's Critique
    of Racial Profiling Research in Canada," *Canadian Journal of Criminology
    and Criminal Justice* 47 (2005): 601 ["Inflammatory Rhetoric"]. See also
    Linda Slobodian, "Code of Silence Hampers Shooting Investigation," *Cal-
    gary Herald*, 12 July 2005, B2.

33 See *Paying the Price*, 27.

34 See Dorothy E. Roberts, "The Social and Moral Costs of Mass Incarcera-
    tion in African American Communities," *Stanford Law Review* 56 (2004):
    1271.

35 See Royson James, "Hear Our Prayer," *Toronto Star*, 14 August 2005, A6.

36 See, for example, Jack Todd, "Sheer Terror: What Blacks Must Feel When
    Police Approach," Montreal *Gazette*, 4 January 1993, A3. See also *Paying
    the Price*, 30–34.

37 See "Inflammatory Rhetoric," 601, where Wortley and Tanner write: "Be-
    ing stopped and searched by the police seems to be experienced by black
    people as evidence that race still matters in Canadian society — that no
    matter how well you behave or how hard you try, being black means that
    you will always be considered one of the 'usual suspects.'" See also Carl
    James, "Up to No Good: Black on the Streets and Encountering Police," in
    Victor Satzewich, ed., *Racism and Social Inequality in Canada: Concepts,
    Controversies and Strategies of Resistance* (Toronto: Thompson Education,
    1998).

38 See *Paying the Price*, 22–29; "Inflammatory Rhetoric," 601; Scot Wortley,
    "Hidden Intersections: Research on Race, Crime and Criminal Justice
    in Canada," *Canadian Ethnic Studies Journal* 35 (2004): 99; "Usual Sus-
    pects," 32–33; Scot Wortley, "Justice for All? Race and Perceptions of Bias

in the Ontario Criminal Justice System — A Toronto Survey," *Canadian Journal of Criminology* 38 (1996): 457–61.

39 See, for example, Tom Tyler, *Why People Obey the Law* (New Haven: Yale University Press, 1990), who writes: "People obey the law because they believe that it is proper to do so, they react to their experiences by evaluating their justice or injustice, and in evaluating the justice of their experiences they consider factors unrelated to outcome, such as whether they ... were treated with dignity and respect" (178).

40 *Ibid.*, 17, 47. See also "Inflammatory Rhetoric," 601; and Roberto Rocha, "'A Vicious Cycle,' Psychologist Says," *The Gazette*, 29 January 2005, A4.

41 See *Paying the Price*, 42.

42 *Ibid.*, 27.

43 *Ibid.*, 21.

44 See Lawrence W. Sherman, "Defiance, Deterrence, and Irrelevance: A Theory of the Criminal Sanction," *Journal of Research in Crime & Delinquency* 30 (1993): 445.

45 See Anthony J. Lemelle Jr., *Black Male Deviance* (Westport: Praeger, 1995).

46 See, for example, the discussion of defiance theory and "forced criminality" theory in Katheryn K. Russell, "The Racial Hoax as Crime: The Law as Affirmation," *Indiana Law Journal* 71 (1996): 607–11. See also "Usual Suspects," 31–33.

47 See, for example, "Making Toronto a Safer City," editorial, *National Post*, 8 August 2005, A14.

48 See the discussion of an anti-racist model of criminal justice, one that would include decreased reliance on the criminal law, in Kent Roach, *Due Process and Victims' Rights: The New Law and Politics of Criminal Justice* (Toronto: University of Toronto Press, 1999), 244–45; and Kent Roach, "Systemic Racism and Criminal Justice Policy," *Windsor Year Book Access to Justice* 15 (1996): 236.

49 See Stan Josey, "Number of Guns from U.S. Unknown," *Toronto Star*, 10 August 2005, B2; Vanessa Lu, "Smuggled Weapons Fuelling Violence," *Toronto Star*, 9 August 2005, A10; and Neil Boyd, "More Guns Mean More Death," *National Post*, 29 June 2004, A21.

50 See Jim Philips and Bruce Kidd, "Introduction," in *Civic Engagement*, 1.

51 See Royson James, "McMurtry to Head Advisory Panel," *Toronto Star*, 19 February 2004, A1.

52 See Anthony Doob and Rosemary Gartner, "Aim at Crime's Cause," *Globe and Mail*, 15 August 2005, A13. See also Judith Blau and Peter Blau, "The

Cost of Inequality: Metropolitan Structure and Violent Crime," *American Sociological Review* 47 (1982): 114.

53 See Bruce Demara, "Jobs for At-Risk Youth Urged," *Toronto Star*, 10 March 2004, B1; Paul Moloney, "Summer Jobs for Troubled Areas," *Toronto Star*, 14 July 2004, B1; and Catherine Porter, "'At Risk' Youth Get Work with City," *Toronto Star*, 18 October 2004, B1.

54 See John Barber, "Malvern Trades Guns for Jobs," *Globe and Mail*, 13 August 2005, M1; and "Right Moves on Crime," editorial, *Toronto Star*, 20 February 2004, A22.

CHAPTER 7: THE WAR ON TERRORISM

1 See Juliet O'Neill, Jim Bronskill, and Rick Mofina, "Crackdown on Financial Networks: Ottawa Grocery Store Is Linked to Global Terrorist Money Trail in Latest U.S.-Led Dragnet," *Ottawa Citizen*, 8 November 2001, B1.

2 SOR /2001-360. Canada adopted the *Regulations* on October 2, 2001. See online: Department of Justice http://laws.justice.gc.ca/en/U-2/ SOR-2001-360/184351.html (date accessed 23 September 2005). See also E. Alexandra Dosman, "For the Record: Designating 'Listed Entities' for the Purposes of Terrorist Financing Offences at Canadian Law," *University of Toronto Faculty of Law Review* 62 (2004): 10 ["For the Record"].

3 See Andrew Duffy, "Ottawa Man 'Devastated' by Charges of Terror Links," *Ottawa Citizen*, 16 April 2002, D1.

4 See "For the Record," 16.

5 See Jake Rupert, "Man Wanted in U.S. Freed on Bail," *Ottawa Citizen*, 15 November 2001, A7. Hussein had surrendered to police on November 12, 2001. See Jake Rupert, "Man Sought by U.S. Turns Himself In," *Ottawa Citizen*, 13 November 2001, A14.

6 Jake Rupert, "Ottawa Man No Longer a Suspected Terrorist Financier," *Ottawa Citizen*, 4 June 2002, A1.

7 See "For the Record," 18–19. See also "Ottawa Man Removed from Terror List," *Ottawa Citizen*, 17 July 2002, A2.

8 See Jake Rupert, "Government Pays Off Victim of Terror Smear," *Ottawa Citizen*, 2 October 2003, A1.

9 See "Money Transfers Land Canadian in U.S. Jail," *Ottawa Citizen*, 23 July 2002, B3.

10 *An Act to Amend the Criminal Code, the Official Secrets Act, the Canada Evidence Act, the Proceeds of Crime (Money Laundering) Act and other Acts, and to Enact Measures Respecting the Registration of Charities, In Order to Combat Terrorism*, 1st Sess., 37th Parl., 2001. See online: University of

Toronto http://www.law.utoronto.ca/c-36/history.htm (date accessed 23 September 2005) for a history of the legislation.

11 As quoted in Faisal A. Bhabha, "Tracking 'Terrorists' or Solidifying Stereotypes? Canada's *Anti-Terrorism Act* in Light of the *Charter's* Equality Guarantee," *Windsor Review of Legal Social Issues* 16 (2003): 96 ["Tracking Terrorists or Solidifying Stereotypes"].

12 The *Emergencies Act*, RS 1985 c. 22 (4th Supp.). See Kent Roach and Sujit Choudhry, "Brief to the Special Senate Committee on Bill C-36," 5 December 2001 [on file with the author]; and Irwin Cotler, "Thinking Outside the Box: Foundational Principles for a Counter-Terrorism Law and Policy," in Ron Daniels et al., eds., *Security of Freedom: Essays on Canada's Anti-Terrorism Bill* (Toronto: University of Toronto Press, 2001) [*Security of Freedom*]. See also "Terror Bill Silent on Racial Profiling," editorial, *Toronto Star*, 6 December 2001, A36; and Kent Roach, *September 11: Consequences for Canada* (Montreal: McGill-Queen's University Press, 2003), 66, 70–74.

13 SC 2001, c. 41.

14 On the twentieth anniversary of the bombing, two men who Canadian prosecutors claimed were behind the bombings, Ripudaman Singh Malik and Ajaib Singh Bagri, were acquitted. See *R .v. Malik*, [2005] BCJ No. 521 (SC).

15 See Anne Dawson, "Canada Potential Threat, PM Says," Montreal *Gazette*, 30 July 2005, A4; Mohammed Adam, "Canada Must Expect Attack," *Ottawa Citizen*, 12 July 2005, A1; James Gordon, "Terrorism Threat Worse Than Ever," *National Post*, 15 February 2005, A6. See also Tonda MacCharles, "McLellan Defends Reach, Scope of Anti-Terror Law," *Toronto Star*, 15 February 2005, A15 ["McLellan Defends Anti-Terror Law"]. Occasionally, there will be a media report of allegations of terrorist cells operating in Canada. See, for example, Andrew Duffy, "Terrorist Leader Says Canada Has Sleeper Cell," *Vancouver Sun*, 14 July 2005, A9.

16 See Campbell Clark, "Canadians Want Strict Scrutiny, Poll Finds," *Globe and Mail*, 11 August 2005, A1.

17 See Transcript of Proceedings, 30 June 2005, 8184–86 and 8187, ll. 3–8, online: Commission of Inquiry into the Actions of Canadian Officials in Relation to Maher Arar http://www.stenotran.com/commission/maherarar/2005-06-30%20volume%2033.pdf (date accessed 23 August 2005).

18 See the discussion in Reem Bahdi, "No Exit: Racial Profiling and Canada's War Against Terrorism," *Osgoode Hall Law Journal* 41 (2003): 293; Sujit Choudhry, "Protecting Equality in the Face of Terror: Ethnic

and Racial Profiling and s. 15 of the *Charter*," in *Security of Freedom*; Sujit Choudhry and Kent Roach, "Racial and Ethnic Profiling: Statutory Discretion, Constitutional Remedies, and Democratic Accountability," *Osgoode Hall Law Journal* 41 (2003): 1 ["Racial and Ethnic Profiling"]; and "Tracking Terrorists or Solidifying Stereotypes."

19 See, for example, Campbell Clark, "Racial Profiling Denounced by Opposition," *Globe and Mail*, 22 March 2005 A10; Neal Hall, "They're Paying the Price," *Vancouver Sun*, 3 July 2004, A4 ["They're Paying the Price"]; Monique Beaudin, "'Singled Out' for Car Check: Customs Officers Accused of Racial Profiling," *The Gazette*, 6 August 2002, A3; Norm Ovenden, "Arabs Face Unfriendly Skies," *Edmonton Journal*, 28 October 2001, A1; "Customs Admits Targeting Muslims Entering Canada," Saskatoon *StarPhoenix*, 20 September 2001, A1.

20 See "McLellan Defends Anti-Terror Law"; and Scott Anderson, "Feds Play the Race Game," online: NOW Toronto http://www.nowtoronto.com/ issues/2001-12-06/news_story.html (date accessed 5 November 2004).

21 See Rita Trichur, "Muslims Distribute Pocket Guide to Civil Rights: What-to-Do Booklet if Detained by Police," *Edmonton Journal*, 26 April 2004, A1.

22 See Christian Cotroneo, "Cartoon Critique of Iraq War Kept Under Wraps," *Toronto Star*, 4 November 2003, A16.

23 See Michelle Shephard, "How Did This Man Land on a 'No-Fly' List?" *Toronto Star*, 15 June 2004, A20. See also Shahid Mahmoud, "Why This Man Cannot Earn Frequent Flier Points," *Toronto Star*, 21 June 2005, A13.

24 See Simon Tuck and Shawna Richer, "No-Fly List in the Works, Transport Minister Says," *Globe and Mail*, 6 August 2005, A5.

25 See Allan Woods, "Critics Fear 'No-Fly' List Will Reinforce Racial Profiling," *The Gazette*, 22 March 2005, A12.

26 See *Paying the Price: The Human Cost of Racial Profiling* (21 October 2003), 33, on-line: Ontario Human Rights Commission www.ohrc.on.ca/ english/consultations/racial-profiling-report.pdf (date accessed 17 August 2005) [*Paying the Price*]. See also Bruce Campion-Smith, "The Trouble with This List Is Simply Getting Off It," *Toronto Star*, 20 August 2005, F1; and "No-Fly List Is a Bad Idea for Canada," editorial, *Toronto Star*, 10 August 2005, A18.

27 See *Presumption of Guilt: A National Survey on Security Visitations of Canadian Muslims*, online: CAIR-CAN http://www.caircan.ca/downloads/ POG-08062005.pdf (date accessed 7 August 2005) [*Presumption of Guilt*].

28 *Ibid.*, 3.

29 *Ibid.*

30 *Ibid.* This was also the experience of the Ontario Human Rights Commission Inquiry on the impact of racial profiling. As it noted in its report, "There was a significant reluctance on the part of members of this community to come forward with their accounts due to a fear of potential consequences." See *Paying the Price*, 32.

31 See Presumption of Guilt, 3.

32 See Ontario Human Rights Commission, *Policy and Guidelines on Racism and Racial Discrimination* (9 June 2005), 7, online: Ontario Human Rights Commission http://www.ohrc.on.ca/english/publications/racism-and-racial-discrimination-policy.pdf (date accessed 9 August 2005).

33 See *Presumption of Guilt*, 6. See also Riad Saloojee, "Life for Canadian Muslims the Morning After: A 911 Wake-up Call," paper presented to the 7th Annual Metropolis Conference "Togetherness in Difference: Citizenship and Belonging, 9–13 September 2002, 7–17 [on file with the author].

34 See *In the Shadow of the Law*, Report by the International Civil Liberties Monitoring Group (May 14, 2003), 7, online: http://www.waronterrorismwatch.ca/In_the_shadow_of_the_law.pdf (date accessed 8 August 2005).

35 These men include Mohmoud Jaballah (Toronto), Mohamed Zeki Mahjoub (Toronto), Hassan Almrei (Toronto), Mohamed Harkat (Ottawa), and Adil Charkaoui (Montreal). Charkaoui was released on bail with strict conditions in February 2005. See "Security Certificates: Time for Reform," online: Amnesty International Canada http://www.amnesty.ca/take_action/actCertificates_300305.php (date accessed 31 July 2005).

36 See Presumption of Guilt, 16–18.

37 See "McLellan Defends Anti-Terror Law," quoting Public Safety Minister Anne McLellan as saying, "We do not racially profile ... That would be a firing offence."

38 See John Ibbitson, "McLellan Becomes 'Minister No' to Visible Minorities," *Globe and Mail*, 6 April 2005; and John Ibbitson, "Police Said to Be Cool to Racial-Profiling Report," *Globe and Mail*, 17 March 2005, A4.

39 See, for example, David Gelernter, "Profiling Only Makes Sense," *The Gazette*, 4 August 2005, A19; Bruce Garvey, "Finally, Canadians Begin to Wake Up," *National Post*, 27 July 2005, A16; "Profile in Silliness," editorial, *Globe and Mail*, 18 March 2005, A6; "Racial Profiling a Proper Weapon Against Terrorism," *Vancouver Sun*, 7 June 2002, A14; Ed Morgan, "Terrorism Challenges the Profiling Taboo," *National Post*, 2 January 2002, A14; "Profiling Is No Crime: Properly Used, This Investigative Tool Can Help Stop Law-Breakers," editorial, *Ottawa Citizen*, 6 November 2002, A18; Scott McKeen, "Is Racial Profiling Acceptable?" *Edmonton Journal*, 10 November 2001, A17 ["Is Racial Profiling Accept-

able")]; Profiling: Beyond the Usual Criticism," editorial, *Windsor Star*, 15 October 2001, A6; and "Profiling Makes Sense," editorial, *National Post*, 6 October 2001, A16. For academic commentary, see Samuel R. Gross and Debra Livingston, "Racial Profiling Under Attack," *Columbia Law Review* 102 (2002): 1437; William J. Stuntz, "Local Policing After the Terror," *Yale Law Review* 111 (2002): 2163–64; and Stephen J. Ellman, "Racial Profiling and Terrorism," *New York Law School Journal of Human Rights* 22 (2003): 337, 359–60.

40 See "Is Racial Profiling Acceptable?"

41 See Andrew Duffy, "Ontarians Approve Racial Profiling, Poll Suggests," *National Post*, 24 May 2003, A8.

42 Ressam was assisted by Samir Ait Mohamed, who is currently in Vancouver awaiting extradition to the United States, and Mokhtar Haourari, who was convicted in New York, largely on Ressam's testimony, of conspiring to provide material support to a terrorist act and sentenced to 288 months. See *United States v. Meskini*, [2003] CA2-QL 137 (2d Cir.). See also Rod Mickleburgh, "Terror Suspect Likely to Go Free Because Ressam Won't Testify," *Globe and Mail*, 27 July 2005, A4. A third accomplice, Abdelghani Meskini, pleaded guilty in New York.

43 See National Commission on Terrorist Attacks upon the United States, The 9/11 Commission Report: Final Report of the National Commission on Terrorist Attacks upon the United States (New York: W.W. Norton, 2004), 178 [The 9/11 Commission Report].

44 See Mike Carter, "Clarke Book Has Errors About Arrest of Ahmed Ressam," *Seattle Times*, 12 April 2004, ["Clarke Book Has Errors"].

45 *United States v. Ressam* (July 27, 2005) [unreported, on file with the author] at 31 [*Ressam*]. See also "22 Years for Millennium Bomb Plot," 27 July 2005, *CBS News*, online: CBS News http://www.cbsnews.com/stories/2005/07/27/national/printable712240.shtml (date accessed 29 July 2005).

46 See "A Lesson for Canada in Ressam Case," editorial, *Toronto Star*, 29 July 2005, A22 ["A Lesson for Canada"].

47 See *Ressam*, 32–33; and "A Lesson for Canada."

48 See "Clarke Book Has Errors."

49 This is also the view of David A. Harris. See "New Risks, New Tactics: An Assessment of the Re-Assessment of Racial Profiling in the Wake of September 11, 2001," *Utah Law Review* 2004 (2004): 913.

50 See David A. Harris, *Profiles in Injustice: Why Racial Profiling Cannot Work* (New York: New Press, 2002), 18–19.

51 See, generally, Sharon L. Davies, "Profiling Terror," *Ohio State Criminal Law Journal* 1 (2003): 52, 64–66.

52 See Sandro Contenta, "Paradigm of Terror Changing," *Toronto Star*, 16 July 2005, A4.

53 See Riad Saloojee, "When Security Triggers Insecurity," *Toronto Star*, 9 June 2005, A19.

54 See "Islam in the United States," online: Answers.com http://www. answers.com/topic/islam-in-the-united-states (date accessed 7 August 2005).

55 See "Islamic World," online: Wikipedia http://en.wikipedia.org/wiki/ Muslim_world#Demographics (date accessed 7 August 2005).

56 See Richard C. Paddock, "Before 9/11, One Warning Went Unheard," *Los Angeles Times*, 7 June 2004 , A1; and Jamie Tarabay, "Austrialian Pleads Guilty to Embassy Plot," *Globe and Mail*, 29 May 2004, A17.

57 See "Who Is Richard Reid?" 28 December 2001, BBC News, online: BBC http://news.bbc.co.uk/1/hi/uk/1731568.stm (date accessed 7 August 2005); and "'Shoe Bomber' Pleads Guilty," 4 October 2002, BBC News, online: BBC http://news.bbc.co.uk/1/hi/world/americas/2298031.stm (date accessed 7 August 2005).

58 See "The Case of the Taliban American," online: CNN http://www.cnn. com/CNN/Programs/people/shows/walker/profile.html (date accessed 7 August 2005); Jamie Tarabay, "Australian's Father Doubts Fair Trial Likely," *Globe and Mail*, 12 June 2004, A23; and "David Hicks," online: Wikipedia http://en.wikipedia.org/wiki/David_Hicks (date accessed 8 August 2005).

59 See "Feds Defend Incarceration of 'Dirty Bomb' Suspect," online: CNN News, Law Center http://archives.cnn.com/2002/LAW/06/27/dirty. bomb.suspect/ (date accessed 8 August 2005); and Jose Padilla, online: Wikipedia http://en.wikipedia.org/wiki/Jose_Padilla (date accessed 8 August 2005). See also *Rumsfeld v. Padilla*, 542 U.S. 426 (2004).

60 See Norman Inkster, "The Problem with Profiling," *Ottawa Citizen*, 20 September 2001, A15.

61 See Lorne Waldman, Marlys Edwardh, and Barbara Jackman, "CSIS, RCMP Must Create Trust with Muslims," *Toronto Star*, 28 July 2005, A19.

62 See "Report Cites FBI's Pre 9/11 Intelligence Lapses," 10 June 2005, online: MSNBC http://www.msnbc.com/id/8163203 (date accessed 9 June 2005). See also Tim Harper, "New Revelations About 9/11," *Toronto Star*, 11 August 2005, A10; and Philip Shenon and Eric Lichtblau, "CIA Failed to Act on Pilot-School Alert," *Toronto Star*, 15 April 2004.

63 For an overview of Canada's National Security Policy, see "Making Canada Safe: The National Security Police," 27 April 2004, online: CBC News http://www.cbc.ca/news/background/cdnsecurity/securitypolicy. html (date accessed 12 June 2005). In her 2004 report, the auditor general identified a number of gaps in airport security. See Allison Dunfield, "Auditor General Finds Gaps in National Security," *Globe and Mail*, 30 March 2004. See also Sean Gordon and Tonda MacCharles, "Passport System Flawed," *Toronto Star*, 6 April 2005, A1.

64 See "Summary of Reviews, 2002–2003 and in the Matter of Ahmed Ressam," online: Security Intelligence Review Committee http://www. sirc-csars.gc.ca/bkgrs_reviews_e.html (date accessed 7 August 2005). See also SIRC Report 2002–2003, Appendix C: Key Findings and Recommendations, online: Security Intelligence Review Committee, http// www.sirc-csars.gc.ca/annual/2002-2003/annxc_e.html (date accessed 29 July 2005). The Security Intelligence Review Committee is "an independent, external review body which reports to the Parliament of Canada on the operations of the Canadian Security Intelligence Service (CSIS or the Service)." See online: Security Intelligence Review Committee http:// www.sirc-csars.gc.ca/index_e.html (date accessed 7 August 2005).

65 See *They're Paying the Price*; and "Ahmed Ressam's Millennium Plot," online: PBS http://www.pbs.org/wgbh/pages/frontline/shows/trail/inside/cron.html (date accessed: 29 July 2005) ["Ressam's Plot"].

66 See "Ahmed Ressam: The Would-Be Millennium Bomber," online: CBC News http://www.cbc.ca/news/background/osamabinladen/ressam_ timeline.html (date accessed 29 July 2005).

67 See "Ressam's Plot."

68 See SIRC Report 2002–2003, "In the Matter of Ahmed Ressam," online: Security Intelligence Review Committee http://www.sirc-csars.gc.ca/annual/2002-2003/sec1a_e.html (date accessed 29 July 2005). See also "Ressam's Plot."

69 See *The 9/11 Commission Report*, 177–78.

CHAPTER 8: LITIGATING CASES

1 See (1) *Kelly v. Palazzo*, [2005] OJ No. 5363 (SCJ); (2) *Molnar v. Beausoleil*, [2005] OJ No. 5115 (SCJ); (3) Tracy Huffman, "Man Claims Peel Police Beating," *Toronto Star*, 10 August 2005, A1; (4) Shannon Kari, "Real Estate Broker Files $3-million Suit Against Police for Alleged Racial Profiling," *National Post*, 14 May 2005, 13 (this lawsuit was filed by Kevin Khan); (5) Richard Foot, "Lawsuit Accuses RCMP, CTV of Racial Profil-

ing," *National Post*, 21 September 2004, 9 (the lawsuits of Rasim Karela and Kerry Bevis in Halifax) ["Lawsuit Accuses RCMP, CTV of Racial Profiling"]; (6) John Duncanson, "Officer Sued for 'Racism,'" *Toronto Star*, 12 February 2003, B5; (7) "Halifax Cops Deny Racial Profiling," *The Gazette*, 26 December 2002, A11 (a lawsuit filed by Ahigbe James, who alleged that two Halifax police officers racially profiled him when they stopped his rented Lincoln Navigator. The suit was dismissed because James failed to attend scheduled court appearances and could not be found. See "Suit Against Cops Dropped," Halifax *Daily News*, 18 February 2005, 5; and (8) *Peart v. Peel (Regional Municipality) Police Services Board*, [2003] OJ No. 2669 (SCJ) [*Peart*].

2 See "Lawsuit Accuses RCMP, CTV of Racial Profiling."

3 *Ibid.*

4 See Andrea MacDonald, "Just Following Orders, Mountie Says in Terror Defamation Trial," *Daily News*, 24 September 2004, 9.

5 See, Richard Foot, "Trucker Sues RCMP," *Edmonton Journal*, 21 September 2004, A8.

6 See Andrea MacDonald, "Man Wins Lawsuit Against ATV-CTV," *Daily News*, 30 September 2004, 7. The trial judge also ordered CTV Inc. to pay $27,516 in legal costs for Karela. See Kim Moar, "CTV Ordered to Pay Court Costs," *Daily News*, 1 December 2004, 10.

7 See, for example, *Arnold et al. v. Arizona Department of Public Safety* (No. 03-15915, United States Court of Appeals for the Ninth Circuit 2005), where, in accordance with the terms of the settlement agreement, the Department of Public Safety agreed to collect traffic-stop data, install video cameras in all police vehicles, and create a citizen advisory board. See also *Rodriguez v. California Highway Patrol*, 89 F. Supp. 2d 1131 (ND Cal. 2000) (the case subsequently settled with terms that included a ban on consent searches until 2006 and comprehensive data collection regarding stops); *Johnson v. City of Tulsa* (No. 94-C-39-H(M), ND Okla. 2003); and *Wilkins v. Maryland State Police* (Civil Action No. CCB-93-468 D.Md. 1994). The details of these and other state and federal cases can be found at "Legislation and Litigation," online: Racial Profiling Data Collection Resource Center (at Northeastern University) www.racialprofilinganaly-sis.neu.edu/legislation/litigation.php (date accessed 29 July 2005).

8 *Peart v. Peel (Regional Municipality) Police Services Board*, [2003] OJ No. 5979 (SCJ) at para. 16.

9 See Parker Barass Donham, "Sued into Silence," *Daily News*, 13 May 2001, 23, discussing the lawsuit for defamation brought against Anne Derrick and Rocky Jones by a police officer. See also "Saskatoon Police

Association Says It Will Sue People Who Make False Complaints," *Canadian Press Newswire*, 9 July 2004.

10 See *Gauthier v. Toronto Star Daily Newspapers Ltd.*, [2003] OJ No. 2622 (SCJ, Cullity J) upheld [2004] OJ No. 2686 (CA). Leave to appeal to the Supreme Court of Canada dismissed January 27, 2005. See [2004] SCCA No. 411.

11 See *Campbell v. Jones*, [2002] NSJ No. 450 (CA) [*Campbell*]. See also Rachel Boomer, "Defamation Verdict Overturned," *Daily News*, 25 October 2002, 3.

12 See *Campbell*, paras. 52–74.

13 A civil suit launched by the girls and their parents settled. See Andrea MacDonald, "Strip-Search Settlement Upsets Mom," *Daily News*, 5 February 2002, 7.

14 I acted for Ian Golden in the Supreme Court of Canada.

15 *R. v. Golden* (2001), 47 CR (5th) 1 at 35 (paras. 81 and 83) (SCC) [*Golden*].

16 *R. v. S.(R.D.)* (1997), 118 CCC (3d) 353 (SCC) [*S.(R.D.)*]. Some additional facts are taken from *R. v. S.(R.D.)*, [1994] NSJ No. 629 (Fam. Ct.); *R. v. S.(R.D.)*, [1995] NSJ No. 184 (SC); and *R. v. S.(R.D.)* (1995), 102 CCC (3d) 233 (NSCA). See also Carol A. Aylward, "'Take the Long Way Home': R.D.S. v. R., The Journey," *University of New Brunswick Law Journal* 47 (1998): 249 ["The Journey"].

17 This fact comes from "The Journey," 276.

18 See "Judge Corrine E. Sparks," online: Dalhousie University website (James Robinson Johnston Chair in Black Canadian Studies) http://jamesrjohnstonchair.dal.ca/johnston_6827.html (date accessed 25 August 2005).

19 *S.(R.D.)*, 381 (para. 74).

20 In summarizing the Crown's position at the first level of appeal, the Summary Conviction Appeal Court judge observed: "The Crown suggests that ... the Trial Judge's conclusions on credibility flow from a racially based bias against the police, and not from the evidence. Further, the Crown submits that this creates an appearance of unfairness. ... The Crown goes further and alleges that the remarks exhibit real bias." See *R. v. S.(R. D.)*, [1995] NSJ No. 184 at para. 15 (SC). Chief Justice Glube disagreed but concluded that Justice Sparks's reasons had demonstrated a reasonable apprehension of bias.

21 Using the Canadian Criminal Cases, a law reporter series, I could find only four other criminal cases where actual bias was raised on appeal: *R. v. Elliott* (2003), 181 CCC (3d) 118 (Ont. CA); *R. v. Curragh Inc.* (1997), 113 CCC (3d) 481 (SCC); *R. v. Zundal (No. 2)* (1990), 53 CCC (3d) 161 (Ont.

CA) [*Zundal*]; and *R. v. Toth* (1991), 63 CCC (3d) 273 (BCCA) [*Toth*]. In the first two cases, the applications were brought by the Crown. The first case involved a judge whose fitness is currently being assessed by the Canadian Judicial Council. See *Cosgrove v. Canadian Judicial Council*, [2005] FCJ No. 1748 (Fed. Ct.). The second case involved a judge who called the provincial Attorney General's Office during the course of a trial to complain about the conduct of the prosecutor and to ask that he be removed from the trial; otherwise, the judge would "secure that end." The third and fourth cases involved appellants who were a Holocaust denier (*Zundal*) and an anti-abortionist (*Toth*). The allegations in both cases were brought by the same defence lawyer.

22 *Ibid.*, 25.

23 See Richard F. Devlin, "We Can't Go on Together with Suspicious Minds: Judicial Bias and Racialized Perspective in *R. v. R.D.S.*," *Dalhousie Law Journal* 18 (1995): 422–29.

24 The six were Justices LaForest, L'Heureux-Dubé, Gonthier, Cory, McLachlin, and Iacobucci. Justices Cory and Iacobucci were the two swing votes because they agreed with the dissenting justices that there was no evidence to link the social context with the officer's conduct. They ultimately concluded, however, that there was no apprehended bias because, first, the comments were made in response to the Crown's suggestion that there was "absolutely no reason to attack the credibility of the officer"; second, before making the comments, Justice Sparks had already given reasons for accepting the evidence of R.D.S. based on the evidence; third, Justice Sparks raised only the possibility of a link between race and the officer's conduct and testimony; fourth, to the extent that she concluded he probably did overreact, she linked that to his statement to R.D.S., "Shut up, shut up, or you'll be under arrest too"; and, fifth, given the burden of proof on the Crown to prove its case, there was no need for her to resolve the issue of why the officer might have overreacted. See *S.(R.D.)*, 401–3 (paras. 146, 153–55). The other four justices of this majority of six concluded that there was an evidentiary foundation for linking systemic racism and the officer's overreaction. *Ibid.*, 375 (para. 55).

25 *Ibid.*, 362 (para. 6).

26 *Ibid.*, 401 (para. 149). Justices L'Heureux-Dubé and McLachlin (with Justices LaForest and Gonthier concurring) made similar observations. *Ibid.*, 372–73 (para. 47).

27 *Ibid.*, 401 (para. 149).

28 *Ibid.*, 402 (para. 150) (emphasis in original). The majority I speak of included Chief Justice Lamer and Justices Sopinka, Cory, Iacobucci, and Major.

29 *Ibid.* See also the discussion at 395–97 (paras. 128–34) on the use of social context evidence in assessing credibility.

30 *R. v. S.(R.D.)*, [1994] NSJ No. 629 (Fam. Ct.) at paras. 6, 10.

31 *R. v. Hamilton* (2004), 186 CCC (3d) 129 at 168 (para. 126) (Ont. CA).

32 See, for example, the discussion in *R. v. Brown* (2003), 9 CR (6th) 240 at 254 (Ont. CA) [*Brown*].

33 See Lawrence W. Williamson Jr., "Profiling, Pretext, and Equal Protection: Protecting Citizens from Pretextual Stops Through the Fourteenth Amendment," *Washburn Law Journal* 42 (2003): 657; Sherry F. Colb, "Stopping a Moving Target," *Rutgers Race and Law Review* 3 (2001): 191 ["Stopping a Moving Target"]; Wesley M. Oliver, "With an Evil Eye and an Unequal Hand: Pretextual Stops and Doctrinal Remedies to Racial Profiling," *Tulane Law Review* 74 (2000): 1409; Abraham Abramovsky and Johnathan I. Edelstein, "Pretext Stops and Racial Profiling After *Whren v. United States*: The New York and New Jersey Responses Compared," *Albany Law Review* 63 (2000): 725; Kathleen M. O'Day, "Pretextual Traffic Stops: Protecting Our Streets or Racist Police Tactics?" *Dayton Law Review* 23 (1998): 313 ["Pretextual Traffic Stops"]; David A. Harris, "Car Wars: The Fourth Amendment's Death on the Highway," *George Washington Law Review* 66 (1998): 556 ["Car Wars"]; Angela J. Davis, "Race, Cops, and Traffic Stops," *University of Miami Law Review* 51 (1997): 425; David A. Harris, "Driving While Black and All Other Traffic Offences: The Supreme Court and Pretextual Traffic Stops," *Journal of Criminal Law & Criminology* 87 (1997): 544; and Sean Hacker, "Race and Pretextual Traffic Stops: An Expanded Role for Civilian Review Board " *Columbia Human Rights Law Review* 28 (1997): 551 ["Race and Pretextual Traffic Stops"].

34 See William J. Closs, "Unlawful Profiling/Bias-Based Policing," presentation to Kingston Police Services Board, May 15, 2003 [unpublished, on file with the author].

35 Gary Webb, "DWB," *Esquire* 131 (April 1999): 123; and David A. Harris, *Profiles in Injustice: Why Racial Profiling Cannot Work* (New York: New Press, 2002), 19–23, 30–33, 48–72. These indicators include the use of rental cars, the presence of air fresheners, fast-food wrappers, a single key in the ignition, and tools and maps. Vogel was himself judicially rebuked by the 11th Circuit Court of Appeals for his use of pretext stops in a number of decisions, including *U.S. v. Smith*, 799 F.2d 704 (11th Cir. 1986).

This rebuke did not, however, deter him, and he was soon elected sheriff of Volusia County.

36 *R. v. Ladouceur* (1990), 56 CCC (3d) 22 (SCC) [*Ladouceur*].

37 *Brown v. Durham Regional Police Force* (1998), 131 CCC (3d) 1 (Ont. CA) [*Durham Regional Police*].

38 *Ibid.*, 13 (para. 25). The court also observed, however, that there is nothing wrong with the police using a valid traffic stop as an opportunity to facilitate a criminal investigation, provided that the investigation does not go beyond the scope of a valid traffic stop by conducting unreasonable searches.

39 *Ibid.*, 17 (paras. 38–39). The Ontario Court of Appeal came to a similar conclusion in the context of a licence demand in *R. v. Richards* (1999), 26 CR (5th) 286 at 293–94 (Ont. CA) [*Richards*]. I acted for Clifton Richards on his appeal.

40 517 U.S. 806 (1996). The Court held that the appropriate place for such a challenge would be under the 14th Amendment's Equal Protection Clause. The problem with the Equal Protection Clause is that it requires litigants to establish a discriminatory intent. See "Stopping a Moving Target," 192–93, 201. See also "Car Wars"; "Race and Pretextual Traffic Stops," 571–83; and Janet K. Levit, "Pretextual Traffic Stops: *United States v. Whren* and the Death of *Terry v. Ohio,*" *Loyola University of Chicago Law Journal* 28 (1996): 145.

41 *Brown*, 254.

42 This objective approach has been applied in a number of state cases in the United States that have rejected the *Whren* approach. See the discussion in *People v. Robinson*, 767 NE2d 638 at 658–61 (2nd Cir., 2001) as per Levine J (in dissent).

43 See *R. v. Watson* (2005), 191 CCC (3d) 144 (Ont. CA). Despite this fact, the trial judge concluded that there was no racial profiling because he was satisfied that the officers had not seen that Watson was Black until after they had pulled him over. The conviction was overturned on appeal because of the trial judge's improper conduct during the hearing. The Court of Appeal did not discuss the merits of the allegation.

44 In *Richards*, the officer testified that he just wanted to issue the driver a caution. The racial-profiling claim was dismissed at trial and on appeal.

45 *R. v. Martin*, [2004] OJ No. 3174 (CJ). The officers testified that they wanted only to speak to the driver to "talk to them about speeding." The racial-profiling allegation failed.

46 *R. v. Singh* (2003), 15 CR (6th) 288 (Ont. SCJ) [*Singh*]. The decision was upheld on appeal: see *R. v. Edgar*, [2005] OJ No. 4505 (CA) [*Edgar*]. The racial-profiling claim was dismissed at trial and on appeal.

47 *Richards.*

48 *Singh.*

49 *R. v. McIntosh*, [2003] OJ No. 5716 (SCJ). In *McIntosh*, a claim of racial-profiling failed.

50 In *Richards*, for example, a call for back-up was made while the officer was conducting surveillance of the accused's vehicle as it was getting gas at a gas station.

51 This circumstance was one of those relied upon in *Brown*, 254, to support the allegation of racial profiling.

52 *R . v. Davis*, [2000] OJ No. 1795 (SCJ) [*Davis*]. Although the Summary Conviction Appeal Court judge found that the search of the accused's vehicle was unconstitutional, he declined to interfere with the trial judge's conclusion that the purported traffic stop was a valid one.

53 See, for example, *R .v. Gyimah*, [2005] OJ No. 1064 at para. 16 (CJ), where the first question asked of a Black driver of a Mercedes was "Where did you get this car?" In *Gyimah*, the trial judge rejected the profiling allegation.

54 *R. v. Safadi*, [2005] AJ No. 559 (QB) [*Safadi*].

55 *Brown*, 254.

56 *Davis*, para. 12.

57 See, generally, the discussion in *Brown*, 254.

58 *R. v. Khan* (2004), 24 CR (6th) 48 (Ont. SCJ) [*Khan*].

59 *R. v. Mann* (2004), 21 CR (6th) 1 (SCC) [*Mann*].

60 See, for example, Tim Quigley, "Brief Investigatory Detentions: A Critique of *R. v. Simpson*," *Alberta Law Review* 41 (2004): 946–49.

61 See, generally, James Stribopoulos, "A Failed Experiment? Investigative Detention: Ten Years Later," *Alberta Law Review* 41 (2003): 335.

62 *R. v. Simpson* (1993), 20 CR (4th) 1 (Ont. CA). See also *R. v. Ferris* (1998), 126 CCC (3d) 298 (BCCA).

63 A Quicklaw (QL) search revealed that *Simpson* has been cited in more than 400 cases since 1993.

64 *Mann*, 15–16, 18.

65 *Ibid.*, 15.

66 *Durham Regional Police*, 25, 28. For further discussion of the issue of policing future crimes, see the discussion in David M. Tanovich, "The Colourless World of *Mann*" (2004), 21 CR (6th) 47 at 54–55; and Steve

Coughlan, "Annotation to *R. v. Calderon*" (2004), 23 CR (6th) 3 at 5–6, and "Annotation to *R. v. Aldridge*" (2004), 23 CR (6th) 33 at 33–34.

67 *Mann*, 19.

68 See *Khan* (Mercedes); *R. v. Stephen*, [2003] OJ No. 634 (SCJ) (Infinity QX4); *Safadi* (BMW).

69 See *R. v. W.(K.)*, [2004] OJ No. 5327 (CJ).

70 See *R. v. B.(K.)* (2004), 186 CCC (3d) 491 (Man. CA).

71 See *R. v. Burgher*, [2002] OJ No. 5316 (SCJ) [*Burgher*]; *R. v. Snape*, [2002] OJ No. 714 (SCJ); *R. v. Peck*, [2001] OJ No. 4581 (SCJ) [*Peck*]; *R. v. Ramdeen*, [2000] OJ No. 5350 (CJ); *R. v. Nicely* (2000), 39 CR (5th) 340 (Ont. CA); *R. v. Powell* (2000), 35 CR (5th) 89 (Ont. CJ) [*Powell*]; and *R. v. Carty*, [1995] OJ No. 2322 (Prov. Div.).

72 See *R. v. S.(C.)* (1997), 13 CR (5th) 375 (Ont. CJ).

73 See *R. v. Heslop*, [2005] OJ No. 2072 (SCJ); *R. v. Campbell*, [2005] QJ No. 394 (Court of Quebec, Criminal and Penal Division) [*Campbell*]; *R. v. Griffiths* (2003), 11 CR (6th) 136 (Ont. CJ) [*Griffiths*]; and *R. v. Johnson* (1995), 39 CR (4th) 78 (Ont. CA).

74 When this happened, I confirmed this fact with trial counsel.

75 See the discussion of cultural competence in Rose Voyvodic, "Advancing the Justice Ethic Through Cultural Competence," presented at the Fourth Colloquium (Windsor, 2005), online: Law Society of Upper Canada http://www.lsuc.on.ca/news/pdf/fourth_colloquium_voyvodic.pdf (date accessed 18 April 2005); Michelle S. Jacobs, "People from the Footnotes: The Missing Element in Client-Centered Counselling," *Golden Gate University Law Review* 27 (1997): 345; and Clark D. Cunningham, "The Lawyer as Translator, Representation as Text: Towards an Ethnography of Legal Discourse," *Cornell Law Review* 77 (1992): 1298.

76 "Racial Profiling and Law Enforcement." See online: Canadian Bar Association http://www.cba.org/CBA/resolutions/pdf/04-07-A.pdf (date accessed 25 July 2005).

77 *Ibid.*, 2–3.

78 See "Racial Profiling," online: Canadian Bar Association http://www.cba.org/CBA/Equality/Equality/Racial%20Profiling.aspx (date accessed 25 July 2005).

79 See Jewel Amoah, *Critical Race Theory Bibliography* (Ottawa: Canadian Bar Association, 1999), for a summary of some of the Canadian writing in this area.

80 These tenets are taken from the helpful summary provided by Richard F. Devlin, "Jurisprudence for Judges: Why Legal Theory Matters for Social Context Education," *Queen's Law Journal* 27 (2001): 193–98.

81 Carol A. Aylward, *Canadian Critical Race Theory: Racism and the Law* (Halifax: Fernwood Publishing, 1999), 34–35 [*Canadian Critical Race Theory*]. See also Aylward, "The Journey," 249.

82 Resolution 00-01-M, online: Canadian Bar Association http://www.cba. org/CBA/Racial/PDF/Resolution00_01_M.pdf (date accessed 1 August 2005).

83 Professor Aylward offers some important and helpful advice on critical race praxis for lawyers. See *Canadian Critical Race Theory*, chapter 4: "How to Engage in Critical Race Litigation."

84 *R. v. Mills*, [1999] 3 SCR 668.

85 *Ibid.*, 727–28.

86 *Golden*, para. 83. Appellate courts have also recognized equality principles in interpreting provisions of the *Criminal Code*. See, for example, *R. v. Parks* (1993), 84 CCC (3d) 353 (Ont. CA) [*Parks*]; *R. v. Williams*, [1998] 1 SCR 1128 [*Williams*], in the context of jury selection; and *R. v. Gladue*, [1999] 1 SCR 688, and *R. v. Borde* (2003), 8 CR (6th) 203 (Ont. CA), in the context of sentencing.

87 See *Ladouceur*, 30.

88 Ladouceur was convicted of driving while his licence was suspended, contrary to the provisions of the *Highway Traffic Act*, RSO 1990, c. H.8 [*Highway Traffic Act*], and fined $2,000.

89 For example, this power is legislated in section 216(1) of the *Highway Traffic Act* and in similar provisions across the country.

90 *Ladouceur*, 38. In the United States, the Supreme Court rejected the necessity argument and limited the power of the police to stop vehicles to situations where the officer has some basis to believe that a traffic violation has been or is being committed. See *Delaware v. Prouse*, 440 U.S. 648 (1979).

91 *Ladouceur*, 43–44.

92 *Ibid.*, 29 (emphasis added).

93 *R. v. Belnavis* (1997), 118 CCC (3d) 405 at 434 (para. 66) (SCC) (emphasis added) [*Belnavis*]. Racial profiling does not appear to have been raised in the case.

94 *Ladouceur*, 44.

95 See David A. Harris, "The Stories, the Statistics, and the Law: Why 'Driving While Black' Matters," *Minnesota Law Review* 84 (1999): 311.

96 See, for example, the suggestion in "Stopping a Moving Target," 209–11, that the police should be entitled to stop a vehicle only in cases where the driver poses a real safety hazard. In other cases, a ticket should simply be issued by mail.

97 *Singh.* See also David M. Tanovich, "Annotation" (2004), 15 CR (6th) 289.

98 See *Edgar.*

99 See *Parks* (establishing the right to challenge jurors for Black accused); *Williams* (establishing the right to challenge jurors for Aboriginal accused); *R. v. Koh* (1998), 131 CCC (3d) 257 (Ont. CA) (establishing the right to challenge jurors for all racialized accused). See also *R. v. Campbell* (1999), 139 CCC (3d) 258 (Ont. CA); *R. v. Gayle* (2001), 154 CCC (3d) 221 (Ont. CA); *R. v. Spence*, [2005] SCJ No. 74; and *R. v. Rogers* (2000), 38 CR (5th) 331 (Ont. SCJ).

100 See *Parks,* 369.

101 *R. v. Ferdinand* (2004), 21 CR (6th) 65 at 75 (para. 35) (Ont. SCJ).

102 *R. v. McKennon*, [2004] OJ No. 5021 (Ont. SCJ).

103 *Ibid.,* para. 33.

104 See *R. v. Haas*, [2005] OJ No. 3160 (CA). Indeed, the Supreme Court of Canada has frequently resorted to shifting burdens: see, for example, *R. v. Harper*, [1994] 3 SCR 343 at 354; *R. v. Stillman*, [1997] 1 SCR 607, in the context of section 24(2). See also *R. v. Daviault*, [1994] 3 SCR 63; *R. v. Stone*, [1999] 2 SCR 290. In this latter context, the Supreme Court has imposed an evidentiary burden on the accused because of the difficulty of disproving a claim of extreme intoxication or other form of automatism.

105 John Sopinka et al., eds., *The Law of Evidence in Canada,* 2d ed. (Toronto: Butterworths, 1999), 420–21.

106 See *R. v. Therens*, [1985] 1 SCR 613 at 638–45.

107 See the thorough discussion in *Powell.*

108 See, for example, *R. v. H.(C.R.)* (2003), 11 CR (6th) 152 (Man. CA), and the cases cited therein.

109 *Mann,* 12 (para. 19).

110 See David M. Tanovich, "Using the *Charter* to Stop Racial Profiling: The Development of an Equality-Based Conception of Arbitrary Detention," *Osgoode Hall Law Review* 40 (2002): 184–86; David M. Tanovich, "E-Racing Racial Profiling," *Alberta Law Review* 41 (2004): 932; and David M. Tanovich, "*R. v. Griffiths:* Race and Arbitrary Detention" (2003), 11 CR (6th) 149. See also Robert L. Bogomolny, "Street Patrol: The Decision to Stop a Citizen," *Criminal Law Bulletin* 12 (1976): 560–67.

111 *Griffiths.*

112 *R. v. Pinto*, [2003] OJ No. 5172 (SCJ). See also *R. v. Savory*, [2002] OJ No. 2715 (CJ). See further the discussion in "Pretextual Traffic Stops," 331–32, where the author urges the application of the "reasonable African-American standard" to determine whether a person is seized so as to trigger

the application of the Fourth Amendment. See also the dissenting opinion of Justice Mack in *In re J.M.* 619 A.2d 497 at 509 (DC Cir. 1992) (*en
banc*), and Randall S. Susskind, "Race, Reasonable Articulable Suspicion,
and Seizure," *American Criminal Law Review* 31 (1994): 346.

113 *Belnavis*, 376 (in dissent).

114 See Kirk Makin, "Lawyerless Litigants Slow Wheels of Justice," *Globe and
Mail*, 14 January 2002, A1.

115 For similar views, see Herbert Packer, *The Limits of the Criminal Sanction*
(Stanford: Stanford University Press, 1968); and Alan Young, "All Along
the Watchtower: Arbitrary Detention and the Police Function," *Osgoode
Hall Law Journal* 29 (1991): 329.

CHAPTER 9: RETHINKING THE USE OF RACE IN SUSPECT DESCRIPTIONS

1 *Carter v. Rafferty*, 621 F. Supp. 533 at 534–35 (NJ Dist. Ct.). For a more
detailed look at Carter's long and arduous journey, see James S. Hirsch,
Hurricane: The Miraculous Journey of Rubin Carter (Boston: Houghton
Mifflin, 2000).

2 Carter was released for a short period in 1976, when his convictions were
set aside by the New Jersey Supreme Court. See *State v. Carter*, 354 A.2d
627 (1976). The retrial commenced on October 12, 1976, and ended on
December 22, 1976, when the jury returned with a verdict of guilty.

3 *Carter v. Rafferty*, 621 F. Supp. 533 at 534, 538–48 (1985), upheld *Carter v.
Rafferty*, 826 F.2d 1299 (1987).

4 See Susan Kastner, "The Crazy Idealists," *Toronto Star*, 21 April 1991, D1.

5 See Tracey Tyler, "Hurricane Carter Arrested by Mistake," *Toronto Star*, 12
April 1996, A22. See also "Another Bad Round for Rubin Carter," editorial, *Toronto Star*, 18 April 1996, A26 ["Another Bad Round"]; Tracey Tyler,
"Ex-Boxer 'Hurricane' Carter Angered by 2nd False Arrest," *Toronto Star*,
13 April 1996, SA2; and Tracey Tyler, "Ex-Boxer Fights Police 'Disrespect':
'Gangsterism Prompted False Arrest,' He Says," *Toronto Star*, 16 April
1996, A6.

6 See "Another Bad Round."

7 *Report of the Aboriginal Justice Inquiry of Manitoba*, vol. 2: *J.J. Harper*
(Winnipeg: Queen's Printer, 1991), 1–4 [*Manitoba Aboriginal Justice Inquiry*].

8 *Ibid.*, 5.

9 *Ibid.*

10 *Ibid.*, 30.

11 *Ibid.*

12 *Ibid.*, 39.

13 *Ibid.*, 32, 94.

14 Glenn Cheater, "Constable Who Shot Harper Keeps Job," Montreal *Gazette*, 4 November 1992, B1.

15 "Case Based on Fatal Shooting in July 1991," *The Gazette*, 21 February 1997, A8.

16 Eric Siblin, "Police Racism Endangers Lives, Coroner Says," *Ottawa Citizen*, 8 May 1992, A3 ["Police Racism Endangers Lives"].

17 Bart Kasowski, "The Shooting of Marcelus François: Chronology Tells Tale of a Case of Mistaken Identity," *The Gazette*, 13 July 1991, B5.

18 Geoff Baker and Tu Thanh Ha, "Police Racist Toward Blacks," *The Gazette*, 7 May 1992, A1.

19 "Police Lost Suspect's Car Before François Was Shot: Tape," *The Gazette*, 21 May 1993, A4.

20 Albert Noel, "I Never Saw His Face, Cop Who Shot François Says," *The Gazette*, 21 September 1993, A3. See also "Cop Tells Inquest Why He Shot Wrong Man Dead," *Calgary Herald*, 24 October 1991, A13.

21 See "Good Reason to Stop Car with François in It: Cop; Detective Sure Suspect Was in Vehicle," *The Gazette*, 22 October 1993, A3; and "Cop Contradicts Other Officer," *Edmonton Journal*, 26 October 1991, E11 ["Cop Contradicts Officer"].

22 "Police Racism Endangers Lives."

23 See "Cop Contradicts Officer."

24 Albert Noel, "2 Cops Suspended for Abusing Authority in François Case," *The Gazette*, 15 September 1994, A3 ["Cops Suspended for Abusing Authority"].

25 Irwin Block and Lisa Fitterman, "18 Police Officers Found Blameless in François Shooting," *The Gazette*, 15 June 1994, A1. The Montreal Urban Community Police (MUC) did eventually agree to settle a civil suit for $218,000. See See Irwin Block, "MUC to Pay François Family $218,000," *The Gazette*, 21 February 1997, A1 ["MUC to Pay"].

26 "Cops Suspended for Abusing Authority."

27 Gabriella Pedicelli, *When Police Kill: Police Use of Force in Montreal and Toronto* (Montreal: Véhicule Press, 1998) [*When Police Kill*].

28 Griffin was nineteen years old. See *When Police Kill*, chapter 5.

29 Lawson, who was seventeen years old, was shot in the back of the head by one of the six bullets fired at the car he was driving. See Farrell Cook, "Officers Shot Fleeing Lawson Deliberately, Prosecutor Says," *Toronto Star*, 3 April 1992, A30.

30 The officers involved in both cases were all eventually acquitted of all criminal charges. See *R. v. Gosset*, [1993] 3 SCR 76, and "Crown Won't Appeal Gosset's Acquittal," *The Gazette*, 30 April 1994, A3. See also Paul Todd, "Province Decides Against Appealing Officers' Acquittals," *Toronto Star*, 9 May 1992, A4. Griffin's mother, Gloria Augustus, civilly sued the MUC and eventually settled for $25,000, the amount suggested by Justice L'Heureux-Dubé, writing for the Court, in *Augustus v. Gosset*, [1996] 3 SCR 268. See "MUC to Pay," 60.

31 The day before the shooting, two officers posing as journalists were caught on videotape making racist comments about Aboriginals and Blacks. See Peter Edwards and Harold Levy, "Ipperwash Tapes Raise Questions," *Toronto Star*, 22 January 2004, A4. Following the shooting, mugs and T-shirts mocking the shooting were produced by other officers. See "Commissioner's Ruling Re Motion by the Ontario Provincial Police and the Ontario Provincial Police Association," online: The Ipperwash Inquiry http://www.ipperwashinquiry.ca/li/pdf/Commissioner_Ruling_Aug15.05.pdf (date accessed 24 September 2005).

32 See Peter Edwards and Harold Levy, "Activist's Death Remembered," *Toronto Star*, 6 September 2005, A17. See also "Who Was Dudley George?" *Toronto Star*, 8 September 2001, K1; and *R. v. Deane*, [1997] OJ No. 3057 (PD).

33 See *R. v. Deane*, [1997] OJ No. 3057 (Ct. J. (Prov. Div.)). See also *R. v. Deane* (2000), 143 CCC (3d) 84 (Ont. CA) affd. [2001] 1 SCR 279.

34 The officer was given a conditional sentence of two years less one day. See *R. v. Deane*, [1997] OJ No. 3578 (Ct. J. (Prov. Div.)). The Crown's appeal of the sentence was dismissed: see *R. v. Deane* (2000), 143 CCC (3d) 84 at 127–28 (Ont. CA). On January 1, 1996, Parliament enacted a new criminal negligence-causing-death sentencing provision for cases involving firearms. Under this new regime, an accused who commits the offence with a firearm is subject to a four-year mandatory minimum sentence. See *Firearms Act*, SC 1995, c. 39, s. 141. The officer escaped this mandatory minimum because he committed the offence before this section came into force.

35 See *R. v. George* (18 May 2000), Ontario C29482 (CA).

36 See Peter Edwards, "Indians Get Ipperwash Back," *Toronto Star*, 19 June 1998, A1.

37 See Scot Wortley, "Hidden Intersections: Research on Race, Crime and Criminal Justice In Canada," *Canadian Ethnic Studies* 35 (2003): 105.

38 See *When Police Kill*, 64.

39 See, generally, Cynthia Lee, "'But I Thought He Had a Gun': Race and Police Use of Deadly Force," *Hastings Race and Poverty Law Journal* 2 (2004): 1.

40 See Doug Sanders, "Shoot-to-Kill Error Causes U.K. Uproar," *Globe and Mail*, 18 August 2005, A2; Rosie Cowan, Duncan Campbell, and Vikram Dodd, "London Police Subdued Man, Then Shot Him Point-Blank," *Globe and Mail*, 17 August 2005, A1; Mike Blanchfield, "Killing Was a 'Tragedy,'" *The Gazette*, 24 July 2005, A1; and Sandro Contenta, "Fatal Error by Police Heightens Tensions," *Toronto Star*, 24 July 2005, A3.

41 This area was described as encompassing the Keele and Eglinton corridor, extending to Tretheway Drive and towards Caledonia, as far north as Lawrence Avenue. See *R. v. Walker* (18 October 2004) at 5 (Ont. Ct. Jus.) [on file with the author] [*Walker*].

42 *Ibid.*

43 *Ibid.*

44 *Ibid.*

45 *Ibid.*, 12.

46 *Ibid.*, 10.

47 See Dale Anne Freed, "Officer Escapes Criminal Record," *Toronto Star*, 18 January 2005, B5.

48 See, for example, Sujit Choudhry, "Protecting Equality in the Face of Terror: Ethnic and Racial Profiling and Section 15 of the *Charter*," in Ronald J. Daniels et al., eds., *The Security of Freedom: Essays on Canada's Anti-Terrorism Bill* (Toronto: University of Toronto, 2001), 6; Sheri L. Johnson, "Race and the Decision to Detain a Suspect," *Yale Law Review* 214 (1983): 242–43 ("Race and the Decision to Detain a Suspect"); and David A. Harris, "Using Race or Ethnicity as a Factor in Assessing the Reasonableness of Fourth Amendment Activity: Description, Yes; Prediction, No," *Mississippi Law Journal* 73 (2003): 423. See also the concerns expressed by Bela A. Walker, "The Color of Crime: The Case Against Race-Based Suspect Descriptions," *Columbia Law Review* 103 (2003): 662 ["The Color of Crime"]; and by R. Richard Banks, "Race-Based Suspect Selection and Colorblind Equal Protection Doctrine and Discourse," *UCLA Law Review* 48 (2001): 1075 ["Race-Based Suspect Selection"].

49 *Paying the Price* (21 October 2003), 6, online: Ontario Human Rights Commission, http://www.ohrc.on.ca/english/consultations/racial-profiling-report.pdf (date accessed 22 November 2004) (emphasis added).

50 See See Bill C-296, *An Act to Eliminate Racial Profiling*, 1st. Sess., 38th Parl. (first reading 18 November 2004), online: Libby Davies website

http://www.libbydavies.ca/pdf/c-296-racial-profiling-bill.pdf (date accessed 14 August 2005).

51 *R. v. Smith*, [2004] OJ No. 4979 at para. 36 (SCJ) (emphasis added). See also *R. v. Clayton* (2005), 194 CCC (3d) 289 (Ont. CA).

52 *R. v. Mann* (2004), 21 CR (6th) 1 (SCC) [*Mann*].

53 *Ibid.*, 8–9.

54 *Ibid.*, 19.

55 *Ibid.*, 9 (para. 4).

56 See Tim Quigley, who makes a similar observation in "*R. v. Mann*, It's a Disappointing Decision" (2004), 21 CR (6th) 41 at 44–45.

57 "Race-Based Suspect Selection," 1081, n. 16.

58 See "Race and the Decision to Detain a Suspect," 242–43.

59 See "Race-Based Suspect Selection," 1093–94.

60 *Ibid.*, 1107–8.

61 The problem of cross-racial identification has been recognized in *R. v. McIntosh* (1997), 117 CCC (3d) 385 at 394–96 (Ont. CA), and *R. v. Richards* (2004), 186 CCC (3d) 333 at 342–43 (Ont. CA). See also John P. Rutledge, "They All Look Alike: The Inaccuracy of Cross-Racial Identifications," *American Journal of Criminal Law* 28 (2001): 207.

62 *Manitoba Aboriginal Justice Inquiry*, 94–95. See also the discussion in "Race-Based Suspect Selection," 1111–12; "The Color of Crime," 669–70; Don Sellar, "When Racial Labels Do No Good," *Toronto Star*, 17 July 2004; and Deborah A. Ramirez, Jennifer Hoopes, and Tara L. Quinlan, "Defining Racial Profiling in a Post-September 11 World," *American Criminal Law Review* 40 (2003): 1229–30.

63 "The Color of Crime," 675.

64 *R. v. Moosvi* (13 October 2004) (Ont. Ct. Jus.) [on file with the author] [*Moosvi*]. See also Gail Abbate, "Two Constables Found Not Guilty of Assaulting Deaf Man in 2002," *Globe and Mail*, 14 October 2004, A2; Peter Small, "Officers Acquitted of Beating Deaf Man," *Toronto Star*, 14 October 2004, B5; and Carol Goar, "Peter Owusu-Ansah's Nightmare," *Toronto Star*, 21 July 2004.

65 *Moosvi*, 45.

66 See "Cops Cleared in Mistaken Black Arrests," Vancouver *Province*, 19 April 1995, A8. According to the media reports, the reasons given were that Muojewke "is a black man in his 20s."

67 See Paul Minvielle, "Skin Color Alone Can't Justify Arrest," Victoria *Times-Colonist*, 19 April 1995, 1.

68 See Kim Bolan, "Arrest of 2 Blacks Defended on Basis Few of Race in City," *Vancouver Sun*, 19 April 1995, A3 ["Arrest of 2 Blacks Defended"].

69 See Kim Bolan, "Police Board Member Should Quit, Blacks Say," *Vancouver Sun*, 20 April 1995, B7 ["Police Board Member"].

70 See "Arrest of 2 Blacks Defended."

71 See "Police Board Member."

72 *R. v. Yamanaka* (1998), 128 CCC (3d) 570 at 573 (para. 4) (BCCA) (emphasis added).

73 *Ibid.*, 575–76 (para. 15).

74 These additional facts about the location of the stop were provided to me by Eric Gottardi, one of Greaves's appellate counsel.

75 See Tim Quigley, "Annotation" (2004), 24 CR (6th) 17.

76 See *R. v. Greaves* (2004), 189 CCC (3d) 305 at 315 (para. 9) (BCCA).

77 *Ibid.*, 323 (para. 39).

78 *Ibid.*, 324 (para. 42) (emphasis added).

79 *Greaves*, 324.

80 Erika Johnson, "'A Menace to Society': The Use of Criminal Profiles and Its Effects on Black Males," *Howard Law Journal* 38 (1995): 655–57.

81 [2004] SCCA No. 522 (3 March 2005).

82 See "The Color of Crime," 664.

83 *Manitoba Aboriginal Justice Inquiry*, 95.

84 Walker comes to a similar conclusion in "The Color of Crime," 682–83.

85 See "Race-Based Suspect Selection," 1117–18.

86 *Ibid.*, 1096, 1096–1108.

87 *Ibid.*, 1123.

CHAPTER 10: LEGISLATIVE REFORM

1 *International Convention on the Elimination of All Forms of Racial Discrimination*, 21 December 1965, 660 UNTS 195 (entered into force, 4 January 1969; accession by Canada, 14 October 1970).

2 *International Covenant on Civil and Political Rights*, 16 December 1966, 999 UNTS 171 (entered into force 23 March 1976; accession by Canada, 19 May 1976).

3 See Susan Delacourt, "'Not Our Canada,' Martin Says," *Toronto Star*, 6 April 2004, A1.

4 See Elizabeth Thompson, "$2 Million to Fight Racial Profiling," Montreal *Gazette*, 29 March 2005, A1; and Salim Jiwa, "Police Program Takes Aim at Ethnic Profiling," Vancouver *Province*, 30 March 2005, A13. LEAD is an initiative of the Canadian Association of Chiefs of Police designed to develop policing policy that is sensitive to the needs of Aboriginal and racialized communities. See "Part I: The Multiculturalism Program,"

online: Canadian Heritage http://www.pch.gc.ca/progs/multi/reports/ ann2003-2004/2_e.cfm (date accessed 15 August 2005).

5 See Government of Canada, *A Canada for All: Canada's Action Plan Against Racism* (2005), 26, 29, 31, online: Department of Canadian Heritage http://www.pch.gc.ca/multi/plan_action_plan/pdf/action_long_e.pdf (date accessed 15 August 2005).

6 See Bill C-296, *An Act to Eliminate Racial Profiling*, 1st Sess., 38th Parl. (first reading 18 November 2004), online: Libby Davies website http:// www.libbydavies.ca/pdf/c-296-racial-profiling-bill.pdf (date accessed 14 August 2005) [*Eliminate Racial Profiling*]. See also Ian Bailey, "Davies Wants End to Racial Profiling," *The Province*, 21 November 2004, A44. The Act was first introduced as Bill C-476 on February 12, 2004, and had to be reintroduced because of the June 28, 2004, election.

7 See Campbell Clark, "Racial Profiling Denounced by Opposition," *Globe and Mail*, 22 March 2005, A10.

8 See Tracey Tyler, "Senator Calls for Racial-Profiling Law," *Toronto Star*, 18 August 2004, A16; and Jack Aubry, "Senators Call for Law to End Racial Profiling," *Ottawa Citizen*, 23 June 2003, A4.

9 See "Opposition Parties Call for Ban on Racial Profiling," *Globe and Mail*, 21 March 2005. See also "Racial Profiling and Law Enforcement," a Canadian Bar Association Resolution (04-07-A) (August 2004) calling for anti-profiling legislation. Online: Canadian Bar Association http:// www.cba.org/CBA/resolutions/pdf/04-07-A.pdf (date accessed 15 August 2005).

10 As of August 2004, twenty-three states in the United States had passed legislation banning racial profiling. See *Threat and Humiliation: Racial Profiling, Domestic Security, and Human Rights in the United States* (New York: Amnesty International USA, 2004), online: Amnesty International http://www.amnestyusa.org/racial_profiling/report/rp_report.pdf at 28 (date accessed 11 August 2005) [*Threat and Humiliation*].

11 *Ibid.*, 29.

12 See section 5(2)(b) of *Eliminate Racial Profiling*, which calls for data collection.

13 See *Paying the Price: The Human Cost of Racial Profiling* (21 October 2003), 71, online: Ontario Human Rights Commission http://www.ohrc. on.ca/english/consultations/ racial-profiling-report.pdf (date accessed 11 August 2005) [*Paying the Price*]. One of the earliest calls for data collection came from the *Report of the Commission on Systemic Racism in the Ontario Criminal Justice System* (Toronto: Queen's Printer for Ontario, 1995), 405–6.

14 Ontario Human Rights Commission, *Policy and Guidelines on Racism and Racial Discrimination* (9 June 2005), 44–48, online: Ontario Human Rights Commission http://www.ohrc.on.ca/english/publications/racism-and-racial-discrimination-policy.pdf (date accessed 11 August 2005) [*Policy and Guidelines*].

15 *Ibid.*, 46.

16 See "Background and Current Data Collection Efforts: Jurisdictions Currently Collecting Data," online: Racial Profiling Data Collection Resource Center at Northeastern University http://www.racialprofilinganalysis. neu.edu/background/jurisdictions.php (date accessed 14 August 2005) [Racial Profiling Data Collection Resource Center]. See also *Threat and Humiliation*, 41–44.

17 See "New 'Stop' System for Met Police," BBC News, 17 November 2004, online: BBC News http://news.bbc.co.uk/1/hi/england/london/4017809. stm (date accessed 11 August 2005).

18 John Saunders, "Black Traveller Calls Search Racial Profiling," *Globe and Mail*, 4 June 2001, A16 ["Black Traveller Calls Search Racial Profiling"].

19 See "New Rules for Customs Officers after Human Rights Complaint," CBC News online: CBC News Online http://cbc.ca/cgi-bin/templates/ view.cgi?category=Canada&story=/news/2002/02/06/customs_settle020206 (date accessed 14 July 2005).

20 See "Black Traveller Calls Search Racial Profiling."

21 See Canadian Human Rights Tribunal, *Minutes of Settlement*, Selwyn Pieters and Department of National Revenue (now Canada Customs and Revenue Agency) File no. T650/3801 (30 January 2002) [on file with the author].

22 See John Duncanson, "Customs to Gather Race Stats," *Toronto Star*, 7 February 2002, B2; and John Saunders, "Traveller Wins Customs Fight," *Globe and Mail*, 6 February 2002, A1.

23 See Action 1, *Paying the Price*, 68. See also Appendix A, for a list of all systemic racism Ontario reports.

24 The ban was imposed on February 23, 1989. The Board Policy Prohibiting the Keeping of Race-Based Statistics states: "It is the policy of the Board that the Board and the Force not compile or publish statistics relative to the race, colour or creed of individuals involved in criminal activity, except as approved by the Board. This policy does not affect the releasing of descriptions of suspects wanted for criminal acts." None of the other police services boards in Ontario appear to have a similar prohibition. See "Minutes of the Public Meeting of the Toronto Police Services Board," 20 February 2003, 15, online: Toronto Police Services Board

http://www.torontopoliceboard.on.ca/minutes/2003/030220pma%20full.
pdf (date accessed 11 August 2005).

25 Fantino's speech was given at a time of very strained relations between the police and the Black community, particularly in light of the police shootings of Lester Donaldson in February 1989 and Wade Lawson in December 1988. See "Analysis Raises Board Hackles," *Toronto Star*, 20 October 2002, A9; and Jim Rankin and John Duncanson, "Fantino Still Shoots from the Lip," *Toronto Star*, 6 March 2000, 1.

26 Many of the methodological issues surrounding data collection are discussed earlier in the book at chapter 4. See also "Planning, Training, Implementation: Data Collection Elements," online: Racial Profiling Data Collection Resource Center at Northeastern University http://www.racial-profilinganalysis.neu.edu/planning/ (date accessed 11 August 2005).

27 See *Policy and Guidelines*, 47–48. See also *Guidelines for Collecting Data on Enumerated Grounds under the Code* (24 September 2003), online: Ontario Human Rights Commission http://www.ohrc.on.ca/english/publications/data-collection-guide.pdf (date accessed 11 August 2005).

28 A number of pilot projects are now investigating the impact of having cameras in cruisers. These projects include a group of fifteen patrol vehicles of the Toronto Police Service (which began in September 2005), twenty-two OPP vehicles in the Greater Toronto Area, and twelve OPP vehicles in Kenora. See Timothy Appleby, "Police Cruisers to Be Fitted with Cameras," *Globe and Mail*, 11 June 2005, A13. See also Action 15, *Paying the Price*, 72. Global Positioning Systems (GPS), which track the movements of police vehicles, is another important monitoring mechanism. See Chantal Eustace, "Police Cars Equipped with GPS," Regina *Leader-Post*, 12 June 2004, A9.

29 See Cindi John, "London Police Called to Account," BBC News, 17 November 2004, online: BBC News http://news.bbc.co.uk/1/hi/uk/4017167.stm (date accessed 14 August 2005); and "'Receipts' Keep Track of Police Stops," BBC News, 1 April 2003, online: BBC News http://news.bbc.co.uk/1/hi/england/2903377.stm (date accessed 14 August 2005).

30 See, generally, the discussion in Richard V. Ericson, *Reproducing Order: A Study of Police Patrol Work* (Toronto: University of Toronto Press, 1982), 200–1.

31 See Nick Bland, Joel Miller, and Paul Quinton, *Upping the PACE? An Evaluation of the Recommendations of the Stephen Lawrence Inquiry on Stops and Searches* (Police Research Series, Paper 128), ed. Carol F. Willis (London: Home Office Research, Development and Statistics Directorate,

2000), 78, online: U.K. Home Office http://www.homeoffice.gov.uk/rds/ prgpdfs/prs128.pdf (date accessed 14 August 2005).

32 This point is recognized by Scot Wortley and Julian Tanner, "Inflammatory Rhetoric? Baseless Accusations? A Response to Gabor's Critique of Racial Profiling Research in Canada," *Canadian Journal of Criminology and Criminal Justice* 47 (2005): 599 ["Inflammatory Rhetoric"].

33 *Ibid.*

34 *Ibid.* See also Nick McCabe-Lokos, "Police Can't Be 'Politically Correct,'" *Toronto Star*, 11 November 2002, A1; and Heather Macdonald, *Are Cops Racist? How the War Against the Police Harms Black Americans* (Chicago: Ivan R. Dee Publishers, 2003). See also Thomas Gabor, "Inflammatory Rhetoric on Racial Profiling Can Undermine Police Services," *Canadian Journal of Criminology and Criminal Justice* 46 (2004): 457. Gabor's concern appears to be the impact of imprecise definitions of racial profiling and false allegations on police effectiveness.

35 See "Inflammatory Rhetoric," 599–600.

36 See *Policy and Guidelines*, 46.

37 See Greg McArthur, "Force Will Be First in Canada to Collect Stats on Race," *Kingston-Whig Standard*, 20 June 2003, 1; and James Mennie, "Police Adopt Policy Against Racial Profiling by Officers," *The Gazette*, 23 March 2004, A1.

38 See Action 12, *Paying the Price*, 72. See also Scott Roberts, "Test Police to Oust Racists, Top Black Officer Suggests," *Toronto Star*, 22 May 2005, A2. See also "Bias-Free Policing," *Calgary Herald*, 6 May 2005, PA01.

39 See also Sidhartha Banerjee, "Courses to Show Budding Cops How to Avoid Racial Profiling," *The Gazette*, 13 February 2005, D3.

40 See Action 14, *Paying the Price*, 72.

41 See Kent Roach, "Hard to Prove Racial Profiling," *Toronto Star*, 25 November 2002, B2.

42 See Sujit Choudhry, "Laws Needed to Ban Racial Profiling," *Toronto Star*, 25 November 2002, B2. See also Sujit Choudhry and Kent Roach, "Racial and Ethnic Profiling: Statutory Discretion, Constitutional Remedies, and Democratic Accountability," *Osgoode Hall Law Journal* 41 (2002): 22–32.

43 See *Eliminate Racial Profiling*.

44 See John Deverell, "Racial Profiling Seen as Crime," *Toronto Star*, 29 October 2002, B5.

45 The link between racial profiling and hate crimes is made in Lu-in Wang, "'Suitable Targets'? Parallels and Connections between 'Hate' Crimes and 'Driving While Black,'" *Michigan Journal of Race & Law* 6 (2001): 209.

46 See "Police in New Jersey Face 5 Years in Jail, $15,000 Fine for Racial Profiling," *Toronto Star*, 15 March 2003, A20. See also "New Jersey Outlaws Racial Profiling," online: CBS http://cbsnewyork.com (date accessed 6 June 2003).

47 See *Threat and Humiliation*, 29.

48 See "The Need for Civilian Review of the RCMP on National Security Issues," speech delivered to the Access and Privacy Conference, 17 June 2005, 45, 48–49, online: Commission for Public Complaints Against the RCMP http://www.cpc-cpp.gc.ca/DefaultSite/Whatsnew/index_ e.aspx?ArticleID=776 (date accessed 14 August 2005).

49 See *The Police Amendment Act, 2005*, c. 25, amending *The Police Act*, SS 1990, c. P-15.01, online: The Legislative Assembly of Saskatchewan http://www.qp.gov.sk.ca/documents/english/Chapters/2005/Chap-25.pdf (date accessed 18 August 2005).

50 See *Report of the Commission of Inquiry into Matters Relating to the Death of Neil Stonechild* (October 2004), 207–11, 213, online: Stonechild Inquiry http://www.stonechildinquiry.ca/finalreport/default.shtml (date accessed 19 August 2005). See also James Wood, "Police Complaint Process Changing," *Leader-Post*, 7 July 2005, A10; and James Wood, "Complaint System Gets Overhaul," *Leader-Post*, 10 May 2005, A8.

51 For a national look at mechanisms of police complaints, see "Domestic Models of Review of Police Forces," Police Review, 10 December 2004, online: Commission of Inquiry into the Actions of Canadian Officials in Relation to Maher Arar http://www.ararcommission.ca/eng/Domestic %20Models%20of%20Review%20of%20Police%20Forces.pdf (date accessed 14 August 2005).

52 "Report on the Police Complainants System in Ontario," 22 April 2005, 58, online: Ontario Police Complaints Review, http://www.policecomplaintsreview.on.ca/ (date accessed 27 April 2005).

53 *Ibid.*, 66–68, 72–73.

54 *Ibid.*, 80.

55 See "Arar Commission: Policy Review," online: Commission of Inquiry into the Actions of Canadian Officials in Relation to Maher Arar http:// www.ararcommission.ca/eng/12.htm (date accessed 14 August 2005).

56 CPC has reported that it has had difficulty accessing information from the RCMP. See "2004/2005 Annual Report," June 2005, 35–41, online: Commission for Public Complaints Against the Royal Canadian Military Police, http://www.cpc-cpp.gc.ca/app/DocRepository/1/PDF/AR0405_ e.pdf (date accessed 14 August 2005). See also "RCMP Hinders Overseer, Agency Reports," *Toronto Star*, 25 July 2005, A3.

57 See *Submissions of the Commission for Public Complaints Against the RCMP: Regarding the Policy Review of the Commission of Inquiry into the Actions of Canadian Officials in Relation to Maher Arar*, 21 February 2005, 40–52, online: Commission for Public Complaints Against the RCMP, http://www.cpc-cpp.gc.ca/DefaultSite/Whatsnew/index_e.aspx?ArticleID=776 (date accessed 14 August 2005).

58 *Ibid.*, 54–72. A similar recommendation was made by the Canadian Bar Association in its submissions to the Special Senate Committee reviewing the *Anti-Terrorism Act*. See "Submission on the Three Year Review of the *Anti-Terrorism Act*," May 2005, 19–22, online: Canadian Bar Association, http://www.cba.org/CBA/submissions/pdf/05-28-eng.pdf (date accessed 14 August 2005).

59 This outcome could also occur, of course, if the CPC is given the audit and information gathering powers it is seeking.

60 See *Paying the Price*, 17–66. See also Maureen J. Brown, "In Their Own Voices: African Canadians in the Greater Toronto Area Share Experiences of Police Profiling" (commissioned by the African Canadian Community Coalition on Racial Profiling, March 2004), 18–19, 23–30 [on file with the author] ["In Their Own Voices"]; Brenda Branswell, "How Blacks See Encounters with the Police," *The Gazette*, 13 February 2005, D1; and "Voices: Racial Profiling and the Police," *Toronto Star*, 23 October 2002, A6 ["Voices"].

61 "In Their Own Voices," 18–19. See also Margo Varadi, "Youth Feel Picked on for No Good Reason," *Toronto Star*, 24 September 2005, L7.

62 "In Their Own Voices," 17.

63 See John Barber, "Malvern Trades Guns for Jobs," *Globe and Mail*, 13 August 2005, M1.

64 "In Their Own Voices," 16–17.

65 In *Paying the Price*, 37–42, the Ontario Human Rights Commission documented the extent to which racialized communities change their behaviour in an attempt to minimize the likelihood of a police encounter and to better cope with the experience when it does occur.

66 See Jack Todd, "Sheer Terror: What Blacks Must Feel When Police Approach," *The Gazette*, 4 January 1993, A3.

67 See "Racism Was a Gun at His Head," *Toronto Star*, 22 October 2002, A6; and Jennifer Quinn, "New Jersey Shooting Spurred Real Reform," *Toronto Star*, 21 October 2002, A6.

68 Royson James, "Why I Fear for My Sons," *Toronto Star*, 21 October 2002, A1. See also Debbie Parkes, "Black Kids Taught to Beware of Cops," *The Gazette*, 30 January 2005, A3; "Voices."

69 "In Their Own Voices," 19–21.
70 *Paying the Price*, 17.

Acknowledgments

THE WRITING OF THIS book was made possible in large part by the generous support of the Law Foundation of Ontario. This funding allowed me over the last two years to work with a number of bright and energetic Windsor Law School research assistants, including Alex Procope, Sarah Vokey, Michelle Booth, Cherie Daniel, and Tim Morgan. Special thanks to Alex, the book's primary student researcher, whose dedication, thoroughness, and insightful reading greatly improved this book.

Many friends and colleagues supported this project in different ways. Rose Voyvodic and Brian Etherington read the entire manuscript, and Liz Sheehy, Reem Bahdi, Don Stuart, Constance Backhouse, Riad Saloojee, Aaron Dhir, and Dean Beeby commented on parts of it. Dean Bruce Elman ensured that I had all of the research help I required. Many others provided support, including my assistant Mary Mitchell, human rights lawyer Selwyn Pieters, and Saman Wickramasinghe, a third-year student who read the manuscript with a critical eye. The *Ottawa Law Review* allowed me to include parts of chapter 9 from an article I published in volume 36 of the journal.

My publishers, Bill Kaplan and Jeff Miller of Irwin Law, were engaged and enthusiastic about this book. In particular, Bill's role as a mentor and critic went well beyond that expected of a pub-

ACKNOWLEDGMENTS

lisher, and his dedication tremendously improved the book in all aspects. Thanks also to editor Rosemary Shipton and the peer reviewers, whose comments were detailed, cogent, and of tremendous help. Finally, I would like to thank Heather Raven and the rest of the production staff at Irwin Law for all of their hard work in putting the book together.

Most important, I owe a special debt of gratitude to the patience, support, and love of my wife, Melanie, and our three children, Evan, Nicholas, and Mara. I will never forget the sacrifices you made to give me the freedom to write this book.

This book covers relevant events up until Decmber 31, 2005.

David M. Tanovich

Index